# THE WEST COUNT
# LITERARY INVENTION
## Putting Fiction In Its Place

Is the 'West Country' on the map or in the mind? Is it the south-west peninsula of Britain or a semi-mythical country offering a home for those in pursuit of the romance of wrecking, smuggling and a rural Golden Age?

An intellectual journey through history and ideas, this book offers a literary angle on a representative selection of places within the region loosely defined as the West Country—mainly Cornwall and Devon, but also areas of Somerset and Dorset. The chosen texts represent some of the topography characteristic of the region: rocky coasts, wild moors, chalk cliffs, fishing villages and rural towns, and the book is a guide for those who want to travel through the West Country, whether on foot or in their imagination, alert to sights, sounds, place-names and ideas.

Parson Hawker helps you to tread carefully among the airy heights of the cliff paths in North Cornwall; Charles Kingsley takes you in and out of steep-sided combes within an Elizabethan North Devon. R.D. Blackmore guides you among the branching valleys or 'goyals' of a romantic Exmoor before leading you to the place that Thomas Hardy described as 'sad Sedgemoor'. Hardy's readers experience the storms of a semi-real, semi-imagined Egdon Heath, tramp through the midges of Marshwood Vale and listen to the 'sea-mutterings' off Portland Bill. Sabine Baring-Gould tempts you into smugglers' caves on the Devon-Dorset border and enables you to hear the voices of Dartmoor songmen within a 'wild and wondrous region' of tors and granite crosses. Virginia Woolf takes you on a journey to St Ives: the itinerary inclues a boat-trip to Godrevy lighthouse. By the end of the journey you have moved across a territory underfoot, and a territory of the mind, created a map of places and thoughts, circled a peninsula and the idea of a region.

Simon Trezise is a lecturer in literature at the University of Exeter and has worked as a Tutor-Counsellor for the Open University. He has lived and worked in many parts of the West Country. His current research interests include narrative in fiction, drama and film.

*The Cobb, Lyme Regis.*
Here, Tennyson shunned the view of nearby Monmouth Beach to
seek the 'exact spot' where Louisa Musgrove fell.

*Don't talk to me of the Duke of Monmouth.*
*Show me the exact spot where Louisa Musgrove fell.*

Tennyson at Lyme Regis

*25 August, 1867. Lyme Regis . . . We go down to the Cobb, enjoying the sea, the
breeze, the coast-view of Portland, etc., and while we sit on the wall I read to him
[*Tennyson*], out of* Persuasion, *the passage where Louisa Musgrove hurts her
ankle.*

William Allingham

# THE WEST COUNTRY AS A LITERARY INVENTION

## Putting Fiction In Its Place

*Simon Trezise*

UNIVERSITY
*of*
EXETER
PRESS

This book is dedicated to my daughter Demelza and my wife Kate.

I am grateful to all those who have assisted me, especially to my sister Anna, my family and my students. Colleagues at Exeter University have been generous with their advice and their time: especially Brian Edgar, Peter Faulkner and John Travis. I have also benefited from the advice and practical help of Ian Maxted of the Westcountry Studies Library, Exeter.

First published in 2000 by
University of Exeter Press
Reed Hall, Streatham Drive
Exeter, Devon EX4 4QR
UK
*www.ex.ac.uk/uep/*

**British Library Cataloguing in Publication Data**
A catalogue record for this book is available from the British Library

Paperback ISBN 0 85989 538 6
Hardback ISBN 0 85989 537 8

Typeset in 12/13pt Garamond 3 by Kestrel Data, Exeter

Printed in Great Britain by
Short Run Press Ltd, Exeter

# Contents

# Illustrations

All photographs by Simon Trezise.

The cover image (paperback only), the map and the illustrations of Hawker's Vicarage, Plover's Barrows, the 'Hieroglyphic Napoleon' and Dewerstone Rock are all reproduced courtesy of Westcountry Studies Library.

# Foreword

This book came as a very pleasant surprise: it is one of those conspicuously well-researched books that is also very interesting to read. Its general thesis concerns the decision of a number of writers to root their fictions in the landscapes of the West Country, that region seen by most of us as naturally adventurous and romantic. After completing this book's imaginative journey through the folklore and local milieux of the region, you may decide to join those of us who are irretrievably 'hooked' by a characteristic way of writing about the West.

I did myself write years ago about a famous French equivalent, Alan Fournier's *Le Grand Meaulnes*, who almost seems to belong among our own Westcountry writers, in spite of his obviously very different background and upbringing. When I was young, quite a lot of my life was swallowed in dreaming of Lorna Doone and Jan Ridd, as Meaulnes dreamed of his mysterious Yvonne. Later I fell under the spell of Hawker and Exmoor, and I still have a very high regard indeed for his wonderful Tennysonian blank verse. Hawker's 'Sangraal' is to my mind an unjustly forgotten Victorian masterpiece. Since I think of myself as partly Cornish and know Cornwall in so many ways, I find all that this book tells us of Hawker's 'Trelawny Ballad' especially fascinating. Trezise uses all his skills as an academic and combines them with his clear commitment to the region. He portrays his series of subjects, from the colossal shadows of Thomas Hardy and Virginia Woolf down, in ways that reveal the reality of a hidden-domestic world.

All great classics teach us about our own long-lost selves, what we must once have been. We discover in literature the complexities and half-conscious secrets of our own pasts. Sometimes this will be with a smile, more often with a tug of the heart. This well-known almost magnetic and self-revealing charm of the often remote past is part of the rich experience of re-reading. Lucky, those who have a Trezise to guide them back over its fascinating landscapes and prospects, some new, others remembered. He goes a journey we should perhaps all—and always—make, and never forget what we learn from it.

*John Fowles, February 2000*

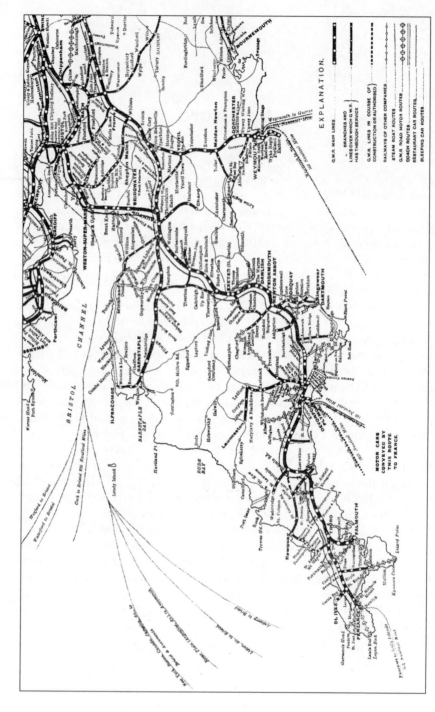

Part of the 1910 Great Western Railway map, reproduced here to show rail routes in the West Country.

# Preface

# The Territory of the Mind and the Territory Underfoot

*The test of imagination, ultimately, is not the territory of art or the territory of the mind, but the territory underfoot.*

Wendell Berry

Why write a literary book about the 'West Country'? This territory of uncertain borders is of understandable interest to local historians, tourists, travel writers, geographers and geologists, but writers of fiction are admired for using their skills with words to give to 'airy nothing' a 'local habitation and a name'. One voice argues:

> Surely, writers should not and cannot be tied to a particular region on the map or features in the landscape? The places that should most concern literary scholars are the places in the reader's mind, places such as the world on the other side of Lewis Carroll's looking glass or Thomas More's *Utopia* (literally 'no place'). These are not regions on the map but regions of imagination, created by the complex interaction between a fictional text and the reader's thoughts.

Another voice replies:

> There are certain fictions which embody a strong sense of place and regional identity, that invite the reader to go from the text to topography and from topography back to the text.

This relationship between the word and the world, the territory of the mind and the territory underfoot, deserves careful consideration. The best place-conscious fictional texts are too subtle and detailed to take the form of a travel brochure, too subjective or eccentric to count as local history, too imaginative to be reliable geography, too profound in their exploration of people and places to be categorized as travel writing, although travel writing of the more complex type approaches their role. Such literary texts have a special role linking imagination and landscape, deriving energy from both sources. Like Antaeus the mythical giant, these texts only have full strength when they are planted firmly at a particular spot on the earth. From that spot of the earth, however, they often engage the reader's feelings wherever he or she may live. Readers can enjoy Wordsworth without visiting the Lakes. Nevertheless, a visit to the Lakes with Wordsworth in mind will enrich one's perceptions of both his texts and the topography which they explore. For many readers, certain texts become inseparable from the regions which they simultaneously reflect, perpetuate and create: the Lake District without Wordsworth, the Potteries without Arnold Bennett, Sligo without Yeats, London without Dickens, Dublin without Joyce, become unthinkable. One of the reasons for writing this book is the belief that some lesser known literary explorations of territory also deserve recognition: that North Cornwall without Hawker, Devon and Somerset without Blackmore, Dartmoor without Baring-Gould, should also be unthinkable.

The regional writer who gains an audience has the power to form perceptions of geographical regions, to become an inescapable part of the region that he or she fictionalizes. Some regional fiction attains the status of fact, its inventions becoming part of our 'mind-map' of where we live. There were six towns in the region called 'The Potteries' but many readers think there were five because of Arnold Bennett's fictions: he decided that 'Anna of the Five Towns' was more euphonious than the more accurate alternative (Drabble 1975: 3–4). When Tennyson was invited to pay attention to local history while visiting Lyme Regis, he is said to have replied: 'Don't talk to me of the Duke of Monmouth. Show me the exact spot where Louisa Musgrove fell' (Powys 1983: 136; cf. Page 1983: 58). There is much meaning to be teased out of this anecdote. Tennyson's supposed comments enable us to appreciate the power of fiction to rival reality and form perceptions of place. The imaginary Louisa seems real partly because she has been artfully inserted in a real location. Louisa does not fall 'anywhere': she falls at an 'exact spot' imagined so vividly by readers that they expect to find it outside the text. Nevertheless, Tennyson is referring to an incident in a novel where the story is actually halted so that the narrator can enthuse about the nature of Lyme, a place that exists separately from the text. Near the Cobb lies Monmouth Beach, the place-name preserving what Tennyson wants to ignore. The history of a West Country rebellion cannot rival the reality invented by Jane Austen as far as Tennyson is concerned, but Monmouth is considered a worthy subject of fiction by those writers with West Country allegiances, R.D. Blackmore and Thomas Hardy. Although the regional writer can toy with the details of a chosen region, the writer's work is unlikely to be remembered unless it convinces the reader as an adequate fictional representation of *those* people in *that* place at *that* period of history. If this is successfully achieved, the text then becomes more than a mirror of topography. It assists us to hold the place in our minds, to imagine it before and after we encounter it, to see it with fresh and clear vision when we do encounter it. Sligo without Yeats is unthinkable; Sligo with Yeats is *thinkable*. Under Ben Bulben, the shadow of Yeats and a mighty mountain combine.

Readers are sensitized by the most effective regional texts to look for particular features in the landscape, and to consider the question of some 'common ground': *geographical* territory that is open to exploration by means of the senses and the mind, *human* territory in which labour and traditions have been and still may be shared. This symbiosis between place and text is a sometimes overlooked feature of past and present life in that part of Britain called South-West England or the 'West Country'. The phrases 'Hawker's West Country', 'Kingsley's West Country', 'Baring-Gould's West Country', do not have the same popular currency and recognition-value as 'Hardy's Wessex': it is because Hardy is the region's literary giant that other interesting writers' work has been lost in his shadow. Famous and lesser known texts have a part to play in the making of the West on the map and in the mind. This book is not based on the argument that all the writers discussed are overlooked geniuses. Charles Kingsley and R.D. Blackmore are mainly remembered as writers of classics for children, not as writers who emulate Tolstoy. Baring-Gould of Dartmoor, fascinating biographically, parallels Hardy's work without achieving his literary excellence; Hawker of

Morwenstow in North Cornwall cannot rival Tennyson's achievements as a poet, despite his fragment of Arthurian genius 'The Quest of the Sangraal'. Nevertheless, the works of these lesser known writers do deserve attention in the specific context of place-conscious writing; their attempt to capture the essence of their localities and region is sometimes as successful as that of other, better known, regional writers. This book is based on the principle that all the writers whose work is explored here have made an important contribution to the marriage between texts and places which contributes to the perceived identity of the West Country. Many of the writers explored in this book have not achieved the eminence of Hardy and Woolf, but their work repays study for its largely unrecognized but seminal influence in creating a 'West Country' unquestioningly recognized by thousands. The nineteenth century and Victorian period is an important part of the background: that was when 'the literary personality' of the West Country was mainly formed. However, the notion of the literary contribution to regional identity is still relevant today. The texts selected for discussion here help us to explore a question of continuing importance: the relationship between fiction, topography and community viewed in a long perspective.

This book is an intellectual journey through history and ideas but it is also an encounter with a varied terrain. It will provide a literary angle on a representative selection of places within the region loosely defined as the West County. The texts are representative of the counties usually assumed to be part of the West Country: mainly Cornwall and Devon, but also areas of Somerset and Dorset. The texts represent some of the topography characteristic of the region: rocky coasts, wild moors, chalk cliffs, fishing villages and rural towns. The book can be used as a guide for those who want to travel through the West Country, whether on foot or in their imagination, alert to sights, sounds, place-names and ideas. Parson Hawker helps you to tread carefully among the airy heights of the cliff paths in North Cornwall; Charles Kingsley takes you in and out of steep-sided combes within an Elizabethan North Devon. R.D. Blackmore guides you among the branching valleys or 'goyals' of a romantic Exmoor before leading you to the place that Thomas Hardy described as 'sad Sedgemoor'. Hardy's readers experience the storms of a semi-real, semi-imagined Egdon Heath, tramp through the midges of Marshwood Vale and listen to the 'sea-mutterings' off Portland Bill. Sabine

Baring-Gould tempts you into smugglers' caves on the Devon–Dorset border; he also enables you to hear the voices of Dartmoor songmen within a 'wild and wondrous region' of tors and granite crosses. Virginia Woolf, perhaps an unexpected guide, takes you on a journey to St Ives: the itinerary includes a boat-trip to Godrevy Lighthouse. By the end of the journey, you have moved across a territory underfoot and a territory of the mind, created a map of places and thoughts, circled a peninsula and the idea of a region.

The contemporary American poet and thinker, Wendell Berry, stresses the importance of remaining in touch with the land. He rejects the attempt to define 'Southernness' or 'blackness' in America without reference to geography, as if they were 'meta-regions' existing in a dimension divorced from the physical world. Berry argues that while the survival of human individuality is threatened by the power of the State and Market Forces, the physical world resists 'homogenization'. Mother Earth, with her varying features and natural boundaries, still survives in recognizably distinctive shapes alongside or underneath the surface of human activity. High street shop-fronts, tower blocks and housing estates often look identical, but the massive features of the land still survive, enabling regions to retain a distinctive visual character. We could add to Berry's argument that features such as climatic difference and 'micro-climates', as well as species of plants and animals found in some habitats and not others, also evade homogenization. Furthermore, land and buildings record varying patterns of labour in the past and present. In Berry's view, it is the role of the regional artist/writer to pay attention to these matters. He takes issue with the argument that there is a 'territory of art' where there is no inherent value in subjects, only the value conferred on them by the artist. In Berry's view, there *is* value inherent in certain subjects and it is the obligation of the artist or writer to 'pay attention' to this. The regional writer's subject is the 'territory underfoot'. The seminal work of Barry Lopez helps Berry to make his case. Influenced by his understanding of Native American culture, Lopez argues that the mind has its own landscape, but this is shaped *in response* to the exterior landscape (Lopez 1988: 64–66). Berry rephrases this in a poet's way, using words engaging with ethics, thought and feeling: the 'invisible landscape' of the psyche is the 'guide' and 'protector' of the 'visible' world; equally, the 'visible landscape' must 'verify and correct the invisible' world of the mind. The territory of art is actually, according to Berry, inseparable from the territory underfoot (Berry 1987: 24–27). The role of regional writers, in this context, is to preserve the locality in words, to 'correct' their texts in the light of the physical world that they can touch and see, to carefully map their chosen territory in a way that remains faithful to a particular environment. Such writers are *attentive* to the minutiae of the local scene although, in the act of writing, they may make it available to a more than local audience.

Many creative writers and some literary critics use language about the physical world in a way that supports Berry's views. George Eliot eloquently states the case: 'A human life, I think, should be well rooted in some spot of native land, where it may get the love of tender kinship for the face of the earth . . .' (Chapter 3, *Daniel Deronda*). Even a writer as focused on social questions as George Orwell included 'love' of 'the surface of the earth' among the inspirations for his literary work (see his well known essay 'Why I Write'). The novelist John Cowper Powys (1967: 151) describes how his father taught him and his brothers to pay attention to the land: 'He brought us up to note every undulation, every upland, every spinney, every ridge, every fen, and the effect produced upon all these by every variety of season or weather'. Powys (1964: 11) put these lessons into practice in his fictions and in his records of the territory of his Somerset childhood: 'I set out with my brother Littleton to scamper home to Montacute Vicarage round the back of Montacute House; our favourite way being always by the Trent Lanes rather than by Babylon Hill and the Slopes. Sherborne was five miles from Yeovil; and Yeovil was five miles from Montacute; so at Sherborne we were ten miles from home if we ran the shortest way.' This local knowledge, dependent on having place names at your fingertips and an exact sense of features in relation to other features, can be shared, if the writer is skilled, by those who do not know the local territory. An admiring reader once said to Hardy about his semi-real, semi-fictional Wessex: 'It seems to me there isn't a contour of the country, from Exonbury to Christminster, that isn't mapped in your mind. You appear to know every copse and common, every elbow of every lane, every "church-hay", every water-mead, every "ewe-leaze"' (Archer 1901: 310). For this reader, Exeter has become Exonbury and Oxford has become Christminster: fiction has changed the place-names of a region. Nevertheless, Hardy is preserving not changing the distinctive character of the land underfoot: he conserves in words the particulars of the landscape, such as an 'elbow' in a lane, and he uses the particular terms in which the land is locally described ('church-hay', 'ewe-leaze').

There is more involved in regional identity than topography and toponymy. A region is also its people. A region cannot be imagined without recognition of the inner world of its observers and residents. Hawker gathered ideas from the inhabitants of his remote rural parish. Baring-Gould braved the Dartmoor weather to gather folk-songs from labourers, and put the anecdotes he heard and the characters he met into his fictions. As the reader will discover, R.D. Blackmore partly derived the plot of *Lorna Doone* from some mysterious Wise Women of North Devon. Hardy's Wessex grows partly from his experience of listening to people. His landscape is filled with people and their stories. Conjurer Trendle, Serjeant Troy, the Tramp Woman and Henchard the hay-trusser are fictional figures with roots in folk memory. Reversing the role of the Dorsetshire landowner who moved an entire village in order to preserve his privacy and his view, the regional writer can ensure that the people are in the scene (Kay-Robinson 1972: 107). Regional fiction can enable the reader to understand that Nature may also be 'nurture', that the landscape is partly the product of centuries of human labour.

The critic and writer Phyllis Bentley stresses the realism rather than the romance of regional writing. For Bentley, this realism has a fundamentally democratic nature, being based on the principle that 'ordinary' men and women and their day to day labour are interesting (1941: 45). The regional writing surveyed in this book is at its most challenging when it sets out, not only to trace the contours of the land, and to capture the spirit of the place, but when it tries to capture the spirit of the people who live and work in a particular area. While the writers surveyed vary in their ability to cross class barriers, sometimes patronizing or failing to empathize with their working-class figures, the literary image of the West attempts to be inclusive. The literary West Country would be seriously depopulated if one removed all its yeoman farmers, artisans and servants. The West Country workers in the fiction of Baring-Gould and Hardy include the tenant, the day labourer and the vagrant, as well as the skilled artisan or copy-holder whose family retains ownership of a house for three generations. The hero of the West Country regional novel is more likely to be a Jan Ridd than an aristocratic Doone, to be a craftsman or a farmer than a Lord.

I hope that this book's focus on the local specifics of a region illustrates an attitude of mind that is also of relevance to the wider world, a world that can still benefit from being viewed in terms of regions. John Cowper Powys not only thought *about* his part of the West Country, he thought *with* it:

> every aspect of the Weymouth coast sunk into my mind with such transubstantiating magic that . . . when I think now of certain things I think *with* St. John's spire and the Nothe, and the old Backwater, and the Harbour Bridge, and the stone groins, and the green pier-posts, and the dead seaweed and the windrow-flotsam, and the stranded star-fish! Yes, it is through the medium of these things that I envisage all of the experiences of my life. . . . (Powys 1967: 151)

The place-names here may mean less to those who do not know this landscape than to those who do, but this passage conveys something of the inspiration of a common territory: the territory of childhood, with its infinite possibility of hope and adventure. This is also a landscape worth mature reflection. The subtleties of relationship between the landscape (Nothe fort, the chalk cliff called the White Nothe) and man-made buildings (the church, the pier), the signs of the border territory where the sea meets the land, and the human meets the elements (seaweed, flotsam): here is a pattern provided by a region, a pattern of solid objects that can inspire solid ideas. It enabled Powys to order his thoughts and interpret his life. Others, whatever their regions and locations, can follow Powys' example, ensuring that the territory of the mind pays the territory underfoot the respect and attention that is its due.

# 1

# The West Country on the Map
# and in the Mind

*We learn to see a thing by learning to describe it.*
Raymond Williams, *The Long Revolution*

*These people could see nothing in 'The Farmer's Wife' because it was rustic,
and dealt with a life of which they knew nothing and for which they cared
nothing. . . . No place . . . is more provincial than the West End.*
Arnold Bennett on the London reception
of a play by Eden Phillpotts, 1924

## Words and Picture-Writing

George Eliot argues that the 'subtle symbolism' of language creates a
'picture-writing of the mind'. If we could see into the minds of
readers and listeners, implies Eliot, we would find that certain words
consistently conjure up certain pictures. However, Eliot is more
concerned to show that the same word may create very different
images, according to the experience and outlook of the word's
receiver. The single word 'railway', she argues, conjures up for the
traveller of 1856 attractive images of a Bradshaw guide and a local
train station. The same word will mean very different things to the
'navvy' who builds the railway, the engineer who designs the engines,
the shareholder who owns the railway and the landowner who accepts
payment for allowing the train to cross his land (Byatt 1990: 107).
What kind of picture-writing, for what kind of readers, is created
by the following words and their sometimes overlapping fields of

meaning: peasant, rustic, Hodge, rural, native, agitator, country, provincial, parochial, regional, dialect, accent? The argument of this book is not only concerned with the individual meanings of these words but with the fact that groups of these terms often appear in association with each other: they are part of the ready-made, already-bolted-together language of cliché. A visitor to Britain in 1852 relied on this ready-to-hand language of cliché when he referred casually, as if the phrase did not need debate, to the 'barbarian Welsh peasant' (Tuckerman 1982: 107). An English commentator of 1838 used this type of language to construct a stereotype of the rural labourer: 'the clod-hopper . . . the hawbuck, the hind, the Johnny-raw, or by whatever name, in whatever district he may be called, is everywhere the same . . .' (Howitt 1838, Vol. 1: 157–58). This person is there to serve you (a hind) but can only do so within limits: this person is clumsy and dirty (a clodhopper), a bumpkin or oaf (a hawbuck), a mere beginner (Johnny-raw). By 1851 these terms or others like them were being used to represent over a million rural labourers and 364,000 farm servants in Britain (Harrison 1984: 60). There are no human individuals visible in this language. As George Orwell warns us in his well known essay 'Politics and the English Language', such names and ready-made phrases deaden perception of contradictions and subtle gradations of difference, those tangible realities encountered when we really grapple with the process of living and working in a particular landscape.

Consider the implied status, within texts written during the Victorian and Edwardian periods, of the 'boorish peasant', the person whose views are 'parochial' or who has a 'provincial' cast of mind. 'Dialect', once used to describe a language, gathers momentum during the eighteenth and nineteenth centuries as a word to describe an inferior way of speaking. A dialect then loses the status of a language and becomes subordinate to an abstraction called 'Standard English' (Williams 1988: 105–6, 231–32). To speak in dialect was to use 'provincialisms', a word that also carries a sense of inferiority to centralized good taste. When Margaret Hale, the heroine of Mrs Gaskell's novel *North and South* (1854–55), moves from the civilized south to the manufacturing town of Milton Northern, she is warned to preserve her southern way of speaking: 'Margaret don't get to use these horrid Milton words. "Slack of work:" it is a provincialism' (Chapter 29). Some soul-searching about intended audiences underlies the changing titles of William Barnes' verse: his first major collection was boldly entitled *Poems of Rural Life in the Dorset Dialect* (1844); his second collection was more carefully offered to the public as *Poems Partly of Rural Life in National English* (1846). To be even 'partly' 'rural' might be perceived as in conflict with a demanding and homogenizing 'national' identity. Both political radicals and genteel people can agree on the use of 'rural' as a term of disparagement. The 1888 Preface to the *Communist Manifesto* assumes that urban living is necessary to rescue the masses from 'the idiocy of rural life'; the popular novelist Eliza Braddon captures the tones of a certain genteel attitude to the term 'rural' in the following phrase: 'Perhaps to keep company—odious phrase—with some rural swain!' (Braddon 1876, Vol. 2: 14).

'Country', as readers of Raymond Williams' seminal work will know, occupies a particularly wide range of conflicting meanings. 'Country' can appear in a heroic light as the unifier of many interests, a term used to indicate a 'nation' or all of the people. To meet a 'fellow country-man' abroad is to recognize a national and common identity. 'Countryside', for many tourists, carries associations of 'rural' bliss and picturesque views, although it too can be used as term for all the people in a rural area (Williams 1985: 1–8; Williams 1988: 81–82). Such people may possess a distinctive character, which is both a fascination and a threat. In 1866 Parson Hawker of North Cornwall describes those of his parishioners who collude with wrecking and smuggling as an 'active and diligent "country-side" '. He thinks his use of the term important enough to explain: it was the 'name allotted to that chosen troop of native sympathisers' who were prepared to cheat the Customs men (Hawker 1893: 95).

Add the term 'bumpkin' to 'country', and it joins a whole family of abusive, patronizing or generalizing terms from the past and present: the 'country cousin', the 'local yokel', the 'rustic', the 'clodhopper', the 'churl', 'Hodge'. These are innocent, ignorant, clumsy characters who cannot behave 'properly' or speak 'proper' English, and can be manipulated by the sophisticated person from the city. ('Bumpkin' may derive from a Dutch word for a little barrel or a little tree: was it transferred from an object to a country person perceived as being as insensible as a tree or as having clumsy movements and a squat figure?)

Underlying the nineteenth-century stereotype of the countryman are human beings who work with their hands so that others may keep their hands clean; these verbal fields of meaning have a relationship

3

with workers in the fields. The 'clodhopper' is one who works with clods of earth. The idea of the clumsy, stupid countryman arises partly from city prejudice misinterpreting an observable reality. Accurate chroniclers of rural life, such as Richard Jefferies of Wiltshire (1848–87), knew that some rural labourers developed a rolling gait because the act of ploughing a field permanently deformed their natural stride. Children wearing heavy boots and labouring on clayey soils grew up with a different gait to the 'man about town' (Looker 1966: 240). The caricature of physical characteristics was combined with assumptions about the rural labourer's mental state. Joseph Arch of Warwickshire (1826–1919), founder of the Agricultural Workers' Union, explains in 1897–98 how the silent countryman was assumed to be stupid or 'boorish':

> If I had been a weak and fearful man, like scores of my class, I might have got lock-jaw when in the presence of my 'betters' . . . The timid labourer did, and his masters thought that he was so dull and slow that he had next to no wits, and so had nothing to say. . . . A man with the weight of many masters upon him learns how to be dumb, and deaf, and blind, at a very early hour in the morning.

Arch suggests how the countryman perceived as a Shakespearean clown was at less risk than a figure who stood up for his rights: 'The peasant might mop and mow before his lord like a monkey, but he stood up as a man at his peril' (Arch 1983: 80, 147).

It is educational to contrast Arch's perspective with George Eliot's. In her essay of 1856 ('The Natural History of German Life'), Eliot shrewdly penetrated idealizations of country poverty. She is convincing in her satire of pastoral imagery:

> The painter is still under the influence of idyllic literature, which has always expressed the imagination of the cultivated and town-bred, rather than the truth of rustic life. Idyllic ploughmen are jocund when they drive their team afield; idyllic shepherds make bashful love under hawthorn bushes; idyllic villagers dance in the chequered shade and refresh themselves, not immoderately, with spicy nut-brown ale.

Eliot is less convincing when she tries to construct the real human being beneath these clichés:

> But no one who has seen much of actual ploughmen thinks them jocund; no one who is well acquainted with the English peasantry can pronounce them merry. The slow gaze in which no sense of beauty beams, no humour twinkles,–the slow utterance and the heavy slouching walk, remind one rather of that melancholy animal the camel . . .

Eliot continues by seeing through the Stage Rustic only to perpetuate that familiar fiction, the countryman who cannot speak 'proper' English and behaves 'improperly':

> The conventional countryman of the stage, who picks up pocket books and never looks into them, and who is too simple even to know that honesty has its opposite, represents the still lingering mistake, that an unintelligible dialect is a guarantee for ingenuousness, and that slouching shoulders indicate an upright disposition.

Eliot avoids the sentimentality of the idealizers of rural life, but then adopts the position of the 'superior person'. Her real countryman is a less than human beast of burden given the predictable signs of inferiority: drunkenness, uncivilized speech and ape-like posture. With one eye on Coleridge's Romantic credo and another on her idea of reality, Eliot pronounces: 'the only realm of fancy and imagination for the English clown exists at the bottom of the third quart pot' (Byatt 1990: 109). Arch interprets all these signs differently: for him, his fellow-workers clown in order to survive, walk in a particular way because their labour has shaped them, pretend to be slow because it is prudent to do so, and have their own legitimate dreams of a better life. Arch disapproves of the labourer's drunkenness as much as Eliot does, but he understands the poverty and desperation which give rise to this problem. Arch does, however, prove Eliot's theory of 'picture-writing' to be correct: the same words can conjure up very different pictures for those 'outside' and those 'inside' the subject they describe.

Regional and rural writers cannot write without becoming tangled in a web of words with mainly pejorative associations. Their choices of expression are limited by the language they inherit. However, one of the fascinations of reading rural and regional writing is that it tests the conventional meanings of these words in various ways, uncovering hidden and suppressed possibilities. Regional writers can accept the conventional words obediently; they can accept them yet undermine them; they can propose alternatives; they can try and rescue the words from their pejorative meanings.

A typical note of obedience can be heard in a story of Welsh life first published in 1828 and republished up to 1873: it was introduced to an English public with the phrase: 'this unpretending little provincial production' (Prichard 1873: 5). Parson Hawker, writing in the 1860s, is fiercely loyal to his Cornish territory but leans towards the values of the dominant discourse when he describes it as a place of 'semi-barbarous life' which may be of interest to 'the reader of a more refined and civilised region' (Hawker 1893: 36, 95). More unusual in this context are the pronouncements made by the young and idealistic Samuel Taylor Coleridge while seeking Utopia in the West Country. He defied and ignored the pejorative aspects of his chosen words when he declared in 1796 that his children would be given a West Country childhood: 'bred up from earliest infancy in the simplicity of peasants, their food, dress and habits completely rustic' (Griggs 1956, Vol. 1: 240). Some writers make concessions to central good taste while they admit to the fascinations of the peripheral. N.T. Carrington, attempting to make the despised region of Dartmoor admired, claimed that he learned about the value of his chosen territory by listening to the rural speech of 'the half-savage peasant' (Carrington 1826: 9). Richard Jefferies accepts the language of the 'urbane' even when pleading the countryman's case in 1889: 'I think there is a great deal yet to be discovered by the diligent observation of localities. The experience of the rudest country rustic is not to be despised; and an observation is an observation, whoever makes it . . .' (Jefferies 1948: 200). R.D. Blackmore, on the other hand, sometimes undermines accepted words through an implied tone and an ironic context. When Jan Ridd, the hero of *Lorna Doone* (1869) refers to 'we clods of Exmoor' (Chapter 4), the reader is invited to see through the term to a human reality underlying it.

Jefferies uses the term 'Hodge' without undermining it, although he can portray labourers as individuals. Hardy specifically sets out to challenge the use of the word 'Hodge'; and in his fictions often makes us see an individual Henchard rather than a stereotypical Hodge. His

6

poem about 'Drummer Hodge' (1899) succeeds in humanizing a stereotype. When Hardy refers to 'workfolk', he is describing hard-working members of his community with a local word free of the associations of 'Hodge', or 'peasant'. According to Hardy, 'workfolk' is the word that these individuals might choose to describe them-selves. He perfectly expresses the tensions between the available choice of terms in his comment about the characters in *Far From the Madding Crowd* (1874): Hardy hoped that 'the rustics, although *quaint*, may be made to appear intelligent, and not boorish at all' (F. Hardy 1986: 97, 313). When Hardy chooses to entitle a novel *The Return of the Native* in 1877, and to make his 'native' hero more sympathetic, dignified and morally upright than some of the out-siders in the local community portrayed, he is ambitiously valuing a potentially negative word. The 'play' in the meaning of 'native' as noun or adjective indicates the complexities of a large field of meaning: to use your native wit, to speak a language as well as a native, to say like Walter Scott 'This is my own, my native land', is to be acceptable or admirable from a central perspective. Yet in the word can still be heard the resonance of the European colonist who calls the indigenous population of another country 'natives', and worries when they are 'restless'.

It is short step in language and thought from 'restless' to 'social unrest', to the idea that 'native sympathisers' were law–breakers, that the rural labourer could become an 'agitator'. Defying the dominant discourse, Arch tried to welcome this latter word and turn it into an accolade: 'Of course I was called an agitator; so I was, because everyone who stirs up people to do things is an agitator, but those who so named me attached a bad meaning to the word' (Arch 1986: 121). When Jefferies was seeking a publisher for his work on rural matters in the 1870s, he felt compelled to distance himself from the rural 'agitator':

> Political matters will be strictly excluded—no bias will be shown on either side . . . Owner, tenant, labourer, clergyman, tinker, gypsy—all will be described just as they are. Nothing of an immoral or unpleasant nature will be mentioned . . . there will be nothing in the book that might not be read aloud in the drawing room. (Looker 1966: 237)

In this context, Hardy's use of 'native' in a book title is brave, as his attempt to rescue the word 'provincial' from the pejorative meaning attributed to it by Matthew Arnold and other influential persons.

'Country' derives from the word 'contrata' meaning 'against'; 'country' or the 'provinces' can be understood as crude, blanket terms for everything *against* which a capital city can be defined. The provinces are merely there as background and not worth mapping in detail; or they are only valuable as a place of escape which enables you to return refreshed to the real business of city life. The land is not a place of work but a landscape to be enjoyed for its views before a return to reality. Within this field of meaning, 'region' occupies an interesting position as a site of contradictions. A region may be viewed both as a distinctive area with its own importance and as a definite part of a more important entity. 'Region' derives from the Latin *regere* meaning 'to direct' or 'to rule'. Consider 'the Roman governor . . . gave charge that Macedonia should be divided into four regions . . . ' (Williams 1988: 265). Similarly, 'province' derives from the Latin *provincia*, meaning 'conquered territory outside Italy but under Roman dominion'. Matthew Arnold thought that his contemporaries in the 1860s would be likely to say of a Welsh person: 'his land is a province, and his history petty' (Super 1973: 293). In these contexts, the region or province is a place to be mapped only in order to be conquered. If its distinctiveness is merely 'quaint', such an area is conquered by travellers, tourists and antiquarians. If its distinctiveness is powerful, if it creates a unity of place, speech and local beliefs, if it cannot be tamed and assimilated by the centre, it may need to be conquered in a more brutal sense. Regional identities can contribute to national identity but they must not rival it. The *Manchester Guardian* of 1881 refers to 'that unfortunate regionalism of Italy'. The idea that a region must be subordinate to a centre is still implicit within attempts at devolution: 'devolution' derives from *devolvere* or 'to roll *down*'. 'Handing down' happens between superiors and inferiors; 'power-sharing' requires equal partners (Williams 1988: 81, 264–66).

There are, however, approbatory meanings for 'region' and 'region-alism', especially within the twentieth century. The person with a 'regional accent' and 'parochial' attitudes is suspected of being blind to the wider world; the 'regionalist' writer or critic wants the wider world to notice the many worlds of which it is constituted. In fact, the regionalist finds the dichotomy between the wider world and the parochial to be false: the wide world only exists because it is made of little worlds. 'Standard English' is a fiction: there are only the many 'Englishes' actually spoken. The regionalist argues that there are valuable, distinctive ways of life which may not be understood from a distant centre. For the child Dylan Thomas, growing up in Wales after the First World War, the whole of England was perceived as London. London is often at the centre of the British cultural mind, although a map reminds us of its true location in the south east of the country. Distance from London in nineteenth-century Britain can be measured in three related ways: in terms of miles, in terms of time and in terms of social class. Parson Hawker claimed in 1862 that for every 100 miles you lived from London, you travelled back a hundred years in time. Morwenstow was 250 miles from the capital and therefore existed in 'the year 1610 in all that relates to agriculture and civilisation'. (Byles 1906: 361–62).

Raymond Williams has argued that the romantic type of regional novel was part of a flight from central social questions (Williams 1985: 253). This is persuasive if we consider the regions as many steps behind the social vanguard, reflecting the class prejudice of the past rather than the human values of a 'democratic' future. It is, however, possible to cast doubt on the present with the aid of the past, and past problems may remain unsolved into the present. Elsewhere, Williams shows that regionalism need not be escapist, that it can confront the issues of class, giving a voice to those excluded from central and dominant discourse. Consider the implications of Williams' searching question: how far do you have to leave London before you enter the provinces or the regions? As he points out, a novel set in Cornwall is 'regional', while a novel set within London, or in the 'Home Counties' near London, is not. He speculates that the term 'Home Counties' owes its existence to the 'Home Circuit' of a judge who organizes the administration of justice within a specified region (Williams 1988: 265–66). He also shows, however, that 'home' is being defined from the London perspective; the twentieth-century reader may add, that 'county' is also a term that slides between geographical location and class associations. The title of Hardy's remarkable story, 'On the Western Circuit' (1891), serves as a reminder of the distinctive nature of his choice of location for his fictions, both in terms of geographical regions and regions of class. He administers poetic justice on a 'circuit' that includes the views of the dispossessed.

Improvements in transport brought the regions closer to London: in 1760 it took three days to reach the South West from London; in 1830 it took one day (Daiches 1979: 179). The migration of labour from country to towns aided by the railways, a process witnessed with some regret by Hardy and Baring-Gould, both broke down regional identity and created opportunities for people to discover their own region by contrast with others. The extraordinarily rapid growth of the railway network during the 1840s increased participation in travel and the speed with which the urban could learn about the rural and vice versa. But how far did this process really result in detailed understanding of regions and capital, how far did it penetrate the walls of class that divided the rural 'workfolk' from the city manufacturer as much as geographical location? Regional writing is one way of exploring answers to this question.

The long debate around these related words and their meanings was especially active during the mid-nineteenth century. In 1865 an article entitled 'Provincialism' appeared in *The Cornhill Magazine*. The literary critic David Masson had already noted the growth of the provincial novel in 1859, and Matthew Arnold had questioned the validity of provincial attitudes in 1864, arguing that the nation suffered from the lack of an Academy of Letters on the French model. The *Cornhill* writer begins with a reference to the increasing 'use of the words "provincial" and "provincialisms" in our popular literature . . .'. This writer is a little drawn to the fascinations of the foreign within his own country, to the idea that 'remote' locations have a part to play in the national picture: 'It seems to us pleasant to think of Shakespeare retiring to Stratford . . . of Cowper at Olney, of Scott in his ancestral border district.' So writers have understandable loyalties to their native places and are permitted to 'retire' there. Also, although his writing is marked by a London perspective, the *Cornhill* author concedes in unconsciously patronizing tones: 'England has a score of little capitals—capitals in miniature—instead of a single big one. York was a capital for the North, Shrewsbury for Wales . . . Bath and Exeter for the West.' There was a time, according to this writer, when 'a man of the country . . . differed from a London man in a way rather piquant than otherwise. He had a stamp of his own about him which compensated, and often more than compensated, for his disadvantages.' So the regional character could be a picturesque part of the past but not a real force in the Victorian present. Throughout the remainder of the article, it is the disadvantages of the provincial that are stressed. Charles Kingsley regretted that his novel *Westward Ho!* had led to the creation of a seaside resort to please the 'cockney' visitor: he respected the rural local, not the city local. The *Cornhill* writer disagrees. For him, 'Provincialism' and 'cockneyism' are equated: they each describe, whether in country or city, the *'local man*, the man all whose prejudices are bred in him by the place, and who measures everything by the place's standard . . .'. Despite this admission that the Londoner can be as prejudiced as the provincial, the argument mainly finds prejudice outside the capital, in the small town and the rural area. Most revealing of all is the writer's distinction between the 'provinces' and the 'counties': 'the very word *counties* retains a dignity which the word *provinces* lacks. There is a fine historical smack about it . . . The county feeling which made Speke proud of being a Somersetshire man, which makes a Devonshire man glory in Raleigh, a Northumberland man in Collingwood, and a Norfolk man in Nelson, is not provincialism' (Anon. 1865: 673–75, 681). Clearly, what allows points west and north recognition on the national compass is the fact that they contain the birthplaces of those who loyally serve the nation as warriors and explorers. The 'counties' contain great men. The 'provinces', on the other hand, may contain troublemakers, eccentrics or dangerously ignorant people.

Arnold's exploration of literary style in 1864 is also hostile to the possibility of a provincial or regional viewpoint. The 'note of provinciality' is 'caused by remoteness from a centre of correct information' and 'correct taste'. It should be contrasted with the superior 'prose of the centre', with 'urbanity, the tone of the city, of the centre'. The 'provincial spirit . . . exaggerates the value of its ideas, for want of a high standard at hand by which to try them' (Super 1973: 245–46, 249). This is to conflate the spatial sense with a sense of values: the urbane, urban person, looks down from the centre on the peripheral, suburban and rural man. If the provincial can succeed, he can only do it with the help of London urbanity. Alphonse Esquiros, writing in the same year as the *Cornhill* article, found that even in remote Cornwall the presence of London as a cultural ideal was inescapable:

> There are classes, I allow, but no distances. The gentleman is the
> same from one end of Great Britain to another . . ., instead of
> going to London, he attracts London to his house. To do this he

receives new books, the reviews and papers. . . . (Esquiros 1865: 26)

Arnold and the Cornhill writer use the terms 'provincial' and 'provincialism' in powerfully pejorative ways. Even the proudly local Parson Hawker accepts the terms of the national debate in 1866 when he contrasts 'the provincial mind' with 'the intellect of cities' (Hawker 1893: 87).

However, Arnoldian influence did not succeed in silencing alternative meanings of 'provincial'. There were many writers from various parts of Britain who did not comply with the central perspective. While John Ruskin and George Eliot criticized idealized representations of rural life by artists and writers, the literary critic David Masson thought that some novelists succeeded in escaping from a superior London outlook on values and language. In 1859 he approvingly noted: 'the representations of previously unexplored tracts of provincial English scenery and life in the novels of Miss Brontë, Mrs Gaskell, Miss Mulock and others' and 'the minute speciality with which these novels [sic] physiognomies and places are described; the range which they take among the different professions, crafts and classes of society, as each possessing its peculiar habits and cast of thinking; and the use in them all, when occasion serves, of the local dialect or of racy provincialisms' (Masson 1859: 259). Miss Mulock (Dinah Craik) is not much remembered today but her novel *John Halifax, Gentleman* (1856) became a Victorian best seller, partly due to its successful evocation of a Gloucester country town. The Brontës, Gaskell, and later writers with a strong sense of place such as George Eliot, Hardy and Bennett, need no introduction: their work is proof that provincial settings can attain universal interest. George Eliot maintained the tradition noted by Masson when she openly subtitled *Middlemarch* 'A Study of Provincial Life' (1871–72). The novel explores an evolving 'provincial society' where 'municipal town and rural parish gradually made fresh threads of connection' (Book 1, Chapter 9); Eliot and her readers found this world just as complex and absorbing as London life to its admirers. Hardy, writing from a more exclusively rural perspective than Eliot, specifically rejected Arnold's argument: 'Arnold is wrong about provincialism . . . A certain provincialism of feeling is invaluable. It is the essence of individuality, and is largely made up of that crude enthusiasm without which no great thoughts are thought, no great deeds done'

(F. Hardy 1986: 146–47). 'Crude' is a concession to the superior, urbane view of the clumsy countryman: everything else here is an attempt to protect and justify the individuality of regional life. Hardy also suggests that what is at issue is not the pettiness of provincial life with its associations of small town gossip; on the contrary, it is in the provinces that you find the 'feeling' and 'individuality' which inspire great thoughts and deeds. This is a clue to Hardy's combination of regional manners with Greek tragedy. That Hardy the rural novelist should identify with the defence of the 'provincial' raises interesting questions. Some critics have stressed differences between the meanings of 'rural', 'provincial' and 'regional' (Keith 1988: 11; Wiener 1993: 42). The evidence explored here suggests that they can also be usefully considered as separate but related terms. They work in the context of a picture-writing of the mind that forms an inaccurate image of life outside of London.

### Compass points: *Where* is the West Country?

Many of the words used to describe outer landscapes are also used to describe inner ones. There is a 'terrain' the walker knows and a 'terrain' which is an area of knowledge. There are 'regions' of countryside and 'regions' of imagination, 'provinces' on the map and 'provinces' of specialist knowledge, 'tracts' of land and 'tracts' of words, 'fields' for labourers and 'fields' of meaning, a 'topography' outside the mind and a 'topography' within it. The latter term, combining *topos* 'place' with *graphé* 'writing', can be used to suggest how a landscape, once recorded in words, combines solid geo-graphical features with interpretation and a textual presence. William Barnes, the Dorset poet, proposed the word 'placewrit' as a Saxon and West Country alternative to 'topography' (Barnes 1830: 395). All these words face both ways: towards the territory we can touch and see and towards the mind with which we respond to that territory. Where do we place the 'West Country' on the map and in the mind, amongst these fields of meaning? What kind of 'picture-writing' does it create in the mind's eye?

If everyone had always agreed with *The Cornhill Magazine* that Britain should best be perceived as divided into counties, a region of the West subsuming counties would never have gained popular currency. There are, however, many potential conflicts covered by the term 'West Country'. As George Eliot's theory of picture-writing prepares us to understand, it means different things to different people in Britain. From the perspective of a native of Cornwall, with its claim to a language and a national identity (to be a country not a county), the 'West' can be perceived as a threat to local identity. Writers such as Sabine Baring-Gould and Charles Kingsley saw no such conflict, and happily joined Cornwall and Devon together in a united region. From the perspective of a native of Gloucester, it may be useful to regard the West as home territory and the peninsula (including Cornwall, Devon and parts of Somerset and Dorset) as the South West. Modern geologists, guided by an understanding of the underlying forces that shape landscapes, and 'bio-regionalists', who wish to preserve 'natural' boundaries, can also see the South West peninsula as a separate region. For Charles Kingsley, the 'West Country' described a territory that mainly consisted of the South-West peninsula. When he referred affectionately to the people of the peninsula as 'those of dear old "Down-along"', he was mapping the shape of the West and linking location in space with cultural identity (Kingsley 1871: 371). 'Down' from the capital and 'along' a neck of land that is surrounded by sea, this West can be perceived as almost an island within the island of Britain. Other writers agree that the peninsula must be accepted as essential to the West Country but extend its borders remarkably far to the east. Edward Thomas stretched it as far as Wiltshire in 1907; Thomas Hughes thought that his novel set in Berkshire should be of special interest to 'west-countrymen' in 1857 (*The Scouring of the White Horse*, Hughes 1892: 19); Thomas Hardy, rooted in central Dorset, orientated himself accordingly: 'citizens dream of the south and west/And so do I' (see his poem 'Weathers'). He did, however, adopt North Cornwall as the territory for many of his poems, prided himself on knowing 'West-country life' and was firm in his belief that he shared a distinctive 'West of England' consciousness with R.D. Blackmore, the writer of *Lorna Doone*, a book rooted in Exmoor, Devon and Somerset (F. Hardy 1986: 56; Purdy 1978, Vol. 1: 37–38). The 'Wessex' described by Hardy, Barnes and others extends the original territory of the *West* Saxons to rival the concept of the West Country.

It is certainly evident that for some observers, the West Country of uncertain borders on the map is connected with a firmly delineated, internal, emotional territory. For some twentieth-century writers, it is the peninsular qualities of a South West that inspire the imagination. John Fowles explains that the compass of his emotions is firmly set South West, towards 'those two counties whose lifeblood has always been the sea, and who point, like a massive arm bicepped by Devon, forefingered by the Land's End peninsula, to some secret centre further south-west still' (Fowles 1978: 1). Prior to choosing to live and work with fishermen of the West Country in 1907, Stephen Reynolds was lured by the prospect of his chosen territory as a projection into a wider world: ' "And stepping westward seemed to be/A kind of *heavenly* destiny". That's the real feeling at the back of my mind. *I want* to go west, towards the sunset; over Dartmoor towards Land's End, where the departing ships go down into the sea.' Reynolds adapts Wordsworth's lines on travelling westward in Scotland to express his own idealization of Devon and Cornwall (Reynolds 1911: 8). He was following the example of Wilkie Collins and Dinah Craik in romanticizing the point where the land of Britain ends and the ocean begins. Edward Thomas, writing in 1909, also finds that promontories such as Land's End, whether in the West of England or West Wales, inspire verbal pictures:

> looking at a map of Britain, the West calls, out of Wiltshire and out of Cornwall and Devon beyond . . . Westward for men of this island, lies the sea . . . In a mere map the west of Britain is fascinating. The great features of that map, which make it something more than a picture to be imperfectly copied by laborious childish pens, are the great promontories of Caernarvon, of Pembroke, of Gower and of Cornwall, jutting out into the western sea, like the features of a great large face, such a face as is carved on a ship's prow. These protruding features, even on a small-scale map, thrill the mind with a sense of purpose and spirit. They yearn, they peer out ever to the sea, as if using eyes and nostrils to savour the utmost scent of it, as if themselves calling back to the call of the waves. To the eyes of a child they stand for adventure. (Thomas 1932: 8–9)

Memories of childhood, echoes of the Age of Discovery, visions of Empire, all combine to create this emotional compass and imaginative map.

It is Charles Kingsley (1819–75) who provides the most emotional of all the responses to the West. Here is a glimpse of the picture-writing in Kingsley's mind: 'The thought of the West Country will make me burst into tears at any moment. Wherever I am it always hangs before my fancy as *home*, and I feel myself a stranger and a sojourner in a foreign land the moment I get east of Taunton Dean, on the Mendips. It may be fancy, but it is most real, and practical, as many fancies are' (F. Kingsley 1891, Vol. 1: 3). The 'bio-regionalist' looks for a massive landscape feature such as a canyon or a river to mark a border: Kingsley has an internal equivalent of this, a psychological fissure between the West and the world, a fancy that is powerful enough to seem real. Kingsley was born at Holne on Dartmoor and although he left there while still a baby, liked to think that this locality had somehow influenced his character. More important to him still were the school days that he experienced in Cornwall, and his memories of Clovelly and Bideford on the North Devon coast. He expresses affection not only for these places but also for their people, claiming to participate and rejoice in the dialect that others despised. He wrote to his wife in 1843, conflating the voices of the Cornish and the Devonians:

> You must love these Cornish men! They are the noblest men in England—strong, simple-hearted, united, working—'One and all,' is their motto. Glorious West Country! . . . You must not despise their accent, for it is the remains of a purer and nobler dialect than our own, and you will be surprised to hear me when I am merry, burst into pure unintelligible Devonshire; when I am very childish, my own country's language comes to me like a dream of old days! (F. Kingsley 1891, Vol. 1: 71–72)

These emotional concepts of place owe much to personal childhood loyalties, tangled with notions of both local identity and national mission; they still retain a link to the map, the terrain, and the people who live and work in it.

## Compass points: *When* is there a West Country?

As I write this in the year 2000 it is possible to go shopping at 'West Country Computers', to watch the 'Westcountry' television news, to go to hospital with the help of 'West Country Ambulances', to visit 'West Country Inns', to plan a holiday with the 'West Country Tourist Board', to buy numerous 'West Country' guide books and to visit a library in Exeter devoted to 'Westcountry Studies'. This geographical term, with its romantic resonance, was not always so pervasive. Travellers and diarists in the South West from the seventeenth century onwards referred more prosaically to the 'Western Counties' or the 'West of England'. For some readers at this period 'West of England' conjured up an image, not of romance, but of woollen broadcloth. The use of the term 'West countrie' to describe the South-West region is at least as early as 1576; the idea that this region has distinctive inhabitants, speaking their own dialect, who are nevertheless loyal to their nation, partly originates in the sixteenth and seventeenth centuries when a national navy and national survival partly depended on West of England sailors and adventurers. Consider the mythology surrounding Walter Raleigh of Devon and Dorset, whom John Aubrey describes as a companion of the 'learnedest and politest persons' but as speaking in a rural accent 'to his dying day' (Clark 1898, Vol. 2: 182). Similar picture-writing is suggested by the representation of the West Country and rural life in the pageants before the Lord Mayor of London from 1678 to 1690. These pageants contained a song referring to the 'dreadful name of Drake' and his glorious part in the defeat of the Armada in 1588 as well as a 'West-Countrymon's Song' sung in a rural accent. The 1690 pageant included a reference to: 'zome honest plain West-Country-mon' (Jordan 1678: 3, 16; 1683: 6 and the OED). The creation of the nineteenth-century West as a specifically literary and romantic region dates from Parson Hawker's 'The Song of the Western Men' (1826) and his desire that the pages of his books of poetry should be turned by a 'Western hand', by a reader who knew the landscapes concerned. His work was followed by a long series of fictions by would-be novelists with titles or subtitles such as 'A Romance of the West', 'By the Western Sea' and 'Tales of the Western Moors', produced between the 1840s and the 1890s. Charles Kingsley was probably the most active promoter of a West of England literary consciousness, referring to Hawker as the 'West Country Poet' in 1849 and to distinctive 'West-country ways' in 1865 (F. Kingsley 1891, Vol. 1: 170; C. Kingsley 1892: 79). *Westward Ho!*, Kingsley's novel of 1855 firmly set in North Devon and Cornwall, was so popular that its title was given to a newly created Devon seaside resort in 1863. R.D. Blackmore's bestseller, *Lorna Doone: A Romance of Exmoor*, turned Devon and Somerset into the West Country for readers at home and abroad from 1870 onwards. Despite influential mid-century warnings against the dangers of 'provincialism', the literary celebration of a rural West continued to grow.

Following the popular success of Kingsley and Blackmore, 'West Country consciousness' reached a high point in the late Victorian, early Edwardian era. Hardy published his early Dorset novels and his Cornish or 'Off-Wessex' novel *A Pair of Blue Eyes* during the 1870s. In 1875 an anthology of verse celebrating 'the poetic mind of the West' was published under the title *The West Country Garland* (Worth 1875: 4). In 1881–82 *The Western Antiquary* was founded, a periodical dedicated to the history and culture of its region. William Borlase introduced the publication with a series of gestures typical of the period. There is the gesture of sentimental pride in home territory: 'this little Western world of ours'. There is the gesture of wonder at the incomplete record of an ancient past that lends itself to imaginative speculation: 'the old Danmonian promontory'. There is the grand gesture, combining history, romance and speculation: Borlase's theory that the South West has a separate destiny and character because of its peninsula, its Celtic inheritance and its mineral wealth. Borlase refers to the 'history of the West Country' as if there is no doubt as to its boundaries and existence (Borlase 1882, Vol. 1: 5–7). Borlase's certainty is reflected in the output of fiction writers. A computer analysis of the 50,326 records in Exeter's Westcountry Studies Library shows that the term 'West Country' and its variations appear most frequently in book titles from the 1880s onwards (Maxted 1998). The accumulated impact of the literary West on the national consciousness by the last decade of the century is indicated by a review of Hardy's work: 'Only Charles Kingsley and Mr Blackmore have rivalled . . . him in bringing that beautiful West Country home to us' (Morris 1892: 219). Kingsley, Blackmore and Hardy were joined by Sabine Baring-Gould, J. Meade Faulkner, Eden Phillpotts and George Gissing, writers who celebrated West Country ways or landscapes in the 1890s and early 1900s.

## Compass points: *Why* is there a West Country?

Why does the term 'West Country' become influential in the nineteenth century? Prior to 1750, there were periods when the West was amongst the most populous and industrialized regions in Britain. After 1750, a gradually declining cloth industry and a lack of coal and iron created a different kind of region, one with some industrial activity, but with two other main sources of employment: agriculture and services, including a growing tourist trade (Havinden 1991: 13, 17). Perceived selectively from the outside, particularly in the railway age from the 1840s onwards, the West was a place for city folk seeking rural solace, painters seeking views and writers seeking plots for romantic fictions. The argument, however, is more complicated than this brief sketch suggests.

Some clues to the mid-Victorian perception of the West can be found in the response to Mrs Gaskell's *North and South* (1859). Mrs Gaskell partially complicates the simple division suggested by her novel's title, but her demarcation was and is a powerful influence. A French reviewer accepted Gaskell's dichotomy between an industrial North and a rural South:

> In the southern counties old English life still remains: there are the monuments and memorials; there lives the agricultural population, submissive for long ages, trained by the aristocracy; there, the *gentleman* still has complete power; the *clergyman* is still honoured . . . It is the land where the soul of old England lives with its mixture of liberalism and aristocracy, it is the country of moderate minds, monarchists and Anglicans . . . —Anglo-Norman England in a word.

In the North, by contrast, can be found:

> complete Saxons, undaunted by the aristocracy and by the moral force of the educated classes, bold, vigorous, pugnacious, anarchic; without intellectual and irrelevant culture, having great practical sense . . . No old towns with historic memories; only towns, completely new . . . instead of upper classes, hardy middle classes . . . The doctrines current in this region are no longer clever liberal theories but radicalism in all its force, —American style democracy amongst the middle classes and the masters, socialist leanings amongst the working mass . . . There, also, the Anglican church is less powerful than in the south, and dissenters more numerous. (Easson 1991: 356–57)

The West Country may seem best perceived as just another part of the South by these rather crude and generalizing measures. The West Country texts investigated in this book were mainly written by clergymen or the descendants of clergymen (consider Parson Hawker, the curate's son R.D. Blackmore, Canon Charles Kingsley, chaplain to Queen Victoria, the Squarson Baring-Gould, writer of 'Onward Christian Soldiers'). The literary and romantic West Country is usually presented as rural: it seldom admits to the industrial character of parts of the region. The figures of the enlightened squire and the obedient peasantry appear in these texts much more often than the figures of Dartmoor tin miners or Cornish mine captains and inventors. Many of the texts are pervaded by the sense that an aristocratic and chivalric past is present in the form of local gentry, feudal loyalties, ancient, abandoned ruins or old mansions still in use. It is therefore tempting to dismiss the literary West as a return to an idealized past, a refuge from an industrial and threateningly democratic present.

More careful inspection reveals, however, that the West as text and terrain does not fit this South so snugly. The West Country bears the marks not only of the Anglican but also of the Celtic Church: it was a stronghold of the religious dissent that the French commentary places in the North. In the terms of crude mid-century notions of racial inheritance, which this French writer shares with Matthew Arnold and Sabine Baring-Gould, the West does not fit the neat division between an Anglo-Norman South and a Saxon North. Insofar as the West is Wessex, it is connected with the territory of the West Saxons; insofar as its place-names and dialects reminded Victorians of a Celtic past, this West is neither Norman nor Saxon. Charles Kingsley celebrated the Celtic regions of the West, although he apparently followed Barnes in respecting the Saxon origins of Dorset dialect. Baring-Gould claimed that the peasants on the west side of Dartmoor were Celts while those on the east were Saxon. Barnes found Celtic influences as far east as Dorset. So, outside the terms of the French commentary, the West Country is perceived as both Saxon and Celtic, and by being Celtic it had links with the underdog, with the loser, with justice, that fugitive from the camp of the conquerors. Parson Hawker's Celtic and Cornish King Arthur belongs in this world. Edward Thomas was sensitive to it, seeing the West in 1909 as a region to which 'the conquered races of the world retreated, and their settlements give those corners a strangeness and charm to our fantastic sympathies' (Thomas 1932: 9).

The construction of this West can be partly understood in relation to the nineteenth-century construction of the Celt. The Victorian

Celt is very likely to be associated with all those pejorative terms linked with the rural: he is often 'savage' and 'barbaric'. While an English peasant is liable to be ignorant, a Celtic one is liable to be both ignorant and violent. This stereotype arises partly from the competition for labour between poor Irish and poor English, after the Irish famine of the 1840s. The violence of the Rebecca Riots in Wales during 1843, thought by some to be linked to Irish unrest, also played a part in making the Celt seem frightening. *The Economist* declared in 1848, that year of revolution: 'Thank God we are Saxons! Flanked by the savage Celt on the one side and the flighty Gaul on the other . . . we feel deeply grateful from our inmost hearts that we belong to a race, which if it cannot boast the flowing fancy of one of its neighbours, nor the brilliant *esprit* of the other has ample compensation in [a] social, slow, reflective, phlegmatic temperament' (Samuel 1998, Vol. 1: 60). A writer claiming expert knowledge of racial characteristics explained that in 'stature and weight' Celts were 'inferior to the Saxon . . .'. The Celts were 'treacherous', 'warlike', work-shy people who despised 'order', 'economy' and 'cleanliness'. On the other hand, paradoxically, they were 'gallant', 'brave' 'warm-hearted', 'full of deep sympathies'. They were 'dreamers on the past' whose sense of their past might threaten the present: 'It is fortunate for mankind that the Celtic race is . . . broken up into fragments' (Knox 1862: 319–22). The *Telegraph* explained in 1862 that the Saxon was qualified to conquer the globe, while the Celt belonged in the past: 'There is that old distinction between the Teuton and the Celt . . . Your Celt cannot colonise' (Samuel 1998, Vol. 1: 59). 'That is because we know how it feels to *be colonised*', the Celt might have replied. Matthew Arnold was less superior than The *Telegraph* but in the terms of *The Economist*, wanted to benefit from the poetic gifts of the Celts without conceding to the idea that they could form independent nations. Arnold's Celts could be trusted to entertain and assist a Saxon or Norman master only so long as their weaknesses were kept under control. Arnold's general view was that England's greatness arose from its ability to assimilate Norman clarity, Teuton industry and Celtic romance (Super 1973: 382–83). The West Country, part Saxon and part Celt, could play its part in this process of assimilation: a loyal Westcountry-man could appear, in the manner of Drake or Raleigh, to help the nation in time of crisis. This is a region far from the centre but not too far, now the railways were available; this is a region different enough to be interesting, without being thoroughly foreign. The West Country can be entertaining, a holiday from Saxon reality; the West Country can be charming as long as you do not mistake it for reality. Like the Celt, it is fine in its place. This is not the whole story. Something more is being smuggled into the national consciousness by the literary representation of the West Country. Some of the texts representing the West consist of a sugar of romance coating a bitter-tasting pill of reality. The writers of these texts cannot be blamed if readers ate the sugar and left the pill.

The loyal West Countryman in texts needs to be contrasted with the South West's actual history: the food riots, the tinners' claim to an independent Parliament, the attempts at rebellion or resistance (consider 'An Goff', the Duke of Monmouth and the Tolpuddle Martyrs). This history does leak into the image of the West Country as a rural romance. Charles Kingsley's work is particularly significant in the context of Celt and Saxon, North and South. He warned visitors to North Devon in 1849 that they were not among 'South Saxon clods, but among wits as keen and imaginations as rich as those of any Scotch shepherd or Manchester operative' (C. Kingsley 1891: 291). Kingsley stereotypes his South in the given, pejorative language about rural life, but he is more original in his presentation of the West Country. He links his chosen countrymen with the romance of Scott's highlanders but also with the sharp wit of the Manchester operatives represented in Mrs Gaskell's fiction. The French reviewer of *North and South* in 1859 pictured an obedient peasantry in the south of England. Kingsley agreed, but distinguished his West Country from this passive condition. Consider Tregarva, Kingsley's fictional portrait of a Cornishman in *Yeast* (1848). Tregarva combines an inherited 'Celtic' character with modern Chartist sympathies. He comments harshly on the southerners even though he wishes to help them: 'they are not like us Cornish; they are a stupid pig-headed generation at the best, these south countrymen. They're grown-up babies who want the parson and the squire to be leading them . . .' (Kingsley 1878b: 60, 195).

Mrs Gaskell's *North and South* encouraged the idea of southern prosperity and northern poverty. Viewed from the perspective of a South-Western, rural labourer, these regions of rich and poor could be reversed. James Caird's research of 1852 shows that the wages for rural labourers were generally lower in the South and West than in the North. In mid-nineteenth century Dorset, the heart of

Hardy's Wessex so prettified in picture-postcards today, wages were particularly low. This was because in the north there were more opportunities for labourers to find higher paid jobs in industry (M. Williams 1978: 3–4). Landowners and tenant farmers had to compete with manufacturers for labour, and consequently paid them higher wages to stay in rural occupations.

West Country poverty was not only a nineteenth-century phenomenon. In the seventeenth and eighteenth centuries, the West was a region where wrecking and smuggling were sometimes an attractive alternative to poverty wages. The West Country became one of several regions of Britain notorious for smuggling. There is a glimpse of this in a Customs report of 1788 which describes the smuggler Isaac Gulliver of Dorset (1745–1822) as 'one of the greatest and most notorious smugglers' in the West of England (Coxe 1984: 63). The Customs commissioners estimated that during the 1780s, of 215 vessels suspected of involvement in smuggling on the southern coasts of Britain, seventy-six came from Cornwall, Devon and Dorset (Jamieson 1992: Vol. 1, 246). The southern and eastern coasts of Britain were much nearer the continent than the long peninsula of the South West: for that very reason these coasts were more thoroughly watched by the Customs men, driving some resourceful smugglers to look westwards. On the northern coasts of the South West were remote and wild islands such as Lundy and Flat Holme, useful to smugglers as bases and hiding places. A thriving 'free trade' existed between the southern coasts of the West and the Channel Islands until 1807; smuggling between the West Country and the coast of France occurred during and after the Napoleonic Wars.

Most of the writers investigated in this book, from Hawker to Hardy, are consistently sympathetic to smugglers. Smuggling began to decline from the 1840s onwards, but it continued to thrive as a subject in West Country fiction. Baring-Gould is most open in his admiration and justifications for it, although Parson Hawker is more successful at putting the smuggler into fiction in his prose story of 'Cruel Coppinger' (1866). Baring-Gould's novel *Winefred: A Story of the Chalk Cliffs* (1900), set on the borders between Devon and Dorset, makes an inadequate attempt to fictionalize the real Jack Rattenbury of Beer (1778–1844), whose face survives today as the label on a brand of West Country cider. Walter Besant's *'Twas in Trafalgar's Bay* (1909), a fiction also set at Lyme Regis and in Rattenbury's territory, is no more convincing than Baring-Gould's work. Much more revealing is the supposed autobiography of Jack Rattenbury (1837). The most eloquent evidence of West Country smuggling is not a fiction nor an autobiography, but the many place-names appearing on the map of the South West or used in oral tradition. On the offshore islands and mainland coasts where smugglers landed their contraband and played 'cat and mouse' with the Customs men, we find 'Smuggler's Leap', 'Brandy Head' and 'Pepper Cove'; the coastal spots where goods were secreted are suggested by names such as 'Tom Crocker's Hole' and 'Ralph's Cupboard'; inland, where the smugglers distributed their goods, we find many a 'Smuggler's Lane'. Some names 'smuggle' their connections with the illegal onto the map. 'Mutter's Moor' near Sidmouth, is named after a smuggling family connected with Rattenbury (Hathaway 1994: 174). 'Gulliver's Farm' at West Moors in Dorset commemorates the 'notorious' smuggler Isaac Gulliver. West Country landscapes, buildings and gravestones bear the signs of smuggling for those that know how to detect them, although it is difficult to disentangle legend and fact. Parson Hawker creates a semi-fictional wrecker and smuggler named Coppinger and gives his name to 'Coppinger's Cave' and 'Coppinger's Tracks', a network used for 'free trade' in North Cornwall.

Smuggling and fiction are inseparable: the writer needs the smuggler to create romance; the smuggler needs stories as a cover for his activities. The West Country ghost story has one origin in smuggling. The supernatural was created to cover the 'natural' desire for gain. The counterpart to smuggling place-names are names such as 'Old Ghost House', just as the twin of the smuggler's tale is the ghost story: smugglers encouraged the ideas of ghosts and monsters to keep people in their beds when there was a need to avoid witnesses (Coxe 1984: 23–24, 65). Such events are accurately reflected in the plot of J. Meade Faulkner's *Moonfleet* (1898), set on the Dorset coast, where smugglers terrify people with stories of a piratical 'Blackbeard' who returns from the past to haunt the present.

Both Hawker and Baring-Gould took a special interest in the figure of Coppinger, as we shall see. He represents the darker side of smuggling that led to physical violence, a side associated with the Sussex and Kent gangs but also sometimes encountered in the South West. It was the more romantic side of smuggling that usually appealed to writers and readers of West Country fictions. When the state is a tyrant, some forms of crime seem legitimate. While the squire may tyrannize over the peasant, both may unite in defying central authority; 'Brandy for the Parson', "Baccy for the clerk', 'Laces for a lady': the words of Kipling's well-known 'Smuggler's Song' suggest the image of class divides being temporarily forgotten in a common interest to cheat the taxman. Gender divides are also crossed in smuggling tales, as the traditional ballad of the 'Female Smuggler', Baring-Gould's essay on smuggling and Hardy's short story about a woman smuggler and religious dissenters remind us (consult Baring-Gould 1895c and Hardy's story of 1879: 'The Distracted Preacher'). A criminal like Robin Hood, a noble who lives among commoners and steals from the rich to give to the poor, can become a hero for a whole community. Robin's region will be forever Nottingham and Sherwood Forest, but, as readers of this book will discover, R.D. Blackmore found a Devon equivalent to him in Tom Faggus of North Devon. Walter Scott's Rob Roy belongs in the Highlands, but the idea of a man who must sometimes resort to violence in order to fight corrupt authority was borrowed by the West Country: the smuggler Rattenbury was known as the 'Rob Roy of the West'. In his idyll of North Devon (1849) Charles Kingsley associated wild moors with wild men, the out-of-doors with outlaws, the uncultivated with a culture of ballads and legends: 'It is so with all forests and moorlands. The spirit of Robin Hood and Johnny of Breadislee is theirs. They are remnants of the home of man's fierce youth, still consecrated to the genius of animal excitement and savage freedom' (C. Kingsley 1891: 211, 216). Here the word 'savage' is turned from an insult into a term for an attractive quality. In 1853 Parson Hawker conjures up similar images to Kingsley in a description of smuggling as one of the 'wild, fierce usages of the west' (1893: 32).

Raphael Samuel shrewdly observes that, despite the increase of centralizing legislation and national educational or political reform, centrifugal forces were in fact more powerful than centripetal ones in nineteenth-century Britain (Samuel 1998, Vol. 2: 60). The West Country is pulled towards a romance that sometimes embodies powerful social protest.

## The Territory seen from the Train Window and the Territory Underfoot

How far do these emotional and ideological compass points really explain what happens when people encounter the varied terrain of the West Country? The expansion of the railways enabled more people of more classes to see places than was possible in the days of the coach. Some of those who previously could only travel to places by means of texts could now see the lie of the land for themselves. The coming of the railway began to transform the relationship between space and time, centres and regions. There were 2,486 miles of railways built between 1846 and 1848; by 1851, the year of the Great Exhibition, 7,000 miles of railway track had been laid. The West did not remain immune from the magnetic influence of the centre spreading through the rail network, as Hardy shows in his story set during the time of the Exhibition: 'The Fiddler of the Reels'. In 1844 the rail link between Bristol and Exeter was completed; in 1846 the South Devon coasts were reached; in 1847 Dorchester joined the modern railway network, long before it was fictionalized by Hardy as the rural market town of Casterbridge. In 1855, Barnstaple in once remote North Devon was linked to Exeter; in 1860 Exeter was pulled even closer to London by the rail link to Yeovil, offering a shorter way to the capital than via Bristol (Pyke 1967: 41–42; Travis: 93–105; Thomas 1966, Vol. 1: 166–68).

The Far West was also drawn into the orbit of the centre. In 1851 Wilkie Collins had tried to attract readers to the idea of an unspoilt, romantic Cornwall in a book entitled *Rambles Beyond Railways*. Collins explained: 'Even the railway stops short at Plymouth, and shrinks from penetrating to the savage regions beyond!' (Collins 1851: 7–8). Readers of Dickens' popular periodical, *Household Words*, were advised: 'The world knows that Westward railways terminate at Plymouth; but no-one save Mr Wilkie Collins, and the readers of his pleasant book, know the wonders that lie beyond them' (Anon. 1852: 598). It was no longer possible to make such an assertion in 1864 when Richard John King, a travel writer familiar with the West, publicized the fact that 'the greater part of Cornwall is now readily accessible by railway' (King 1874: 302). By 1867, increasing numbers could travel by train from Paddington to Cornwall in twelve hours, and by 1871, the famous 'Flying Dutchman' had been extended as a slow train to Penzance. Hawker's conception of space and time, urban present and rural past, had not vanished, but it had been radically altered.

The new phenomenon of rail travel was considered by Carlyle in 1850 as threatening the end of separate places, *dis-locating* the local: 'Much as we love railways, there is one thing undeniable: railways are shifting all towns of Britain into new places . . . Reading is coming up to London, Basingstoke is going down to Gosport or Southampton, Dumfries to Liverpool and Glasgow . . .' (Carlyle 1898: 265–66). In 1856 Parson Hawker noted the difference between his own 'rootedness' and the rootlessness now made possible by the age of the train:

> Lady Acland told Mrs Hawker . . . that these Railways had utterly destroyed the Domestic Character of English People. She said that very few of her Friends were content now to endure the monotony of home—the fatal facility of motion had made everybody restless and impatient—dissatisfied unless they had continual change of scene. How strange all this seemed to us two—for we literally never cross the Parish boundary for years. (Byles 1906: 287–88)

Sabine Baring-Gould and Thomas Hardy, also speaking from a rural and West Country perspective, interpreted the train as the destroyer of local culture. In practice the train both threatened localities and made people aware of the differences between them. The train made accessible the once remote, at a stage when it retained enough of its character to seem interestingly different from the dominant centre. Wilkie Collins' rambles *beyond* railways attracted readers with the lure of the remote, but he was only able to walk in Cornwall because the train took him as far as Plymouth. The myth of being 'far from the madding crowd', of enjoying the pastoral nostalgia associated with Gray's famous elegy, was based on the reality that the madding crowd was travelling to the country. The Far West was no longer too far to reach. An anonymous commentator of 1855 captures the mood of mid-century travel:

> In these busy, jostling, nineteenth century days, when, through the agency of iron and steam, the ends of the earth have been brought together, it may well seem almost impossible to find a quiet primitive spot out of sight and sound of rushing engine

and screaming steam-whistle. Yet for those who diligently seek
them, such nooks and corners do still exist . . .

This commentator goes on to discover rural bliss and the England of
Good Queen Bess still existing in Devon ('the most beautiful of our
south-western counties') although he prefers literary to physical
geography when he calls Ottery St Mary 'Clavering St. Mary' after
Thackeray (Anon. 1855a: 534). The 'quiet primitive spot' was made
accessible by the noisy, modern train and the modern writer's fiction.
In 1864 Richard John King found the train brought him within
reach of the wilderness of Dartmoor: 'If the railways which cover the
face of England have destroyed much of that old secluded life which
was not without its great charms, they have opened for us points of
interest in every direction. But in truth many secluded districts still
remain sufficiently remote from the scream of the engine to preserve
their old characteristics to a great extent' (King 1874: 301). In 1875,
Collins' title again emerged in a description of North Cornwall: 'that
remote "land beyond railways", far more inaccessible than the Land's
End itself' (Byles 1906: 592).

This 'inaccessible' land beyond railways, made accessible by railways, became a place of romance in life and fiction. Thomas Hardy's
famous romance with Emma Lavinia Gifford in the North Cornwall
of the 1870s was made possible by the trains that took him from
Dorset westwards, even if the last part of the journey required
a pony and trap. Charlotte Chanter, sister of Charles Kingsley,
expresses how train travel took one to and from a region of West
Country romance:

> If you love the country, then you know the intense delight it is
> to catch a view of distant hills. At first they are but a purple line
> on the horizon; then as one approaches they gradually rise until
> we make out the tower of some village church, and then a
> stately mansion with its ancient trees around, and the little
> cottage homes nestling hard by! Just so the hills of the West
> appear to us as we rush toward them on the railway . . .

Her farewell to the West is detailed with a similar blend of idealism
and the urge for a genuine encounter with the differences between
places:

You take a last glance from the railway carriage . . . of the hills among which you have been wandering. The giant cliffs fade from view, the sea is left behind, and you sigh as you come in sight of the great city where you dwell,—miles, miles of houses, blackened trees, dingy grass, flagging shrubs in dusty squares; and your thoughts fly back to shady lanes and overarching woods, and your heart sinks, just a little, within you. (Chanter 1856: 8–9, 108)

It is not accidental that most of the famous and lesser known fictions celebrating the West Country were created during and just after the expansion of the railways. These fictions are set in the areas of moor and coastline brought closer by the railways while seeming to defy them. Consider the kind of texts discussed in the argument of this book: Hawker's poems in praise of Morwenstow parish ('The Sea Bird's Cry'), Kingsley's novels inspired by the moors and coasts of North Cornwall and Devon (*Westward Ho!*), Blackmore's fictions mainly within the confines of Exmoor (*Lorna Doone*), Hardy's semi-real, semi-mythical Egdon Heath (*The Return of the Native*) and Sabine Baring-Gould's stories of Dartmoor and Bodmin Moor (*Tales of the Western Moors*). They all take readers on imaginary rambles *beyond* railways made possible *by* railways. Charles Kingsley and his sister believed that God made the West Country and man made the town. Modern readers can perceive that town and country were interdependent, linked together by railway navvies and regional writers.

Nineteenth-century observers of the West Country, whether residents or railway visitors, often look at their region through the spectacles of convention or the rose-tinted spectacles of romance. The literary critic David Masson did not specify the West Country in the following passage, but his choice of words indicates how an idealized version of South-Western topography could fulfil a national need for escape:

is it not medicinal that . . . in the pages of our novelists . . . we should be taken away in imagination from our common social haunts, and placed in situations where nature still exerts upon Humanity the unbroken magnetism of her inanimate bulk, soothing into peace in the quiet meadows, whispering of the unearthly in the depths of the forest, telling tales of the past in some solitary crumbling ruin, moaning her sorrow in the gusts of the moor at midnight, or dashing the eternal monotone of her many voices against a cliff-embattled shore? (Masson 1859: 26)

This owes more to the musings of Wordsworth and the Gothic tradition than to a close encounter with a real terrain. Others did observe the terrain of the West and recorded their response to it in some detail. They came in search of a new version of the picturesque, of a landscape that could both fit into a picture and be pictured accurately. Charlotte Chanter, seeking botanical knowledge on foot, nevertheless had an eye for a landscape. She commented that the high hedges of Devon were: 'doubtless very rich in ferns' but that they were 'anything but agreeable when one wants to see the country' (Chanter 1856: 63). Henry James, the Anglophile American looking for 'England', thought that he could see all the prettiness that he wanted from his carriage window in 1872:

For those fanciful observers to whom broad England means chiefly the perfection of the rural picturesque, Devonshire means the perfection of England. I at least, had so complacently taken for granted here all the characteristic graces of English scenery, had built so boldly on their rank orthodoxy, that before we fairly crossed the border I had begun to look impatiently from the carriage window for the veritable landscape in water-colours. Devonshire meets you promptly in all its purity, for the course of ten minutes you have been able to glance down the green vista of a dozen Devonshire lanes. On huge embankments of moss and turf, smothered in wild flowers and embroidered with the finest lace-work of trailing ground-ivy, rise solid walls of flowering thorn and glistening holly and golden broom, and more strong, homely shrubs than I can name, and toss their blooming tangle to a sky which seems to look down between them, in places, from but a dozen inches of blue. They are oversown with lovely little flowers with names as delicate as their petals of gold and silver and azure—bird's eye and king's finger and wandering sailor—and their soil, a superb dark red, turns to spots so nearly to crimson that you almost fancy it is some fantastic compound purchased at the chemist's and scattered there for ornament. The mingled reflection of this rich-hued earth and the dim green light which filters through the hedge is a masterpiece of produced beauty. A Devonshire cottage is no less striking an outcome of the ages and the seasons and the manners. Crushed beneath its burden of thatch, coated with a rough white stucco of a tone to delight a painter, nestling in deep foliage and garnished at door-step and wayside with various forms of chubby infancy, it seems to have been stationed there for no more obvious purpose than to keep a promise to your fancy, though it cover, I suppose, not a little of the sordid side of life which the fancy likes to slur over. (James 1983: 53)

There are a few concessions to realism; James knows he is a 'fanciful observer' who is ignoring the 'sordid side' of rural poverty. James' aesthetic sensibility and botanical knowledge help him to provide a convincing rendering of the wild flowers, red earth and sunken lanes which comprise the rural 'personality' of Devon. However, his view is also biased by the priorities of the painter: the world of nature is there to produce 'masterpieces'; this is a scene, not a workplace, an art gallery more than a terrain. There are few human figures in the scene; the function of the children in the cottage gardens is to 'garnish' the visual feast for the traveller's eye.

Others travelled west looking for a past that bolstered a sense of national pride. King noted in 1864 that topography could teach history: if foreign tours were an education for gentlemen in this respect, there was more justification in the days of more democratic travel for a tour at home. Knowledge derived 'from a well-planned English tour should be all the more valuable in proportion as a knowledge of English history is more important for us than that of any other country'. One of the regions that best gives us this national history lesson, according to King, is the South and West:

Let the Summer tour extend through such a tract of country as that along the south coast,—from Kent into Hampshire, or further, into Devonshire and Cornwall. In such scenery as is truly characteristic of England—rich, green and tranquil; mingled with much that is wilder and bolder, among granite tors and chalk uplands; and in a coast-line of the most varied beauty—this tract is almost unrivalled; and there is hardly another in which places and relics directly connected with the great events of English history are so closely packed or so easily accessible. (King 1874: 276–79)

After the success of Kingsley's *Westward Ho!*, many travellers followed King's advice, visiting Plymouth and the western coasts in order to hear echoes of the greatness of Elizabethan England. There is evidence too, complying with the map of Britain created in the French response to *North and South*, of travellers escaping the frightening industrial democracy of the present for the comforting, rural feudalism of the past. Henry Kingsley (brother of Charles) betrays mixed feelings about this theme in his novel *Ravenshoe* (1862). His narrator comments: 'In barbarous, out-of-the-way places, like the west of Devonshire, the feudal feeling . . . is still absurdly strong'. Elsewhere this narrator is more confident about the benefits of the past and the notion of *noblesse oblige*: 'I am a very great admirer of the old feudal feeling, when it is not abused by either part. In parts of Australia, where it, or something near akin to it, is very strong indeed, I have seen it act on high and low most beneficially; giving to one side a sense of responsibility, and to the other a feeling of trust and reliance' (H. Kingsley 1894a: 266, 359–60).

Some approached the West with a scientific commitment to seeing what was really there. Consider Edmund Gosse's *A Naturalist's Rambles on the Coasts of Devonshire* (1853), Charles Kingsley's *Glaucus or the Wonders of the Shore* (1855), Charlotte Chanter's *Ferny Combes* (1856) and G.H. Lewes's *Seaside Studies* (1858). Gosse's book helped to inspire a visit to Ilfracombe in 1856 by George Eliot and her companion G.H. Lewes. Eliot too has a painter's eye: she finds every yard of a Devon bank to be a 'Hunt picture'. However, Eliot finds that Pre-Raphaelite attention to detail is required by many subjects, not just pretty ones. Eliot praised Ruskin for teaching a form of realism: 'the doctrine that all truth and beauty are to be attained by a humble and faithful study of nature, not by substituting vague forms, bred by imagination on the mists of feeling, in place of definite substantial reality'. Eliot knew it was important to *pay attention* to the world. It is touching to read the record of Eliot's and Lewes' attempt to combine Gosse's scientific knowledge with Ruskin's theory while looking for minute marine life on the shores of Ilfracombe. Searching for zoophytes in vain, Eliot did not blame the world, but their own shortcomings as observers of the world. Their failure was, she decided, proof of the 'wide difference' between 'having eyes and seeing'. They failed because they could not see what was under their noses: it is 'so necessary for the eye to be educated by objects as well as ideas'. Hardy criticized the visitor who had a cold-hearted curiosity, who wanted to name and collect without respect for local humanity: consider his characterization of Dr Fitzpiers in *The Woodlanders*. Eliot puts scientific curiosity in a more positive light: for her the collecting and naming might serve a human purpose. She explains

> I never before longed so much to know the names of things as during this visit to Ilfracombe. The desire is part of the tendency that is now constantly growing in me to escape from all vagueness and inaccuracy into the daylight of distinct, vivid ideas. The mere fact of naming an object tends to give definiteness to our conception of it—we have then a sign that at once calls up to our minds the distinctive qualities which mark out for us that particular object from all others. (Byatt 1990: 219–20, 228–29, 368)

George Eliot wanted to apply this concept of an exacting 'natural history' not only to specimens collected by the shore, but to people: while staying at Ilfracombe she was working on her essay 'The Natural History of German Life'. Her fictional scenes from midlands provincial life contribute to realizing her aims. Her Ilfracombe Journal provides only glimpses of what she might have achieved with a West Country setting.

Other writers more rooted in the West Country sometimes succeed in providing the vivid ideas and the actual names of plants, animals and places which Eliot recommends, applying this local knowledge in ways that do justice to the territory underfoot. The eyes of these writers were educated by the solid objects and people about them; their evocations of landscape operate beyond the boundaries of cliché and stereotype when they succeed in giving their varied world the attention it deserves. The regional West Country writer best evokes locality with local words. Sometimes, within the same text, the attempt at a set piece description of the western terrain fails while incidental reference conjures up a vivid sense of a region. Charlotte Chanter explains in her West Country novel: '"Hay harvest" as they call it in the west,—"haymaking time," as it is called elsewhere —was a busy, important affair . . .' (Chanter 1860, Vol. 1: 29). Henry Kingsley comments in his West Country novel *Geoffrey Hamlyn* (1859): 'This was the day of the Revels which corresponds pretty well with what is called in other parts of England a pleasure fair . . .' (H. Kingsley 1894b: 34). Writing from the viewpoint of those who earn a living from the sea, Parson Hawker hints at a whole world in his reference to a region of ocean between Hartland Point and Lundy Island: 'Harty Race, the local name of a narrow and boisterous run of sea between Lundy and the land' (Hawker 1893: 55). On some occasions it is both an eye for detail and a sense of moving through a landscape which convinces the reader. Henry Kingsley takes the reader on a journey on horseback from the coast and fertile lowlands of South Devon to the wild uplands of Dartmoor in his novel *Leighton Court* (1866):

> So they rode away from the sound of the sea, through the deep red lanes, through the rich overarching boscage of the first band of country; and through a long drawn valley of yellow clay, through which the blue slate peeped here and there, among the world-old oaks, thickly clustered, underlaid with holly—the home of the woodcock. Then, facing on to the culminating height of the slate hills, they rode across the desolate scratch-and-scramble-farmed, infanticide-producing twenty-acre freehold, ten bushel country, which lies between the thirty bushel civilisation of the red lands, and the vast barbarous granite desert beyond; lastly they came to a country of heather and bleating peewit—to the hot silence of the moor. . . . (H. Kingsley 1895: 358)

On some occasions the West Country observer gives a sense of the interaction between terrain and weather. Charlotte Chanter liked the bleak beauty of the northern coasts of the South West: 'the Atlantic blast sweeps unimpeded over the hills; but few trees are visible, and those that are seen turn their faces from the sea breezes and bend crouchingly towards the east, as if to escape its bitterness'. Her eye was educated by seeing the landscape in the weather that often accompanies it: 'The wind comes sighing over sedgy moorlands, the mist drives up from the sea, and mist and wind seem fit possessors of that desolate region' (Chanter 1860, Vol. 1: 1, 9).

She succeeds in conveying that sense of peril only experienced when physically present on the steep descent or the cliff edge. She concisely explains the encounter between a human stride and the steep gradient of Clovelly: 'Any one who ventures down Clovelly high street must leave his dignity behind him . . .' (Chanter 1856: 30). In her novel, the physical excitement and dangers of a North Devon cliffscape are vividly present. A blow-hole is described as follows: 'it is not above three or four feet across, and about eight feet deep, and may easily be crossed at low tide; but it is a different thing when the sea, boiling and surging in the narrow channel, renders the head giddy and the foot unsteady'. Grace, a partial self-portrait of Charlotte, is described as a mischievous child who likes to 'crawl on her hands and knees, to the edge of the most precipitous part of the cliff, and, dropping a stone over, send the wild sea-birds screaming from the nest they had built in the little chinks and crannies of the rock, making the black cormorant, who had been standing on some jagged rock in the sea, take wing, and sail past with his long neck out-stretched, looking like some messenger from a darker world'. Charlotte also knew how to use scientific knowledge and the power of naming. Her focus reveals the fine detail of her terrain when she discovers Wall Rue growing inside the tower of Hawker's church at Morwenstow or when she succeeds in combining her botanical and local knowledge in a description of the changing flora on the cliff edge: 'now the pink thrift and many-tinted ladies'-fingers took the place of the tiny spring quill or mermaid's blue-bells; these would, as the summer advanced, be succeeded by the pale sea-lavender, the sweet-scented ladies'-tresses, and the dwarf centauries' (Chanter 1860, Vol. 1: 14–15, 33). This is poetic nomenclature, combining scientific specificity and word-music; it occupies that interesting territory between the consciously learned and unconsciously assimilated knowledge of place described by the poet Seamus Heaney (Heaney 1985: 131).

Charlotte Chanter and Henry Kingsley portray landscapes more successfully than they portray people. They do sometimes reveal their affection for the people in the landscape and their ways. At these moments they are not above their region but within it, a point of view seldom achieved by the travel guide. The poet David Jones refers to 'differentiated' sites: places that show the marks of a long history of human occupation, labour and legend-making (1974: 'The Tutelar of the Place'). Charlotte's description of Clovelly would serve the purposes of a tourist guide, except for those curious details only known to those who have lived in a 'differentiated site' long enough to know its idiosyncrasies. We learn, for example, that the New Inn at Clovelly has a sign consisting of a 'soldier and sailor . . . who periodically attack one another in a furious manner with swords, but apparently without doing any material damage; I at least have known them five-and-twenty years . . .' (Chanter 1856: 30). In her novel Charlotte also attempts to give us a glimpse of the connection between place and occupation: 'In those days, too, seaports now nearly deserted sent out many a gallant ship, built in the shipyards of the town by men of the town—the very sails and cordage made in the town—so that the ships seemed part and parcel of the people, so many had had a hand in them' (Chanter 1860, Vol. 1: 60). Henry Kingsley gives us a vivid glimpse of a Clovelly-like port when a member of the local gentry pays a visit:

> It was as neat a street as one ever sees in a fishing village; that is to say, rather an untidy one, for of all human employments, fishing involves more lumber and mess than any other. Everything past use was 'hit,' as they say in Berkshire, out into the street; and of the inorganic part of this refuse, that is to say, tiles, bricks, potsherds, and so on, the children built themselves shops and bazaars, and sold one another the organic orts, that is to say, cabbage-stalks, fish-bones, and orange peel, which were paid for in mussel-shells . . . At high market time, they saw Cuthbert come slowly riding along among the children, and the dogs, and the pigs, and the herring-bones, and brickbats . . . As he came along, picking his way gently among the children, the fishermen and their wives came out right and left from their doors, and greeted him kindly. (H. Kingsley 1894: 265)

The novelist Dinah Craik, while travelling in Cornwall, thought that the encounter with a landscape and its people could be educative in a powerful way: 'along this Cornish coast, life and death seem very near together . . . I cannot advise either rash or nervous people to go travelling in Cornwall' (Craik 1884: 28). Educative travel is possible if there is some genuine meeting of minds between the person passing through and the person rooted to the spot. Occasionally, the genteel commentators looking at the people of the West Country give tantalizing glimpses of the people looking back at them. George Eliot describes how she and Lewes became lost and sought directions at a lonely farm house. They were knocking on the door for some time before a 'woman put her head reluctantly out of an upper window and after some parleying conveyed the half comforting . . .

information the we were on the right way for Ilfracombe, but were still *tu mile* away from it'(Byatt 1990: 223). This is a miniature of the outsider meeting the insider. Eliot is a touch aloof; the example of dialect and the hints of suspicion and reluctance in the woman's response suggest how different people with different priorities can occupy the same spot. There is a similar encounter in Charlotte Chanter's *Ferny Combes*. Charlotte describes how she and her party lost their way while travelling over Dartmoor by coach, and asked for directions from an elderly woman who sat at the door of her cottage, knitting. They explained that they had deliberately taken a circuitous route to Princetown for no other reason than to see the sights. Charlotte describes the woman's response as follows: ' "Oh, my dear soul!" she exclaims, in astonishment at the idea; "well sure! so you came this way to see the country!" ' (Chanter 1856: 58–59). Charlotte's holiday territory, or place of scientific wonder, was a workplace to others. Baring-Gould is also capable of giving us illuminating flashes of comedy that help the reader to reverse roles, to move from being an outsider to an insider. Unlike Eliot, he openly encourages us to identify with the 'native'. He records an interview with an old Cornish woman about the whereabouts of a smuggler's cave:

> 'Did the preventive men never find out this place?'
> 'Never, sir, never. How could they? Who'd be that wicked as to tell them? and they wasn't clever enough to find it them-selves . . . Oh, dear! oh, dear! what is the world coming to— for education and all kinds o' wickedness? Sure, there's no smuggling now, and poor folks ha'n't got the means o' bettering themselves like proper Christians.' (Baring-Gould 1981: 281)

This comical, topsy-turvy world, where what is normally good becomes bad and vice versa, is best created by fictional techniques that tempt the reader into moving out of normality, from central safety to eccentric, educative periphery.

## The Place of Fiction

As George Eliot knew, successful fiction serves as a passport between otherwise estranged people and places. Fiction claims to provide more than a superficial encounter with another's existence: it claims to make you identify with that person, to see the world from another's point of view. None of the romancers, scientists and seekers of the picturesque cited in this chapter consistently create this passport. Henry Kingsley the novelist declares, in defiance of the urbane and educated: 'The whims and oddities of a village; which one has seen with one's own eyes, and heard with one's own ears, are not nonsense' (H. Kingsley 1894a: 311). He was paying attention but he lacked the means to turn his attentiveness into a successful novel. It is to Hardy that we must turn in order to appreciate the true power of fiction to evoke a region, and to show the regions within a region. Hardy's semi-real, semi-fictional Egdon Heath is a pervasive presence not only in the novel *The Return of the Native* (1878), but also in several short stories and poems. He persuades his readers to believe in a heath where heathen qualities survive, a place with its own language (the local ponies are 'heath-croppers'), its own occupations closely linked with the earth (furze cutting and reddle making), its own sense of time in defiance of Greenwich ('On Egdon there was no absolute hour of the day. The time at any moment was a number of varying doctrines professed by the different hamlets . . .' (Book 2, Chapter 5, Hardy 1979: 186). The wedding between two of the heath's people, Thomasin and Diggory is described as follows:

> As the fly passed the group which had run out from the homestead they shouted 'Hurrah!' and waved their hands . . . The driver of the fly turned a supercilious gaze upon them; he even treated the wedded pair themselves with something like condescension; for in what other state than heathen could people, rich or poor, exist who were doomed to abide in such a world's end as Egdon? Thomasin showed no such superiority to the group at the door, fluttering her hand as quickly as a bird's wing towards them, and asking Diggory, with tears in her eyes, if they ought not to alight and speak to these kind neighbours. (Book 6, Chapter 4, Hardy 1979: 468–69)

At this culminating point of the novel, only a reader misreading the text identifies with the supercilious outsider rather than the emotional insider. The novel as a whole enables the reader to identify with these 'heathen', 'peasants' and 'provincials', and revalue the pejorative words in which such people are normally described. The Egdon rustics are comical, but we laugh with them, not at them. We are alongside and within this region, not above it. This is achieved by the use of fictional technique to encourage the identification of the reader with characters and their development in narrative.

The right to cherish a region is not confined to those increasingly rare people who have lived in the same place for several generations. It is possible to learn to be a native, and fiction is one of the means of doing so. Arnold Bennett learned to value his childhood territory amongst the region of the Potteries by reading a novel by George Moore, a stranger to the region (Drabble 1975: 2). John Betjeman learned how to put Cornwall into verse and prose with the help of Sabine Baring-Gould. Betjeman explained 'I know that I am far more indebted to him for a romantic sense of place and local legend that I am to any other writer' (Purcell 1957: v). The regional writer not only *sees* the region but also knows how to *express* the region in ways that influence others. In a continuing process, fiction spreads a contagious understanding of the history of a region, and provides passports for many 'strangers' who wish to become 'natives'. The writer sees the territory; the writer expresses it; others imagine what the writer sees and then visit the actual territory with the writer's vision in mind.

## Types of Territory

Wendell Berry charts the progress from childhood to maturity in terms of different territories. There is the territory of the national or global point of view in which 'one does not pay attention to anything in particular'. This zone is closely related to the territory of abstraction which only deals in generalities and empty phrases. The regional writer Flannery O'Connor knew this territory. She attended a conference of would-be writers and was disappointed to hear stories that 'originated in some synthetic place that could have been anywhere or nowhere'. They were stories that had not been 'influenced by the outside world at all, only by television' (O'Connor 1972: 56). John Betjeman links this idea to the geographical territory of this book when he satirizes the Town Clerk who wants to turn the entire West Country into just two regions: South West Area One and South West Area Two (see his poem with the punning title: 'The Town Clerk's Views').

Then there is the territory of self-righteousness, commonly experienced in an adolescent rejection of 'provincial roots'. We can see

*1) Hawker's Vicarage at Morwenstow.*
The chimneys were built to resemble the church towers of places where
Hawker had previously lived (Oxford and North Tamerton, Whitstone
and Stratton in Cornwall).

this territory in the response of Samuel Coleridge to his native Ottery
St Mary when he returned there as a superior young man. Dickens
leaned toward this territory when he called his native Rochester
'Dullborough town' but he redresses the balance in the scenes in
*Great Expectations* where Pip as a gentlemanly Londoner is mercilessly
criticized for attempting to deny his debt to homely Jo Gargery the
blacksmith. A common symptom of this stage is to enjoy escape from
the gossip of 'small town life'. As Berry points out, gossip is only
possible if people know each other. Berry implies that the
community which the adolescent consciousness needs to reject is
precious to the mature person. Developing from this self-righteous
world is the territory of historical self-righteousness, when we
look back on our ancestors' behaviour and take pride in assuming
that, put in the same circumstances, we would never have made
the same mistakes. This superiority to history makes us unable to
imagine it, to empathize with previous generations whose mistakes
and successes can help us to learn. Kingsley's and Baring-Gould's

*2) Hawker's Vicarage.*
Illustration from R. Thurston Hopkins' *The Literary Landmarks of Devon and Cornwall* (London, 1926).

historical West Country, despite their many prejudices, seldom becomes self-righteous in Berry's sense.

Close to the territory of adolescence is the territory of irresponsibility, a place where selfishness is glorified as heroism. Here are found many movies, set in a synthetic gangland or Wild West, where the tough guy not the nice guy wins. None of the texts studied here are in this territory. Another wrong turning takes you to the territory of despair: here whatever is wrong is 'inevitable' and unavoidable. It needs to be carefully differentiated from the territory of tragedy: here, despite the suffering and death, the community can learn from mistakes, can rise above its failures, can continue in spite of mistakes. There is something 'rotten in the state of Denmark' but its future need not repeat its past. This book explores Hardy's work with this in mind. On this journey is also the territory of art where subjects only have the value conferred on them by the artist. None of the writers explored in this book can be accused of this.

Contrasting with all these territories, guarding us against the temptations they offer, reminding us that we share the earth with other forms of life, telling us that something can be done and should be done to improve our treatment of the world, is the solid presence of territory underfoot. Here, reversing the artist's priorities, subjects demand the attention of the observer. Subjects belong, not in 'meta-regions' divorced from geography, but among the physical environment that actually surrounds us, and is the source of our food and air, even though this fundamental reality is screened from our understanding by modern comforts. In a modern version of the theory of Ruskin and George Eliot, Berry, with help from Lopez, argues that the mind needs to correct its ideas against the visible world. The inner imagination needs to learn from the outer world, but must also be its guardian. It needs to reach out, to nourish and cherish the outer world so threatened by those who live in the world of globalization and abstraction. Berry chooses that epic of the Mississippi, *Huckleberry Finn*, as his example of a 'transfiguring regional book'. He is impressed by the fact that 'Huck speaks of and for and as his place'. He comments, re-interpreting the terms explored in the nineteenth century: 'The great gift of *Huckleberry Finn* . . . is to be regional without being provincial. Provincialism is always self-conscious. It is the conscious sentimentalisation of or condescension to or apology for a province. In its most acute phase it is the fear of provinciality' (Berry 1987: 15–30; Lopez 1988: 66–68). The lesser known writers explored in this book seldom rival Twain's achievements but, in their own ways, they do enable us to navigate through the territories mapped by Berry and Lopez to reach the territory of understanding, a place where we can keep a balance between the world in our heads and the world under our feet.

# 2

# Parson Hawker's Territory

## Trelawny, Cruel Coppinger and a Cornish King Arthur

*A Visitor: 'Mr Hawker, what are your views and opinions?'*
*Hawker: 'There is Hennacliff, the highest cliff on this coast, on the right;*
*the church on the left; the Atlantic Ocean in the middle. These are my views.*
*My opinions I keep to myself.'*

Anecdote about Hawker in Brendon 1983: 148;
Betjeman 1997: 187

### Inventions of The Western Shore: Trelawny

The remote parish of Morwenstow on the rocky, windswept coast of
North Cornwall has a literary *topography*. The *graphé* in this *topos*, the
signature on the landscape, was created by Parson Robert Stephen
Hawker (1803–75). The Reverend William Maskell of Bude had no
doubt in 1863 that Hawker and Morwenstow were inseparable: 'So
long as men have any feeling or love for English poetry, Morwenstow
will ever be remembered as the home . . . of the author of some of the
most beautiful of modern ballads' (Maskell 1872: 16). Hawker's
indelible writing on his surroundings can still be found by those who
know how to read it. The house with a cross-shaped window at the
coastal hamlet of Coombe, the stone bridge linking the parishes of
Welcombe and Morwenstow, the curious wooden hut made from the
timbers of shipwrecks and perched on the heights near Hennacliff,
Morwenstow churchyard containing a lychgate and a grave marked
by the figurehead of a ship, the nearby rectory with ornate chimneys:

all these signs in the landscape bear witness to Hawker's good works and creative imagination. He wrote the famous Trelawny ballad while staying at Coombe; the bridge was built due to his initiative; the figurehead and lychgate in the churchyard commemorate some of the many shipwrecked sailors that he buried; the rectory chimneys imitate the church spires of places associated with Hawker's life; the hut on the cliffside was built by him as a place to watch for ships in distress and compose verse in the presence of God's mighty seas and winds. Hawker might even be said to have 'named' this site: the spelling of 'Moorwinstow' was changed to 'Morwenstow' (Morwenna's place) because he wanted the etymological evidence to prove his theory that the local church was founded in the age of Celtic Christianity by Saint Morwenna, daughter of Saint Brychan of Wales. Sabine Baring-Gould questioned this theory but Hawker trumped his critic's reason with faith, declaring that his story of Morwenna must be true since it was revealed to him in a divine dream (Byles 1906: 41–42; Brendon 1983: 25)! Whoever reads 'Morwenstow' on a signpost or a map is reading a place-name as

3) *Hawker's Cottage at Coombe.*
The cross-shaped window was designed by Hawker. This is one of the places where the 'Trelawny Ballad' was composed.

Hawker intended, on the authority of a supernatural event. Hawker's ability to combine the visionary with practical influence on his world is well symbolized by that cross-shaped window at Coombe: it simultaneously enabled him to honour God and let in daylight for written work, work that combined the quest for divine truth with the quest for a publisher.

It is difficult to find Hawker amongst the tangle of fact and fiction that surrounds him. Some of the fiction was invented by Hawker himself who enjoyed a hoax; other inventions were added by his admirers. Sabine Baring-Gould's popular 1876 biography of Hawker was exposed as mainly fictional soon after its publication but the revised version of this work did little to alter the original inaccuracies. Baring-Gould's semi-fictional biography rivalled the actual history of the man until Piers Brendon's genuine biography of 1975. Hawker's influence on a few people has been long-lasting. During the 1960s one unidentified admirer placed holly on Hawker's grave at Plymouth every year for ten years, perhaps to symbolize an 'evergreen' influence. This ritual inspired a local newspaper headline: 'Mystery Holly on "Mad Vicar's" Grave' (Anon. 1965).

While facts about Hawker often turn out to be fictions, one of the most vivid and accurate contemporary portraits of him is to be found in a novel. In 1875 the popular novelist Mortimer Collins presented Hawker thinly disguised as 'Canon Tremaine' in a three volume romance entitled *Sweet and Twenty*. The surface details of Tremaine's life match Hawker's accurately. Just as Hawker was installed at Morwenstow in 1835 and seldom travelled outside the parish boundaries, Tremaine is described in this novel of 1875 as living in the remote parish of 'Saint Gludoc' for forty years. Like Hawker, Tremaine dresses eccentrically, enjoys battles with officialdom and hierarchy, and is determined to restore his rural church. Tremaine's first name is Lancelot in honour of Hawker's chivalric and medieval outlook, as well as his attempt to rival Tennyson's Arthurian verse.

This fictional portrait of a 'poet-rector' takes us beyond externals towards the reality of Hawker. Tremaine's poetry is presented as unfashionable but as destined for future recognition; it is also presented as part of Tremaine's religious mission. When Tremaine preaches at Northminster (Exeter) Cathedral, he argues that faith needs knowledge: science and literature will be used by atheists for their cause unless the holy employ them for God's work. Tremaine's theological position is also a suggestive guide to Hawker's. Tremaine is neither High Church nor Broad Church: he regards the former as time-serving and the latter as little better than Nonconformists. However, the Bible Christians and Wesleyan Methodists of Cornwall whom Hawker distrusted were know for their reliance on the Bible: Tremaine-Hawker also accepts the Good Book as his guide. The novel explains: 'the worthy old poetic Canon took the Bible literally, and by so doing brought out original views of meaning which are lost to the disputatious theological pedants of the present day' (Collins 1875, Vol. 2: 182–84, 208–16, Vol. 3: 227). Perhaps Hawker was so vehement in his dislike of local Nonconformists partly because he recognized rivals to his own speciality?

*4) Hawker's Hut at Morwenstow, North Cornwall.*
Hawker experienced visions here. The hut is reputedly built from driftwood, including the timbers of wrecked ships.

The novel tells us that while Hawker is close to God he will never make a bishop because he does not pursue preferment at Court in London or follow convention by writing political pamphlets and translating Greek plays: 'Canon Tremaine preferred his Cornish eyrie to S. James's, and his own nervous verse to all Euripides' (Collins 1875, Vol. 3: 225). This fictional version of Hawker is perhaps most accurate in its account of the umbilical connection between the man and his chosen place. Tremaine's inaccessible Saint Gludoc is closely based on Hawker's Morwenstow. The roads leading to Saint Gludoc 'have break-neck hills, which frighten any but a Cornish man'. The churchyard with its figurehead of the wrecked *Caledonia* is sketched accurately: 'Many poor ship-wrecked creatures have been buried in his little churchyard; and in one case, where he buried the whole of the crew of a vessel, he has placed a touching inscription on a simple stone, with the figure-head of the vessel beside it' (Collins 1875, Vol. 2: 212, 216). While partially acknowledging the dark side of Hawker's rural existence next to a cruel coast, the novel also recognizes the poetic potential of this isolated encounter with the elements. Tremaine was surrounded by scenery that 'well suited his poetic moods. Wild moorland, where the falcon floated and the chough chattered of King Arthur: a wide expanse of sea, over which you gazed from cliffs three hundred feet high: altogether a solitary legendary place, where a poet might live with much comfort' (Collins 1875, Vol. 2: 210). This probably refers to Hawker's note in the various editions of his verse that the red-legged choughs of Tintagel near Morwenstow were associated in local tradition with King Arthur.

Finally, the novel vividly recreates the way that Hawker, in his chosen location, could cross the barrier between the worlds of the seen and the unseen, reason and faith:

> The Canon will show you many curiosities, about some of which he will tell you odd mystical stories; indeed all his talk has a mystical and poetic haze over it. Then he will take you to see his retreat, which he has cut in the side of the cliff, and as you are sitting there with him, looking down almost a perpendicular height of 300 feet, he will tell you how he comes there to think, and to consider the works of God; and he points across the sea, where no land is visible, and tells you there is nothing but this great sea between you and Labrador. Then he will point down to

a little bay under the cliff where you are sitting, and tell you he
once saw a mermaid there; and you quite believe him, for you
feel you are in a world of mermaids, and all sorts of odd things.
(Collins 1875, Vol. 2: 213–14)

This fictional Tremaine helps us to understand the Hawker who
wrote:

> Wild things are here of sea and land,
> Stern surges and a haughty strand;
> Sea-monsters haunt yon cavern'd lair,
> The mermaid wrings her briny hair
> ('The Sea-Bird's Cry', Hawker 1928: 41)

Hawker, just like Tremaine, used words to spellbind listeners. Here
is a glimpse of Hawker preaching after a baptism: 'he described most
vividly a scene in heaven as a guardian angel was chosen to care for
the newly baptised infant—the descent of the angel—his hovering
round the font at baptism—it was so vividly described that you felt
it was something the Vicar had seen himself, and one involuntarily
glanced round to look for the presence of the angelic being' (J.F.
Chanter, quoted in Byles 1906: 619).

Tremaine's ideas are described as 'in front of the Age, wherefore of
course the Age could not be expected to understand them' (Collins
1875, Vol. 2: 183). A modern reader agrees that Hawker was out of
step with his own time, but not by being ahead of it so much as
behind it. The idealization and conscious recreation of the medieval
past was a common preoccupation among Victorian writers and
artists: Hawker gives the impression that he had no need to recreate
the Middle Ages, he just lived in them. Morwenstow was a place
where the world of angels and devils seemed a reality. The continual
storms and shipwrecks on his coastline were all the proof Hawker
needed that God and Satan continued their fight regardless of man's
puny, nineteenth-century technology.

Hawker describes his own nineteenth-century condition in his
1867 account of the seventeenth-century West Country clergyman:

> insulated within his own limited sphere, often even without the
> presence of a country squire . . . [he] became developed about
> middle life into an original mind and man, sole and absolute

within his parish boundary, eccentric when compared with his brethren in civilised regions, and yet, in German phrase, 'a whole and seldom man' in his dominion of souls . . . These men were not . . . smoothed down into a monotonous aspect of life and manners by this remote and secluded existence. They imbibed, each in his own peculiar circle, the hue of surrounding objects, and were tinged into distinctive colouring and character by many a contrast of scenery and people. (Hawker 1893: 124)

The atmospheric titles of Hawker's collections of poetry and prose are at one with his limited yet varied environment. His verse commemorates the sea, the wind and oral folk tradition, being entitled 'Records of the Western Shore', 'Reeds Shaken with the Wind' and 'Cornish Ballads'. Hawker's two volumes of 'Reeds' were described to readers as first and second 'clusters', vividly suggesting the affinity between his words and the natural world. His poetry and prose were also collected under the titles 'Echoes from Old Cornwall' and 'Footprints of Former Men in Far Cornwall', suggesting Morwenstow's remoteness, the ancient past and the need to preserve its fading evidence. His unpublished notes, written it seems with Bodmin Moor's granite tors in sight or in mind, were called successively, 'A Thought Book', 'Fragments of a Broken Mind' and 'Stones Broken from the Rocks'. The titles of the poems in *Cornish Ballads* commemorate distinctive landmarks ('The Tamar Spring'), tales of smuggling and wrecking ('Featherstone's Doom') and tales linking Cornwall with Arthurian legend ('Queen Guennivar's Round'), as well as Cornish contributions to seventeenth-century history ('Sir Beville'). As these titles suggest, Hawker's life and work really did take on the 'hue of surrounding objects'. His chosen muse and *genius loci*, rather than a woodland nightingale or a skylark on the downs, was the 'cruel cormorant', one of the 'Dark wanderers of the western wave' whose harsh cry seemed an equivalent in sound of granite rocks or as the poet put it, whose 'sullen accents' sound like 'native echoes' of a wild coast ('The Sea-Bird's Cry'). John Betjeman liked to think of Hawker's work on stormy nights when the thunder of the waves could be heard: Hawker's best verse creates this environment in the mind even on calm nights (Betjeman 1997: 186).

For Hawker, the distinctive colouring created from his interaction with a unique environment was a mainly but not exclusively Cornish experience. True to county boundaries, Devon remembers Sir Richard

Grenville's connections with Bideford while Hawker the Cornish poet records how Sir Richard's grandson, Sir Beville, marched from Stow and Kilkhampton in North Cornwall to participate in the Civil War. However, Hawker was born and buried at Plymouth, his first curacy was at North Tamerton in Devon, and his imagination was shaped by topography rather than administrative boundaries, allowing his poetic mind to rove across the Cornish border to Clovelly and Hartland Point. He did not regard the term 'western' as eliding the Cornish claim to be not so much a county as a country with its own racial and linguistic inheritance. The famous Trelawny ballad, adopted as a Cornish anthem, was to Hawker a song of the 'western men'. When Bishop Phillpotts travelled from his residence at Devon's capital city to Cornwall, Hawker defended him in a sermon that linked the Devonian bishop with the subject of the famous ballad, the Cornish Bishop Trelawny: 'for we can never forget that day of glory in our annals, when the thraldom of the oppressor had shut up, in iron bondage, the spiritual ruler of these fields of the west; and immediately the strength of twenty thousand Cornish hearts arose, like the will of one man, to set their Bishop free? My Lord, if all the land beside were false, there ought to be, here in Cornwall, love and loyalty to your Lordship still!' (Hawker 1845: 1). The 'fields of the west' included Devon but defied London.

Hawker introduced his records of the western shore in 1832 as 'legends connected with the wild and singular scenery of 'his own country' and his footnotes continually remind his readers of these connections. 'Featherstone's Doom' commemorates the wrecker supposedly imprisoned in 'The Blackrock'; Hawker's accompanying note enables the non-local reader to picture this landmark, 'a bold, black, pillared mass of schist, which rises midway on the shore of Widemouth Bay, near Bude'. The evocation of Morwenstow in 'The Western Shore' is accompanied by an explanation of Hawker's role in this remote scene as landowner, and inheritor of Morwenna's Station: 'My glebe occupies a position of wild and singular beauty: its western boundary is the sea, skirted by tall and tremendous cliffs, and near their brink, with the exquisite taste of Ecclesiastical antiquity, is placed the church' (Hawker 1928: 13, 15, 57). Hawker claimed in his 1832 preface to 'Records of the Western Shore' to have composed his verse in the course of his 'solitary rambles in the West', turning prose legends into verse during 'walks and rides'. Much of his verse has the tang of being composed out of doors in a salt-laden, coastal wind (read 'The Sonnet of the Sea' composed at Boscastle while Hawker's family were out in a boat). Many of his poems were inspired by particular localities with historical associations. 'The Song of the Western Men' was inspired by a visit to the territory of the Grenville family near Kilkhampton: he composed it 'under a stag-horned oak in Sir Beville's walk in Stowe Wood'.

Hawker also presents his verse as the last part of a conversation with the inhabitants of North Cornwall. The stories in his poems 'were related' to him by others, and 'chiefly by the common people . . .'. 'Mawgan of Melhuach', 'Featherstone's Doom' and 'The Death-Race' are all presented as oral tales related by locals: Hawker appears, not as the inventor of them, but simply as the man who turned existing, local stories into verse. The legend explaining the absence of bells in 'The Silent Tower of Bottreaux' (Boscastle) was, Hawker explained, brought to light because of his inquiries amongst local people. 'The Sisters of Glen Nectan' (Nighton's Kieve near Tintagel) was told to Hawker 'on the spot', although he 'expanded' the original. The first line of his poem 'The Dirge', about a man who requested singing at his funeral, was always on the lips of a local farmer. It was a 'fragment of some forgotten dirge, of which he could remember no more': at this man's request Hawker completed the song. Similarly, Hawker claimed that he wrote the Trelawny ballad to complete the ancient chorus which had survived in popular memory: 'And shall Trelawny die? Here's twenty thousand Cornishmen, Will know the reason why' (Hawker 1928: xiii, 2, 14–15, 28, 57, 128). In all these ways, Hawker presents himself as a bard in a landscape, a poet speaking for the people, preserving and renovating oral tradition as much as he preserved and renovated Morwenstow church.

Nevertheless, Hawker was proud of the fact that he invented more than he found. His 'records' were also inventions, or records of his inventive response to the lonely environment in which he was cast. When John Blight questioned Hawker's use of the word 'carvure' to describe a curious carving in Morwenstow church, the poet curtly replied 'If no such word, it is time there should be. I invent it'. It was his habit as a mystic to rival the claims of scientific discovery: 'I have discovered among other things a New and another Element: the atmosphere of God and Angels. I have named it "Numyne". Remember I claim the word.' A man who could invent words and discover new elements was fully capable of inventing folk traditions.

After Hawker had admitted the element of fiction in his work, a colleague wrote to him in 1868 'Your naif confession of the manufacture of legends remind me of the reply of the Guide to the seven Churches at Glindalough to a friend of mine, who asked how he employed himself in the winter time when there were no tourists:—"I be invintin' ould traditions" ' (Byles 1906: 254, 265, 575). Dickens added so much to Christmas tradition that he might be said to have invented it. He famously invented a ritual: did obscure Hawker invent a country? It is certainly true that Hawker's Cornish tales in verse were unconsciously borrowed or consciously plagiarized in other writers' evocations of Cornwall: he was the unacknowledged source of the Cornish legends that appeared in popular guidebooks by Murray, Walter White, Cyrus Redding and Wilkie Collins. Similarly, Hawker's semi-fictional accounts of wreckers and smugglers were stolen by Baring-Gould and put without acknowledgement into his two Cornish novels: *The Gaverocks* (1887) and *In the Roar of the Sea* (1892). Hawker complained bitterly about being plagiarized but his fate was the inevitable result of his success as a forger of tradition. He had hidden himself so successfully in the landscape and in native tradition that few people knew he was there. It was inconsistent of him to hide and then complain that no one could find him. The legend of Glen Nectan, for example, appeared in the work of one 'Mr H' of Exeter College: he had found it in Murray's guide, not knowing that Murray had found it in Hawker. Hawker had so effectively attached a legend to a Victorian tourist attraction that he was no longer needed to perpetuate it (Byles 1906: 261).

The paradoxical methods of Hawker are exemplified in the creation of his 'Christ-Cross rhyme', a poem about learning the alphabet in the context of Christian belief. Hawker introduced the poem to the public in 1854 as follows: 'In a book that I have seen there is a vignette of a monk teaching a little boy to read and beneath "A Christ-Cross Rhyme"'. He then proceeded, like a second Chatterton, to quote the poem that he himself had recently invented as if it belonged to a monkish manuscript from the ancient past! When he published his poem in *Willis' Current Notes* the following year, he extended the techniques of forgery from the content to the visual impression of the verse on the page. Hawker explained to the editor of this periodical that in the line 'Teach me letters A B C', the latter three letters should be in 'Old English Capitals' so that the typography should create 'in every mind a piece of their old alphabet risen as it were from the past' (Byles 1906: 259). This shows mastery of the techniques required to invent old traditions.

The story of the 'Christ-Cross Rhyme' may help us to understand the origin of the Trelawny ballad, which is often perceived as part of Cornwall's ancient past. Here follows one version of the ballad recorded in 1889 by J.F. Collier. Collier introduces it as the version he had 'always heard sung in Cornwall and Devon':

'Shall Trelawny Die?'

A good sword and a trusty hand,
A merry heart and true,
And we'll give King James to understand
What Cornish lads can do.

And have they found the where and when;
And shall Trelawny die?
Here's twenty thousand Cornish men
Will know the reason why.

We'll cross the Tamar land to land,
The Severn is no stay,
And then we'll come to London town
And who shall bid us nay?

And will they mind Tre, Pol, and Pen?
And shall Telawny die?
There's twenty thousand Cornish men
Will know the reason why.

Up sake our Captain brave and bold,
A merry wight was he,
Were London's Tower, Michael's hold,
We'd set Trelawny free.

Trelawny he's in keep awhile,
Trelawny he must die,
But there's twenty thousand underground
Will know the reason why.

And then we'll come to London Wall,
A pleasant sight to view,
Come forth, come forth, ye cowards all
To better men than you.

And will they mind Tre, Pol and Pen,
And shall Trelawny die?
There's twenty thousand Cornish men
Will know the reason why.
(Collier 1889: 130–31)

The ballad which Walter Scott and Lord Macaulay thought derived from the seventeenth century was actually mostly invented by Hawker in 1824. Hawker presented his work to the public in 1826 in the form of an unsigned poem with a note asserting its historical accuracy. He belatedly claimed authorship of the ballad in 1832 but by that time it had become anthologized by antiquarians as a genuine relic of the past. Hawker's success as a forger had eclipsed his powers as an inventor. In 1903 a correspondent to *The Times* claimed that Hawker had invented the entire ballad, including the refrain. Hawker would surely have interpreted this as a compliment rather than an insult. However, Hawker's assertion that the chorus of the ballad was genuinely ancient is supported by a source of 1772 which quotes a refrain very like Hawker's. Nevertheless, this source, the earliest historical record of the ballad, attaches it not (as Hawker does) to the imprisonment of Bishop Jonathan Trelawny in 1688 in an argument with James II but to an argument of 1627 between the royalist John Trelawny (the Bishop's grandfather) and Parliament. There is also a Trelawny-like refrain connected to the trial of John Lilbourne in 1653. Hawker further complicated the issue by adapting his ballad to serve as an electioneering song in celebration of Salusbury Trelawny standing to represent Cornwall in Parliament in 1832. According to Hawker, one of the 1832 verses became permanently attached to his 1824 version and henceforth distorted popular versions of the song. Further authors contributed to this continuing process of invention, when several composers added music to the ballad in the 1860s. According to Macaulay, the Trelawny story is less about the religious questions raised in 1688 than Cornish loyalty to a family whose origins predated the Norman conquest and reached as far back as the Celtic past.

None of the complications surrounding Hawker's inventions devalue the ballad's Cornish origins but these evolve all the way from 1627 to 1832 and beyond. Most of the words of the ballad are not a seventeenth-century survival but a nineteenth-century invention. It is, however, intriguing to find Macaulay relying on Hawker for the evidence that the line 'Then thirty thousand Cornish boys will know the reason why' existed in an alternative form as 'Then twenty thousand underground will know the reason why' (Byles 1906: 23–31). Hawker and others memorialized a romantic, Celtic Cornwall, a place of dreamy Christianity and hermits in cells by the sea. The ancient evidence that Cornwall was known to the world as a result of its tin-mining is much less reflected in nineteenth-century fictions. Hawker's note to Macaulay preserves a glimpse of an ancient but industrialized Cornwall which his 1824 version of the Trelawny ballad does not address. In this respect, Hawker was both an inventor and recorder of the Western shore. Whatever the true nature of the ballad's origins, it certainly became part of Cornish tradition *after* Hawker's intervention in Macaulay's famous history. Walter White heard the ballad sung in 1855. It was widely known when J.F. Collier sent his version of it to *The Western Antiquary* in 1889. Collier queried whether the ballad was ancient or created by Hawker, only to be directed by the editor of *The Antiquary* to consult Baring-Gould's semi-fictional biography (Collier 1889: 130)! Hawker was trapped in a labyrinth of fiction made by himself and elaborated by his followers. He had, however, succeeded in trapping Cornish history alongside him.

## Inventions of The Western Shore: Cruel Coppinger

The story of Cruel Coppinger is a narrative combining a little history with a lot of speculation and invention. The story goes that in 1792 a man was washed ashore from a shipwreck and found amongst the surf and rocks at Welcombe Mouth on the border between North Cornwall and North Devon. A local yeoman farmer of Golden Park near Hartland took pity on this fugitive from the sea and gave him shelter. This event apparently took its first written form when the rescued man inscribed on a window pane at Golden Park 'D.H. Coppinger, shipwrecked December 23rd, 1792; kindly received by Mr Wm. Arthur'. It seems that Coppinger succeeded in marrying into the local community within a year of his unexpected arrival. The parish register of Hartland parish church records that in 1793 'Daniel Herbert Coppinger of the King's Royal Navy and Ann Hamlyn mard (by licence) 3 Aug.'. There is no record of Coppinger among the commissioned officers of the navy, but the Hamlyns can be traced. His forty-two-year-old wife, Ann, was daughter of Ackland and Ann Hamlyn of Galsham. When Ann's mother died in 1800, she and her husband succeeded to the property of Galsham. Consistent with the behaviour ascribed to him at Golden Park, Coppinger celebrated his new access to life and property by inscribing his name on a window pane at Galsham. He may have spent his new fortune quickly, since he appears in 1802 as a bankrupt before the King's Bench, together with a Richard Copinger (spelt with one 'p'), a merchant on the island of Martinique. Coppinger's fate after this is unknown: it is said that he was resident in Barnstaple, living on an allowance from his wife. It is known that Ann Hamlyn died at Barnstaple in 1833, aged eighty-two, and was buried in Hartland church next to her mother (R. Pearse-Chope 1908: 301–4).

This is a very scanty historical record, especially since the evidence of the window at Golden Park no longer exists. Nevertheless these few hints about Coppinger's life, some proven and some not, became the foundation of a myth. The very brevity of the story provides ample room for a person of imagination to work. Just a few nudges turn the outline into an adventure story with a victim and a villain: Coppinger is a man of mysterious origins who takes advantage of local hospitality to escape temporarily from his former life. He dupes a woman desperate for a husband into marrying him and with the benefit of her money, returns to his old habits of unlawful living and profligate spending. He has associations with illicit merchandise from Martinique. He soon becomes bankrupt, is estranged from his wife Ann and is allowed to continue living in the area providing he restrains his worst tendencies. Older and wiser, Ann requests in her will to be buried next to her mother, thinking 'how I wish I had listened to her advice and never trusted the stranger from the sea'.

How many contributed to the invention or transmission of a story of this kind during the 1830s is a matter of speculation, but we do have some evidence for believing that two years after the death of Ann Hamlyn, Parson Hawker encountered the narrative that began in 1792. In 1835 Hawker seems to have met a man of ninety-seven years of age who had witnessed criminal behaviour by Coppinger and his followers, and then been abducted by them in order to ensure his silence. Hawker stored this anecdote for future use. His reminiscences published in 1865 connect his knowledge of Coppinger's reputation with the wreck of the *Caledonia* off the coast at Morwenstow in 1842. The figurehead of the *Caledonia* in Morwenstow churchyard commemorates the tragedy. The ship sank with nearly all her crew and Hawker had the gruesome job of organizing the finding and burial of the dead. One person, a Jerseyman called Le Dain, was washed ashore and survived (Hawker 1922: 64). Like Coppinger he was a sailor miraculously saved from the sea; Hawker helped to care for him just as William Arthur had cared for Coppinger. Unlike Coppinger, Le Dain was a grateful guest but in his 'Remembrances of a Cornish Vicar', Hawker makes one of his parishioners refer to the perils of taking in Le Dain:

> You don't know, sir . . . the saying on our coast—'Save a stranger from the sea, And he'll turn your enemy'. There was one Coppinger cast ashore from a brig that struck up at Hartland on the Point. Farmer Hamlyn dragged him out of the water and took him home, and was very kind to him. Lord, sir! he never would leave the house again! He lived upon the folks a whole year, and at last, lo and behold! he married the farmer's daughter Elizabeth, and spent all her fortin rollicking and racketing till at last he would tie her to the bed-post and flog her till her father would come down with more money. The old man used to say he wished he'd let Coppinger lie where he was in the waves, and never laid a finger on him to save his life. (Hawker 1893: 40–41)

Due either to the distortions of a story orally transmitted or to Hawker's powers of invention, the original tale has been both compressed and expanded. William Arthur and Golden Park have been excised, and instead, Coppinger escapes from the embrace of the sea straight into the arms of the Hamlyn family. Ann has become an Elizabeth, and her anxious parent is the father not the mother. Coppinger has become perverse and cruel, extorting money not only by deceit but by violence from the family who had offered him shelter and love.

Hawker, however, had only begun his recreation of Coppinger. In 1866, a year after his first sketch, he was writing to his brother-in-law requesting information: 'Do you remember bold Coppinger the

Marsland Pirate? He died 87 years ago. I am collecting materials for his life for *All the Year Round*. If you know any anecdotes of him or Dinah his wife will you let me know . . .'. Consistent with the origins of the story, this Coppinger is associated with Marsland Mouth, close to Welcombe and Hartland, and appears to have married a local woman (not Ann nor Elizabeth but Dinah). On the other hand, this Coppinger is assumed to have died in about 1779, and is not just a manipulator of the local population but a 'pirate'. Soon after his first letter on the matter, Hawker was again pursuing Coppinger, treating him as a flesh and blood person with relations. He wrote to his brother-in-law: 'Hadn't you an Aunt called Coppinger?' (Byles 1906: 557–58, 550).

The result of Hawker's enquiries, and of his imagination, appeared in December of 1866 in Dickens' periodical *All the Year Round*. Like his original, the 1866 Coppinger swims ashore from a ship in a storm and marries a local farmer's daughter. Expanding his short 1865 version of the tale, Hawker makes the forty-two-year old farmer's daughter a young woman and develops the Coppinger who inscribed his name on glass into a man who signs his name on a deed 'in stern, bold, fierce characters, as if every letter had been stabbed upon the parchment with the point of a dirk'. The foreign and strange qualities of Coppinger are emphasized: he comes ashore from a 'strange vessel of foreign rig', no longer a Daniel Herbert, he is simply 'Coppinger', a Dane whose features have 'a fine stately resemblance of one of the old Vikings of the northern seas'. Some time after Coppinger's unexpected arrival, a ship mysteriously appears off the coast: it was built to Coppinger's requirements in a Danish shipyard and assists him in his activities as Viking plunderer, pirate and smuggler. Hawker brilliantly contrives in a compressed form to suggest Coppinger's hidden life. At one point, he has somehow gained enough money to buy a local farm; he pays for it in 'dollars and ducats, doubloons and pistoles, guineas—the coinage of every foreign country with a sea-board'. Hawker then sets about making this exotic foreigner at home in the distinctive landscape of North Devon and Cornwall. Coppinger's smuggling gang take over the footpaths by night: they become known as 'Coppinger's tracks'. He stores his booty in 'Coppinger's Cave' within a towering cliff called Steeple Brink. In a blasphemous parody and inversion of normality, the cave inside the 'Steeple' is said by local people to be as big as the tower of Kilkhampton church. This adventure story rooted in local topography also touches the world of folk-tale. Coppinger not only comes from Viking territory, he is sent by the Devil. He is not simply washed ashore like his original: he chooses to swim ashore. The boat from which he came is not wrecked but 'strange to say' mysteriously disappears. The ship that later appears in connection with him is called *The Black Prince*. Coppinger takes a whip to the local Parson and terrifies a local tailor by telling him that he has arranged for him to make and mend for the Devil. Coppinger does not die like a mere mortal: he leaves as mysteriously as he came on a ship that vanishes 'out of sight in a moment, like a spectre or a ghost'.

Linked to the folk-tales about wreckers and death ships at other parts of the Cornish coast, Hawker's Coppinger also touches pagan myth and Nature worship. Cruel Coppinger incarnates the cruel weather and cruel coast of North Cornwall: his swift steed has hooves which sound like the progress of a storm; he uses his 'sea-cat' or double-thonged whip on his victims like wind and hail lashing a walker in the open air. His arrival is signalled by a 'terrific hurricane' and his departure is followed by thunder, lightning and hail. Just after he has gone a 'storm-bolt' pierces the roof of his former house and falls at the feet of his empty chair. Hawker tempts his readers into smelling the Devil's sulphur, hearing echoes of Odin and seeing the unseen. Coppinger's sudden existence and non-existence is not so much a 'bolt from the blue' as a bolt from Hawker's imagination, a synthesis of Scandinavian mythology, local topography and tradition. Hawker synthesizes influences of local landscape and the Gothic literary tradition when he gives Coppinger and Dinah a son: this creature is born deaf and dumb, is reputed to have no soul and delights in cruelty to animals and children. Remonstrating with him is obviously as pointless as talking to the savage weather that indiscriminately killed so many sailors on Hawker's coast (Hawker 1893: 95–107). The unnamed, unnatural boy, a product of humanity (Dinah) forcibly wedded to wild nature (Cruel Coppinger), belongs in North Cornwall as much as Heathcliff belongs to the Yorkshire moors.

It is important not to underestimate the element of forgery in this invention. In the 1870 revised version of his tale, Hawker introduces Coppinger as a real creature with an existence in the popular mind: 'There was a ballad in existence within human memory which was founded on the history of this singular man, but of which the first verse only can now be recovered.' Hawker then 'quotes' the surviving verse:

> Will you hear of the Cruel Coppinger?
> He came from a foreign kind:
> He was brought to us by the salt-water,
> He was carried away by the wind.

In his 1866 version of the tale, the ballad has different words and consists of two verses:

> Will you hear of the bold, brave Coppinger?
> How he came of a foreign kind?
> He was brought to us by the salt-water,
> He'll be carried away by the wind
>
> For thus the old wives croon and sing,
> And so the proverbs say,
> That whatsoever the wild waves bring
> The winds will bear away.

Was Hawker playing his customary trick of quoting his own creation as if it belonged to an old tradition? The second verse, bearing all the hallmarks of Hawker's sense of rhythm and choice of vocabulary, was probably excised because it seemed less effective as poem and forgery. It is also significant that the 1866 Coppinger is bold and brave, whereas the 1870 Coppinger has found his true name: 'Cruel', a word whose sound and visual impact on the page is well suggested by Hawker when he describes it as 'that weird and graphic epithet' (Hawker 1866: 537–40; 1893: 97). On close inspection, other elements of Coppinger prove to be reworkings of tales heard or invented by Hawker about wreckers and smugglers in general. 'The Remembrances of a Cornish Vicar' and 'The Gauger's Pocket', two Hawker stories of 1853, refer to a group of smugglers whose ship is called *The Black Prince* and to a cruel excise man who has a black dog called Satan. This excise man beheads a smuggler by severing his neck over the gunwhale of a boat. In 1866 Hawker transfers the satanic associations to Coppinger and the violence is committed by the smugglers against the excise men or gaugers: 'No revenue officer durst exercise vigilance west of the Tamar; and to put an end to all such surveillance at once, it was well known that one of the "Cruel" gang had chopped off a gauger's head on the gunwhale of a boat, and carried the body off to sea' (Hawker 1893: 100). The very last glimpse of Coppinger shows him swiftly and mercilessly using his cutlass on a rower caught slacking at his work.

The success of Hawker's renovation and forging of tradition is clear. When Baring-Gould repeated the Coppinger story in his 1876 biography, including a variation on the Dane's feud with the parson, he explained that his version differed from Hawker's because he had told the story as it was related to him 'in the neighbourhood' (Baring-Gould 1899a: 113). If Coppinger was not widely known in oral tales before Hawker's intervention, he seems to have become so afterwards. Hawker's Coppinger attained the status of a myth for some readers. The Hartland Dane began to diversify in nature and locality, like a seagod who could be found wherever there were dangerous coasts, coves or seaports associated with smuggling. One writer claimed to have met an 'informant' in 1890 who located Coppinger's exploits near Newquay (Courteney 1890). Baring-Gould moved Coppinger to Saint Enadoc, the setting of his novel *In the Roar of the Sea* (1892) and then daringly abducted Coppinger from Hawker's landscape in an article presenting him as a spy and smuggler of the Napoleonic wars whose ill-gotten gains allowed him to purchase estates at St Austell and Roscoff (Baring-Gould 1892a and 1895c). That same year a guidebook put Coppinger back near Welcombe and Hartland, presenting him as an accepted part of the landscape and tradition of the Cornwall/Devon borders (Page 1895: 179–82). Coppinger was still on the move in the twentieth century: one commentator linked Coppinger's supernatural associations with a tale about a notorious wrecker near Saint Just (Hamilton-Jenkin, 1932).

The historical reality underlying this mobile Coppinger remains confused with fiction. It is possible to suggest in broad terms, without chasing the elusive individual called Coppinger, what motivated Hawker's inventions. Hawker was frank in his description of the parishioners of Morwenstow: 'My people were a mixed multitude of smugglers, wreckers and dissenters of various hue'. However he was more ambivalent when explaining what wrecking involved. As a parson he disapproved of past tradition, of 'the cruel and covetous natives of the strand, with whom it was a matter of pastime to lure a vessel ashore by the treacherous light, or to withhold succour from the seaman struggling with the sea'. On the other hand, Hawker was also capable of telling the famous tale whereby the local parson holds the lantern so his parishioners can loot a wreck. Wreckers are also described by Hawker half-admiringly as 'daring gleaners of the harvest of the sea'. One of his parishioners is described as a wrecker for forty years only in the sense of being a 'watcher of the sea and rocks for flotsam and jetsam, and other unconsidered trifles which the waves might turn up to reward the zeal and vigilance of a patient man' (Hawker 1893: 37–38). There is an element of tongue in cheek irony about the latter description, suggesting that Hawker knows he is idealizing an activity which could be ruthless. Legal precedent which determined that a wreck was only available to all if no one survived it actually gave an incentive for the wrecker to ignore drowning men. On the other hand, Hawker knew from experience of the heroism shown by those many Cornishmen who risked their own lives to save sailors in peril. Hawker's own contribution to the rescue and decent burial of wrecked sailors was used to counter the stereotype of the cruel Cornish wrecker. After two ships had been wrecked near Morwenstow in 1843, a local newspaper commented on the rescue efforts of the Cornish: 'Conduct like this will soon redeem their country from whatever stigma the misconduct or slanders of past times may have attached to its name. Fifteen shipwrecked sailors have been buried in the churchyard of Morwenstow, in little more than thirteen months . . .' (Byles 1906: 164–65).

Hawker knew some of the facts at first hand: it was due to him that the only authentic contemporary record of the wrecks off the north coast survives. He made one John Bray record his dealings with no less than thirty-seven wrecks. Bray's account makes no mention whatever of men deliberately luring ships to disaster, although it does show a continual war between magistrates and gaugers on the one hand and wreckers and smugglers on the other for control of wrecked or untaxed property (Bray c.1860). Hawker knew from Bray and his own experience that the illegal activity was not motivated by greed and cruelty but by poverty. Many local folk rhymes tell us the truth behind the romance of wrecking. A ship wrecked north of Bude in 1846 inspired the following rhyme: 'The *Eliza* of Liverpool came on shore,/To feed the hungry and clothe the poor'. Those eking a living in a harsh landscape valued the timbers, valuables and food that a wreck could provide. In 1862, Hawker gives a glimpse of a particularly bad year at Morwenstow: 'Never yet during my incumbency of 27 years did the prospects of farmers and labourers and poor assume so dark a hue. They come to me for advice. If they have a few pounds from the wreck my advice always is "Emigrate!" ' (Byles 1906: 63, 401). Whether these pounds were earned legally or not mattered less to Hawker than the fact that they might give the poorest a chance of a new start. The poetry and cruelty of Hawker's Coppinger emerges from this background. Behind Cruel Coppinger, stands Cruel Poverty.

## Inventions of The Western Shore: A Cornish King Arthur

Parson Hawker's remote parishes of Morwenstow and Welcombe were close to a place which was at the very centre of nineteenth-century thought about the past: Tintagel. Its topography irresistably invites invention. An airy headland so surrounded by sea that it is almost an island, its precipitous paths, dark caves, wave-battered shores, vivid sunsets and mist-bound ruins conspire to make legends seem true for any visitor of imagination. This remains so today despite commercialization of the area: in the nineteenth century when choughs and seals could still be seen near Tintagel and before modern archaeology could question myth, the sense of an encounter with another world was even stronger. William Howitt needed little persuasion to use Tintagel as a gateway to an idealized past: 'As the sound of the billows came up from below, and the cliffs stood around in their dark solemn grandeur, I gradually lost sight of the actual place, and was gone into the very land and times of old romance' (Howitt 1835: 335–36). Elihu Burrit, an American visitor to Cornwall, suggests the link between Tintagel Island's distinctive topography and symbolic role in the Victorian period: 'The history of Tintagel Castle conforms itself to the natural features of the place. It is equally wild, grand, and incoherent. It is a headland standing almost insulated in a sea of mystery. The narrow neck of fact that connects it with the mainland of real human life and authentic chronicle, is thinned almost to a thread, and weak and knotty at that' (Burrit 1868: 257).

Tintagel Castle may be partly understood as a monument to invention, particularly the inventive powers of the Norman-Welsh cleric, Geoffrey of Monmouth. He began the long process of creating an Arthurian Tintagel in his famous twelfth-century 'history'. Although there is evidence of Dark Age occupation at Tintagel, we know that Tintagel castle does not belong to the period when King Arthur supposedly lived, but to the twelfth century. Its foundation is associated with the Earls and Dukes of Cornwall. Since one of his patrons was related to these dignitaries, Geoffrey may have invented Tintagel's link with King Arthur in order to cast Arthurian glamour on the Earls' territory even before the castle was built. It is possible that instead of the castle preceding the legend, the legend was one of the reasons why the oddly sited castle was created. From Geoffrey's twelfth-century invention, amplified by Sir Thomas Malory in his fourteenth-century but much reprinted Arthurian classic, the subsequent history of the area follows: the changing of the name of the local village from Trevenna to Tintagel, the numerous local place-names linking caves and rocks to Arthur and Merlin, the story that the red-legged choughs of Tintagel were King Arthur's birds, the legend that this 'isle' associated with Merlin's magic vanishes twice a year, the continued pilgrimages by artists, writers and tour guides seeking inspiration or commercial gain. Tintagel's national and international reputation in the Victorian period is suggested by Burrit's description of the place from an American perspective: 'the very fountain head and focus of Cornish romance and legendary chivalry . . . it has been written upon, engraved and photographed, and sung in noble rhyme, until nearly every English and many an American reader have become familiar with it' (Burrit 1868: 255–56). Burrit refers to the Arthurian poems by Tennyson and his many admirers, to the images of Tintagel by William Clarkson Stanfield, John William Inchbold and Thomas Creswick, to the photographs, engravings and quotations from literary sources that feature in the numerous guide books to the area from William Peneluna and John Murray onwards. One visitor described the relationship between Tintagel and the myths attached to it as follows: 'How all the wondrous legend comes crowding back on the mind when you are on the spot which gave it birth!' (White 1855: 316). A modern reader would argue that the opposite case was equally valid: how much has legend contributed to the 'birth' of Tintagel?

Hawker was one of the many who regarded Tintagel as a place of pilgrimage and inspiration. In 1863 he recalled his first romantic association with Tintagel in 1824: 'I was married, and we went . . . to Dundagel in Lodgings for a Month—close to the Castle of King Arthur and amid the legends of his life and deeds. There we used to roam about and read all that could be found about those Old-World Histories, and often was the legend of the Sangraal talked of as a fine subject for Verse. Often I have said "If I could but throw myself back to King Arthur's time and write what he would have said and thought it would make a good Cornish book" . . . It seems to me so striking and so strange that after nine and thirty years of travel thro' life I come back to the same old scene, circling like some hunted animal to die where my life was born' (Byles 1906: 412–13). The assumption that Tintagel is Arthurian is due to tradition, but Hawker brings his own powers of invention to bear on the recreation of the past. In 1824, long before Tennyson's famous Arthurian Idylls were created, Hawker had already begun both to join the legend and to change the legend. He calls the Holy Grail a 'Sangraal' in an imitation of medieval language, he conceives Arthur in a specifically Cornish context and, characteristically, he asserts the right to tamper with the very name of the place so revered by others, calling Tintagel 'Dundagel'. He had some success in putting his mark on the legend in this respect. Tennyson temporarily included Hawker's version of the name in his *Idylls* and Hardy quoted it in his Cornish novel, *A Pair of Blue Eyes*.

Hawker's imagination continued to circle around Tintagel and Arthur, even when he was overtly writing of other matters. He collaborated with his first wife, Charlotte L'Ans, to write 'The Wreck', a poem of 1840 commemorating her ancestor's role in saving the crew of a ship wrecked off Bude in 1790. The poem is written from the viewpoint of a sailor on the doomed ship looking at Tintagel from the sea:

> Thou seest dark Cornwall's rifted shore,
> Old Arthur's stern and rugged keep:
> There, where proud billows dash and roar,
> His haughty turret guards the deep.

> And mark yon bird of sable wing,
> Talons and beak all red with blood:
> The spirit of the long-lost king
> Pass'd in that shape from Camlan's flood!

> And still, when loudliest howls the storm,
> And darkliest lowers his native sky,

> The king's fierce soul is in that form:
> The warrior's spirit threatens nigh!
> (Hawker 1928: 288–91)

This was the Hawkers' first attempt to make an Arthur at one with the landscape, seas and legends of Cornwall. The L'Ans family crest included a chough and its Arthurian associations were apparently conveyed to Hawker in dialogue with the inhabitants of the northern coast: 'The common people believe that the soul of King Arthur inhabits one of these birds, and no entreaty or bribe would induce an old Tintadgel [sic] quarry-man to kill me one' (Hawker 1928: 17). The legend that Slaughter Bridge near Camelford was the site of the Arthurian battle of Camlann was not unanimously agreed: this did not prevent the Hawkers appropriating the legend for their cause. Their Cornish Arthur fights his last battle with Modred near Camelford and has a fierce, unforgiving character like the stormy seas and rocky coasts near Tintagel. This fierce King is the antithesis of Tennyson's 'modern gentleman of stateliest port'. On the other hand, although the narrator of Hawker's poem fears Cornish wreckers, he is actually saved from the cruel sea by the Arthurian chivalry and bravery of the L'Ans family of Bude.

The Arthur legend was connected in Hawker's imagination with the task of finding a language and imagery appropriate to the Cornish landscape. In 1841, he created a verse called 'Queen Guennivar's Round', attempting to combine the aural and musical qualities of a roundelay with literary legend. By calling Arthur's Queen 'Guennivar' rather than the better known 'Guinevere', Hawker is linking her to the world of Gwenhwyfar of *The Mabinogion*, the Welsh tales of varying historical periods then being translated by Lady Charlotte Guest. Hawker's mind-set linked Morwenstow and Arthurian legend with Wales: he was inspired by a vision of a Celtic past. He was consciously trying to revive and create a tradition and mythology that would flourish on a wild Celtic shore rather than in a Greek setting:

> Naiad for Grecian waters!
> Nymph for the fountain-side
> But old Cornwall's bounding daughters
> For grey Dundagel's tide.
> (Hawker 1928: 102)

Although there are many Welsh and Cornish place-names and legends connected with Arthur, he also has links with many other parts of England. A legend associated with 'Pendragon Castle' near Kirkby Stephen in Cumbria, tells how the famous King Uther attempted to divert the course of the local river Eden to make a moat. The 'local' rhyme goes: 'Let Uther Pendragon do what he can, Eden will run where Eden ran' (Ashe 1980: 167). It is intriguing to find Hawker inventing a Cornish version of the rhyme in his Arthurian ballad of 1851 'The Doom Well of St Madron': 'Now let Uter Pendragon do what he can,/Still the Tamar river will run as it ran' (Hawker 1928: 146).

Hawker was well aware, however, that he was working in the shadow of Tennyson, the Poet Laureate. Writing in 1855, after Tennyson's first Arthurian pieces had caught the public imagination, Walter White found it natural to describe Tintagel with the aid of Tennyson's 'Sir Galahad' and 'Morte d'Arthur'. Hawker accepted that Cornwall was becoming known to the rest of the nation dressed in an Arthurian costume chiefly tailored by Tennyson. In a poem of 1858, dedicated, like Tennyson's *Idylls*, to Prince Albert, Hawker even presents Cornwall as an empty, nameless place until the language of Arthurian legend brought it to life:

> Void was the land in days of yore,
> Of warrior-deed and minstrel song:
> The unknown rivers sought the shore,
> The nameless billows rolled along:—
> Till Arthur, and the Table-round,
> Made stern Tintadgel storied ground
> ('Lines of Dedication to H.R.H. the Prince of Wales,
> 1858' in Hawker 1928: 159)

In 1859 Hawker wrote a poem attributing King Arthur's immortality not to the magic powers of the Isle of Avalon, but to Tennyson's poetic capacity to immortalize the King in verse ('To Alfred Tennyson'). By 1865, as the popularity of the *Idylls* continued to gain momentum, Murray's guide could not introduce King Arthur and Tintagel without indicating Tennyson's authoritative role: 'Of his origin as the great hero of romance there are many versions, but on this spot we shall of course prefer that given by the Laureate' (Murray 1865). When Emma Lavinia Gifford, the first wife of

Thomas Hardy, rendered Tintagel in fiction, she accepted the tradition made famous by Tennyson that this was the place where the King was born. Her heroine assumes that Tintagel is 'the traditionary spot of King Arthur's birth' and proposes 'to look for . . . a grave of some giant knight of King Arthur's Table' (Emma Lavinia Gifford *c*.1870). While Tennyson had imposed himself on Tintagel, he had not completely excluded Hawker. In 1868 Burrit illustrated his account of Tintagel with a quotation from Tennyson's 'Guinevere', an Idyll which refers in Hawker's manner to 'wild Dundagil by the Cornish Sea'. As this survival of Hawker's influence suggests, the Cornish poet was in the Laureate's shadow but not eclipsed by it.

Tennyson's words owe their inspiration to his meeting with Hawker in 1848, while visiting Bude in search of Arthurian inspiration. It is tempting to read between the lines of Tennyson's record of the event: 'Took a gig to Rev. S. Hawker at Morwenstow, passing Comb valley, fine view over sea, coldest manner of vicar until I told my name, then all heartiness. Walk on a cliff with him, told of shipwreck' (Tennyson 1897, Vol. 1: 274). Tennyson's mis-spelling of Coombe hints, like his reference in the *Idylls* to Boss rather than Bos (the logical abbreviation of Boscastle, near Morwenstow), at the limitations of a visitor attempting to capture local colour in a short time. Nevertheless, he had the opportunity to gain genuine local knowledge from Hawker. Hawker's account of the meeting gives more detail of their conversation:

> We . . . talked about Cornwall and King Arthur, *my* themes, and I quoted Tennyson's fine acct. of the restoration of Excalibur to the Lake . . . Then seated on the brow of the Cliff, with Dundagel full in sight, he related to me the purpose of his journey to the West. He is about to conceive a Poem—the Hero King Arthur . . . Much converse then and there befel of Arthur and his Queen, his wound at Camlan and his prophesied return. Legends were exchanged, books noted down and reference given . . . He went next day to the Castle of his hero King, and traced I think, the route I had marked out for him by the Lower Sea. (Byles 1906: 190–94)

Tennyson's encounter with Arthurian landscapes here and elsewhere in Cornwall certainly influenced the genesis of the *Idylls*.

Caroline Fox recorded that Tennyson spoke of the Cornish scenery 'with rapture'; she also noted: 'The Welsh claim Arthur as their own but Tennyson gives all his votes to us . . .' (Fox 1882, Vol. 2: 138, 274–75). We can speculate as to Hawker's part in the exchange of legends with Tennyson by using a boyhood memory from J. Harman Ashley. He records a glimpse of Hawker's contribution to the Arthurian oral tradition: 'None knew so well, nor could relate so delightfully as he, the exquisite legends of the "Morte d'Arthur", Tristram and Isolde, Guinevere and Lancelot, Merlin and Vivien, Sir Kay the Seneschal, Sir Galahad and the Sangraal—how full of life each of these became under the magic of his vivid story-telling!' (Burrows 1926: 78). The titles Ashley uses are both Tennysonian ('Morte d'Arthur') and Hawkeresque ('Sangraal'): Hawker's imagination, his conviction that a Cornish Arthur was his theme, survives alongside Tennyson's influence.

Hawker's major contribution to the Arthurian literary tradition was the astounding 'Quest of the Sangraal' (1863). This was planned to be an epic consisting of five 'chants', a term suggesting the tradition of poetry as a verbal performance. Hawker only completed the first chant and the first few lines of the second: had he completed his project the world might remember Hawker's work as well as Tennyson's. Tennyson's *Idylls* were much admired by Prince Albert. Hawker wrote a carefully worded letter to Queen Victoria in 1863, acknowledging Prince Albert's admiration for Tennyson's *Idylls* while implying his own privileged access to the Cornish dimension of the epic: 'I have been assured that His Royal Highness the Prince your revered and lamented husband took an interest in our Cornish King Arthur, his Castle here by the sea, and the local legends of his life' (Byles 1906: 453). Despite its Cornish flavour, Hawker expected his Arthurian work to be recognized and understood: he uses the well-known stereotypes of Arthur's Court made famous in Malory and Tennyson. Following tradition, Hawker's Merlin is all-seeing, his Bedivere loyal, his Gauvain passionate, his Modred treacherous, his Kay cynical, his Galahad and Percival devout, his Lancelot and Tristram flawed but courageous. In major respects, however, his 'Quest' departs from the Victorian stereotype and therefore could not attain royal or popular approval on a Tennysonian scale.

King Arthur was resurrected in the early to mid-nineteenth century partly because he engaged with that much discussed Victorian topic: the nature of a true gentleman. When William

Howitt visited Tintagel he mused on the moral example set by poets of the past: 'Their heroes did not seek to recommend themselves by dressing, and lounging, and affecting the fine gentlemen—it was only by a self-renouncing course of noble and patriotic action that they could win acceptance.' Past ideals were a way of exhorting the present to do better: Arthurian chivalry represented 'a far more rational and better tone of morals and manners than prevails amongst large classes of the present day . . .'. In exact antithesis to the effete dandy, Arthur stands for 'every thing great, generous, and dignified, every thing calculated to catch the better spirit and kindle a noble ambition . . .' (Howitt 1835: 343, 345). Howitt's Tintagel musings were created not long after one of the principal symbols of the British State was destroyed, not by revolutionaries but by accident: in 1834 the Houses of Parliament burned down. The jokes amongst the large crowds which witnessed the destruction were a cause of anxiety. Before and during the period when Tennyson sought to resurrect Arthur in Cornwall, it was a matter of vital importance that Parliament should be resurrected in London. The new-old building was built in a style redolent of Arthurian/medieval chivalry and contained a series of Arthurian frescoes. Prince Albert headed the commission which requested Pugin and Dyce to make idealized images of the past into the material reality of a new building. If the twelfth-century Dukes of Cornwall built Tintagel Castle in accordance with the blueprint of a legend, the nineteenth-century builders of Parliament followed their example. William Dyce's images owe much to Malory, but so did Tennyson's verse and his series of *Idylls* helped to create the milieu in which the long drawn-out parliamentary project was completed. Tennyson certainly prophesied the national mood when the original inspiration of the *Idylls*, probably in 1833, took the form of connecting ancient Arthurian symbols with nineteenth-century political realities: the Round Table, for instance, was conceived as representing modern 'liberal institutions' (Tennyson 1897, Vol. 2: 123). To this day, the Queen is robed and prepared for her symbolic role in the opening of Parliament in the presence of Dyce's Arthurian frescoes. They continue to play their symbolic part in combining feudal past and modern present, House of Lords and House of Commons, monarchy and democracy.

The newly built Victorian Parliament had some new occupants representing classes hitherto excluded from the machinery of government. The Reform Act of 1832 was part of the process by which power relations between landowners and the rising middle classes were renegotiated. Several novels of the period attempt to answer the problem of the 'Condition of England' by showing how Trade and Nobility could form alliances. The leader class was subjected to scrutiny but only by those who wanted to improve it and join it. In this context the gentleman-dandy of the Regency period, the man who had power without responsibility, was no longer acceptable. His idleness and flippancy could not be tolerated in the new age of earnestness and self-improvement. He was a follower of fashion who was out of fashion. Whereas he had once been the bearer of wit and the subject of wit, he was now no laughing matter: he was a villain. Dickens' Harthouse in *Hard Times* embodies his new fate. However, this was evolution rather than revolution: the gentleman could stay as long as he did his job properly.

The person who embodied the new gentleman in literature was Tennyson's King Arthur: an earnest, patriotic, respectable figure who knows some sins are unforgivable (see his treatment of adulterous Guinevere) but also knows that an excess of idealism can damage the State (see his disapproval of the Grail quest). Hawker has no interest in this Victorian gentleman. His King Arthur is 'the son of Uter and the Night', a stern, fierce, Cornish warrior like his predecessor in 'The Wreck'. He demands extreme action from his followers: far from counselling caution about the Grail, he actively encourages the mission to find it. Tennyson could have created, under Hawker's influence, a warrior-Arthur in a specifically Cornish setting. He knew that his protagonist could have been:

> . . . that grey king, whose name, a ghost,
> Streams like a cloud, man-shaped, from mountain peak,
> And cleaves to cairn and cromlech still.
> (Warren 1989: 441)

Instead, although his Arthur has a strange and Hawker-like Dundagel birth, throughout much of the *Idylls* he is 'Ideal manhood', a Victorian gentleman in medieval costume. As the *Idylls* develop, Arthur becomes less like a warrior and more like Prince Albert (Swinburne referred to Tennyson's work as 'Morte d'Albert'). Hawker's Arthur, by contrast, stays in a Celtic world of cairn and cromlech. His poem is headed by an epigraph proudly explaining its Celtic character when read on the page or aloud: 'As in the title, so in the Knightly Names, I have preferred the Keltic to other sources of spelling and sound' (Hawker 1928: 171). Referring to the forest of 'Brocelian', calling his Grail a 'Sangraal', his Tristram 'Tristan', and his Guinevere 'Guenivvar', Hawker linked his story in terms of sound and etymology to Breton and Celtic sources. Hawker's Grail owes much to the Christian mysticism of Malory but also, through Malory and other sources, derives a little from the pagan, magic cauldrons of ancient Welsh and Irish tales. Hawker takes pleasure in thinking that his Quest is 'Monumental Morwenstow throughout' and also typical of much of Cornwall: 'I have touched on every Cornish feature in existence, Our Rock Altars, Barrows—Moors and etc.'. Elsewhere he explains 'I have given the Record and the Rationale of Keltic Cornwall, The Rock, Barrow, Moor, Mountain, all there, with the spirit of our Fathers rehearsing their intent' (Byles 1906: 440, 446). Hawker's Arthur is lonely like Tennyson's, but his loneliness is expressed in terms of a Cornish landscape:

> But he, the lofty ruler of the land,
> Like yonder Tor, first greeted by the dawn,
> And wooed the latest by the lingering day,
> With happy homes and hearths beneath his breast,
> Must soar and gleam in solitary snow.

While Tennyson's Arthur has a medieval court, Hawker's Arthur lives in a world combining the medieval with the pagan and early Christian, two elements that seemed to Hawker to suffuse the Cornish terrain. The pagan landscape is vividly present when King Arthur's men prepare to start their quest for the Christian Grail at 'craggy Caradon':

> Fit scene for haughty hope and stern farewell.
> Lo! the rude altar, and the rough-hewn rock,
> The grim and ghastly semblance of the fiend,
> His haunt and coil within that pillar'd home.
> Hark! the wild echo! Did the demon breathe
> That yell of vengeance from the conscious stone?

An Early Christian world is evoked at Nectan's Kieve (cauldron) near Tintagel where a St Nectan-like figure is imagined as:

One of the choir, whose life is orison.
They had their lodges in the wilderness,
Or built them cells beside the shadowy sea,
And there they dwelt with angels, like a dream:
So they unroll'd the volume of the Book,
And fill'd the fields of the Evangelist
With antique thoughts, that breath'd of Paradise.
(Hawker 1928: 172, 184–85)

It was the convention for Medieval Grail legends to involve a hermit figure; Hawker integrates this literary figure with the landscape he knew and loved.

Hawker does not relate the Arthurian past to the Victorian present in the same way as Tennyson. Unlike Tennyson, who found sensuality and adultery to be the root cause of the Round Table's destruction, Hawker shows little interest in the tale of Lancelot and Guinevere. In his ballad of 'The Doom Well of St Madron', all of Arthur's followers are put to the test: the well-water reveals the innocent and the guilty. Modred is condemned as treacherous but Lancelot is allowed to go unquestioned. Guinevere's behaviour is sensitively left as a matter for modern Cornish women to judge:

How the fountain flashed o'er King Arthur's Queen
Say Cornish dames, for ye guess the scene.

In 'The Quest', 'the sad Sir Lancelot of the lay' is introduced with a characteristically local reference:

Ah me! that logan of the rocky hills,
Pillar'd in storm, calm in the rush of war,
Shook, at the light touch of his lady's hand!
(Hawker 1928: 145, 172–73)

The mighty Logan or shuddering stone of Cornish tradition could be moved by a child or an innocent person; a strong but guilty man could not budge it. Hawker explains this in a footnote but assumes the reader will know the Arthurian tradition well enough to understand his reference to the lady. She is not the Guinevere who shares Lancelot's guilt, but the Elaine, whose pure and unrequited love for Lancelot leads to her own death. Guilty Lancelot cannot budge

73

the stone which Elaine can move. Adulterous Tristan is presented in an equally subtle manner: 'Did Ysolt's delicate fingers weave the web,/That gleamed in silken radiance o'er her lord?' (Hawker 1928: 183). Since this web is linked to a heavenly rainbow, the reference is to the pure Ysolt of the White Hands, honourably married to Tristram. Nevertheless, it is only on second reading that the reader is able to distinguish this Ysolt from her namesake, wife of Mark, who is part of a web of a more human and harmful kind. Although we only have one of the five projected 'chants' of his work, it is clear from the first chant that Hawker mostly followed the conventions from Malory to Tennyson in his moral ranking of the knights. Sinful Tristram and Lancelot will not find the Grail: this is reserved for pure Galahad whose shield reflects Hawker's holy, 'Numynous' light. However, Hawker compresses his treatment of the sins of Lancelot and Tristram so that he only has to glance at infidelity and sensuality before focusing on his main theme.

Whereas for Tennyson the cause of all evil was the old sin of sexual desire, for Hawker it was modern materialism. It was this conviction that prompted the choice of his Arthurian theme: the quest for a spiritual Grail. He expressed his fears about the poem's reception in a biting satire: 'I do not think it will win with the public. I fear that there will be a want of relish for such a theme and that those who do like the Subject would rather I had discussed the money value of the Vase and its array of jewels and dealt with the Quest as a lucky speculation of Sir Galahad' (Byles 1906: 440). For Tennyson, private wantonness leads to public wars: for Hawker war was the inevitable result of an age combining technological mastery with spiritual impoverishment. Despite the medieval cast to his work, Hawker claimed his poem applied to 'modern history'. Long before the First World War and the work of T.S. Eliot, this is Hawker's prophetic view of a wasteland without the Grail:

> The shrines were darkened and the chalice void:
> That which held God was gone: Maran-atha!
> The awful shadows of the Sangraal, fled!
> Yet giant-men arose, that seemed as gods,
> Such might they gathered from the swarthy kind
> The myths were rendered up: and one by one,
> The Fire—the Light—the Air—were tamed and bound
> Like votive vassals at their chariot-wheel.

Then learnt they War: yet not that noble wrath,
That brings the generous champion face to face
With equal shield, and with a measured brand,
To peril life for life, and do or die;
But the false valour of the lurking fiend
To hurl a distant death from some deep den:
To wing with flame the metal of the mine:
And, so they rend God's image, reck not who!

'Ah! haughty England! lady of the wave!'
Thus said pale Merlin to the listening King,
'What is thy glory in the world of stars?
To scorch and slay: to win demoniac fame,
In arts and arms; and then to flash and die!'
(Hawker, 1928: 188–89)

Hawker's argument is that modern man has a giant's powers without a god's compassion and wisdom. His wars are not just and chivalrous in the Arthurian tradition; technical ingenuity means that long-distance slaughter can take place without the murderer facing the moral or emotional consequences of his actions. The myths which encouraged reverence for God's creations have been forced to surrender to the world of technology: but Hawker attempts to resuscitate these myths in the poetic form and imagery of his condemnation of modern war and materialism. Exactly the opposite diagnosis of the national mission was offered by Prince Albert, Tennyson's modern King Arthur, when introducing the Great Exhibition of 1851 which celebrated Victorian progress and achievement. He found no conflict whatsoever between the pursuit of markets and the preservation of peace, between the laws of science and the values of religion (Golby 1986: 1–2). Hawker despised the Exhibitions of 1851 and 1862 and disapproved of those of his parishioners who joined the masses travelling to London to enjoy the displays. According to Hawker, they were Vanity Fairs, inciting competition and materialism instead of the Christian way. He was more than eccentric in interpreting his Arthur against the grain of the thinking of his time: he was courageous and prescient. In Hawker's coherent visual imagery, the scorching fire of war and the 'flash' of momentary and superficial national greatness could not compare with the divine light of the Grail.

The territory of 'The Quest' is Cornwall plus eternity: the landscape and atmosphere is limited to Hawker's West but the historical period is limitless. When Merlin shows Arthur a vision of all human history the scene is firmly Dundagel but 'whole ages' glide in a 'blink of time'. Hawker pictured space and time as a circle with God at the centre: his Christian faith enabled him to place history next to the unchanging reality of God (Lee 1876). While Hawker's Christian mysticism has Medieval qualities, it also has affinities with the Rosicrucian mysticism of that pioneer of Modernism, W.B. Yeats. Like Yeats, Hawker played with time and space in terms of cones, and like Yeats he compressed much meaning in single phrases and words. Hawker's literary criticism of 'The Quest' makes it seem like an anticipation of the techniques used in 'The Second Coming' (1921) and the famous Byzantium poems (1928–33). He intended Merlin's prophecy to show three visions or periods of time: 'The first, England under Arthur and his wars, the second the Saxon and Norman times of Sangraal light, third from 1536 to 1863 with my notions of the Battle of Waterloo and the Armstrong Gun—Gas, Steam, Electric Telegraph'. He uses the single word 'Libbard' for 'Leopard' to conjure up the atmosphere of the past, the shield of William the Conqueror and the entire Norman period of history (Byles 1906: 437, 446). Hawker's main criticism of Tennyson's *Idylls* was aimed at their typographical form: the print did not seem to belong to the past. Hawker wanted his Quest's words and typography to seem genuinely ancient but only because he wanted to use the past to judge the present. The climax of his chant is very specifically aimed at his contemporaries: the Grail of Christian faith is neglected by the modern age at its peril.

Nine years after Hawker's death in 1875, the novelist Dinah Craik and her family visited Cornwall. As the writer of the popular novel *John Halifax, Gentleman* (1856) and as one who had long idealized King Arthur, Mrs Craik was in tune with Victorian thinking about a gentlemanly Once and Future King. She and her family read and discussed Tennyson's *Idylls* during their travels and interpreted Cornwall as 'King Arthur's country'. Nevertheless, and in a typically anonymous way, Hawker rivalled Tennyson as her travel guide. King Arthur was a Cornishman whose job was

> to uphold right and to redress wrong. Patience, self-denial,
> tenderness to the weak and helpless, dauntless courage against

the wicked and strong: these, the essential elements of true manliness, characterise . . . the kingly Arthur. And the qualities seem to have descended to more modern times. The well-known ballad:—'And shall they scorn Tre, Pol, and Pen? And shall Trelawny die? There's twenty thousand Cornishmen Will know the reason why?' has a ring of the same tone, indicating the love of justice, the spirit of fidelity and bravery, as well as of the common sense which is the root of all useful valour. (Craik 1884: 2–3)

Mrs Craik begins under the influence of 'The Idylls' but she ends quoting without acknowledgement Hawker's 1832 election ballad written for Salusbury Trelawny, and which itself uses lines from Hawker's other ballads of Sir Beville and Bishop Trelawny. Her comment serves as an ironic epitaph to Hawker, the anonymous inventor of literary Cornwall. Hawker's tombstone in Plymouth bears a line from 'The Quest': 'I would not be forgotten in this land'. Hawker's work is not forgotten, but it deserves to be better remembered. He paid the price for inventing traditions and hiding inside them; his religious duties stifled his literary aspirations. The religious faith that inspired 'The Quest' prevented him from finishing it. Nevertheless, Hawker's contribution has been recognized by some influential authors with West Country connections (consult Fowles 1975, Rowse 1986, Betjeman 1997).

It is intriguing to think that some of Hawker's prose pictures of the Western Shore were published in Dickens' *Household Words*, the same economically priced periodical that published *North and South* and *Hard Times* with the intention of reaching a mass readership. These two fictions explored a very different world to the one that Hawker created: his Western shore with its wilderness and religiosity, could not be more different to the world of manufacturing districts and trade disputes set in Milton Northern and Coketown. As David Masson suggested in 1859, there was an appetite for exploring the character of Britain's regions and provinces, whether they were urban or rural. *All the Year Round*, the successor of *Household Words*, included an article with an affectionate bur rather patronizing portrait of a Cornishman called 'Pendraggles', and a burlesque treatment of the Trelawny ballad (Anon. 1860: 188). The tone of this article is similar to the tone of Matthew Arnold describing his charming but weak Celt. Hawker's work, also published in the same magazine, was a reminder to the careful reader of the reality underlying 'Pendraggles': the tough and enduring character of a people formed by the struggle with poverty and the struggle to earn a living from the sea. Despite his occasional deference to London's cultural superiority, Hawker's true self was drawn to the idea of Cornishmen storming London in order to rescue Trelawny. At his best, he makes no concessions to a superior centre and rejoices in peripheral eccentricity and freedom. His literary inventions belong in a unique territory that educated some of his contemporaries and can educate many of us today.

Using the ideas of literary thinkers from Tennyson to Berry and Lopez, it is possible to be specific about Hawker's contribution. In the terms of Tennyson's literary pilgrimage to Lyme Regis, Hawker's characters are as much part of their locale as Louisa Musgrove is attached to an 'exact spot' on the Cobb. Hawker's creation of Trelawny remains a vital part of the 'mind-map' of Cornwall. His lesser known creations such as Coppinger and King Arthur deserve to be better known: they are rooted in 'Monumental Morwenstow' and a cruel coast, they help the reader to *see* this place and its people. His 'Keltic' Arthur offers a fascinating alternative to Tennyson's better known Victorian gentleman. Avoiding those territories of irresponsibility, abstraction and self-righteousness outlined by Berry (see Chapter 1, pp. 39–42), Hawker takes us to the territory underfoot and the territory of understanding. Readers who will never visit Cornwall can take an important quality from the Cornwall in his work. Many modern citizens have lost the sense of sacred places and sacred time: ours is the world of churches turned into shops, and Sundays that seem like every other day. It is not necessary to share Hawker's Christian faith in order to appreciate what he conveys in poetry and poetic prose: his sense of the miracle of life, whether human or animal, his reverence and respect for the natural world. His territory is sacred: you must not blunder through it or mistreat it; you assume you can control it at your peril. You must, in Berry's terms, pay this place attention. Hawker's neglected work provides a model for a relationship with a region, a model from which other regions can learn.

# 3

# Charles Kingsley's Territory
## Self-Righteousness and Self-Doubt

*Mr Ainsworth . . . writes of places he has evidently seen and studied carefully, not only in the county history, but, we should say, with his own honest eyes; he has brought away notions and names of every rock and ditch; and yet he cannot describe them.*

> Charles Kingsley on the novelist Harrison Ainsworth

*Truly a remarkable boy . . . a genuine out-of-doors English boy. His account of a walk or a run would often display considerable eloquence; the impediment in his speech, rather adding to the effect.*

> Derwent Coleridge, son of Samuel Taylor Coleridge,
> commenting on Charles Kingsley as a schoolboy

## *Westward Ho!* and The Eastern Question

It is still possible to see today, as Charles Kingsley saw in the nineteenth century, the evidence of that phase in history when the geographically peripheral West became most identified with the central, national destiny. Many of Queen Elizabeth's courtiers and adventurers had West Country accents and origins. Walter Raleigh's birthplace at Hayes Barton and his house at Sherborne, Humphrey Gilbert's fortified manor at Compton, near Paignton: these are solid reminders of an Elizabethan past that Kingsley inherited and had no need to invent. Modern readers, however, read this past with Kingsley's inventive help; they are reading genuine Elizabethan writing through Victorian spectacles. In fact, today's West Country is Elizabethan and Mock Elizabethan. Bideford in North Devon, where Kingsley's Elizabethan novel *Westward Ho!* was written, combines sixteenth-century history with Victorian myth. Nearby Barnstaple arguably played a bigger role in Elizabethan maritime exploits, but Kingsley's novel made Bideford the centre of the tourist's attention. Bideford's bridge, immortalized in the novel, actually dates from the fourteenth century and reached its imposing form in 1810. Bideford's quay, also featured in the novel, owes more to the seventeenth-century tobacco trade than sixteenth-century heroics. Bideford's apparently Elizabethan town hall and crest were Victorian tributes to the age of Elizabeth. The local cannon were retrieved from the river in the Victorian age to conjure up images of Hawkins and the Armada of 1588. The statue of Kingsley on the quay, dedicated to him in 1919, represents him carrying a book: this object is a clue to the real source of much of what can be seen or imagined in this particular place. When you visit 'The Rose of Torridge', a Bideford cafe named after the heroine of Kingsley's story, or when you see a signpost that directs you to a nearby seaside resort called 'Westward Ho!' in honour of Kingsley's work, you are living in history and geography altered by a Victorian novel. It is easy to find the place 'Westward Ho!' on the map; finding its origins in history and fiction involves an imaginative journey which tells you more about the 1850s than the 1580s.

Mid-Victorian Britain built its pride and consensual values on foundations of conflict and anxiety. The Great Exhibition of 1851 successfully celebrated the feudal past and the commercial future, the ideals of chivalry and the wonders of technology, the need to sustain a monarchy and the values of democracy. Employers paid for their workers to travel by train from the West Country and elsewhere to experience a unifying London perspective on the national destiny. The 'hungry 'forties' were, it seemed, to be replaced by the prosperous fifties. However, the 1840s cast their shadow over the future. Carlyle had amplified the echoes of the French Revolution in an influential three-volume history and linked the sansculottes to modern Chartists; in 1848 it seemed to some that revolution in Europe was spreading to England. Despite the reassuring message of the Exhibition, when social protest was feared but did not materialize, events of the 1850s awoke ancient animosities and fears.

Since 1833 the Oxford Movement had argued for a return to Catholic origins; Newman converted to Catholicism in 1845. In

1850 the Vatican restored the Roman Catholic hierarchy in Britain. Some feared that the legacy of a Tudor Protestantism, created by Henry VIII and safeguarded by Queen Elizabeth, was being betrayed. When Holman Hunt painted some sheep straying over the edge of cliffs in a work entitled 'Our English Coasts' (1852–53), the image was interpreted as a parable about the Protestant Church losing its flock and the threat of foreign invasion. Fear of the foreign plagued Britain at home and abroad. Behind the fiction of *Westward Ho!* lurked the 'Eastern Question', or the problem of what to do with the decaying Turkish Empire under threat from the Tsar. In 1854, the year before the publication of Kingsley's novel, Britain went to war to defend Turkey against Russian ambitions to gain a Black Sea port: the Crimean conflict began. Perceptions of national pride and global responsibilities were apparently more important than religious allegiance: Britain was allied with a Muslim country to fight a Christian one. Compounding the religious complications, the British troops in the Crimea facing artillery fire and risking cholera for the national good included many Catholic Irish.

Charles Kingsley's life and work (1819–75) were part of the conundrums of the 1840s and 1850s. He was as contradictory as the times he lived in. He sometimes claimed that his experience as a witness of the anti-Reform riots in Bristol made him sympathize with the aristocracy; he also claimed that the same experience made him a Radical. In his novel *Alton Locke* (1850), partially inspired by the life of the Chartist Thomas Cooper, he defended 'moral force' Chartism but condemned 'physical force' Chartism. He made a very public attack on the Catholic Newman, yet planned a novel that would defend Catholics. He was Christian and Socialist; 'on the outside' defending West Country ways and accents against London snobbery; 'near the centre' as chaplain to Queen Victoria. *Westward Ho!* embodies his own and his age's contradictions.

Kingsley was one of several who responded to the anxieties of the present by looking for inspiration in the Elizabethan past. The Hakluyt Society was formed in 1846 and began making Hakluyt's accounts of sixteenth-century voyages available to nineteenth-century readers. Kingsley admiringly reviewed the volume of Raleigh's works in 1853. As he read the authentic words of the past, he recreated history in his Victorian imagination. His wife noted: 'It was very impressive to observe how intensely he realised the words he read. I have seen him overcome with emotion as he . . . perused the tragic story of Sir Humphrey Gilbert in his beloved Hakluyt' (F. Kingsley 1891, Vol. 2: 220). As a Christian and a patriot, Kingsley was moved by the story that Gilbert died courageously and piously declaring that 'We are as near heaven by sea as by land'. Lord Macaulay added his authority to the rewriting of the Elizabethan age in 'The Armada', a fragment of poetry full of stirring national sentiment and English topography. When the Londoner Walter White visited the West Country in 1855, he did not think it odd to recite Macaulay's poem to a group of local haymakers. According to White, the poem

> completely fixed their attention, and they listened in silence to the end, though here and there an eye brightened, and a face glowed, as the recitation stirred their latent patriotism. Besides the heroic spirit, the poem contains many proper names belonging to Devonshire, and these being familiar to the haymakers, made it more interesting to them. They gave a cheer as I concluded. . . . (White 1855: 108–9)

Kingsley's passion for the West Country's Elizabethan past was influenced by the work of his brother-in-law, the historian J.A. Froude. Froude made the nation remember the Elizabethans whom he called 'England's forgotten worthies'. His 1852 account of the boyhood of Elizabethan heroes on the River Dart was acceptable to those who liked their history connected with a romantic sense of place:

> Some two miles above the port of Dartmouth, once among the most important harbours in England, on a projecting angle of land which runs out into the river at the head of one of its most beautiful reaches, there has stood for some centuries the manor house of Greenaway. The water runs deep all the way to it from the sea, and the largest vessels may ride with safety within a stone's throw of the windows. In the later half of the sixteenth century there must have met . . . a party as remarkable as could have been found anywhere in England. Humfrey and Adrian Gilbert, with their half-brother, Walter Raleigh, here when little boys, played at sailors in the reaches of Long Stream; in the summer evenings doubtless rowing down with the tide to the port, and wondering at the quaint figure-heads and carved

prows of the ships which thronged it; or climbing on board, and listening with hearts beating, to the mariners' tales of the new earth beyond the sunset. And here in later life, matured men, whose boyish dreams had become heroic action, they used again to meet . . . (Froude 1894, Vol. 1: 478–80)

Kingsley made clear his allegiance to Froude's kind of history. During the opening of *Westward Ho!* (1855), he warns his readers against 'those improved views of English history, now current among our railway essayists, which consist in believing all persons, male and female, before the year 1688, and nearly all after it, to have been either hypocrites or fools . . .' (Chapter 1, Kingsley 1878a: 7–8). The Kingsley family were able to visit the West Country partly owing to the growing railway network; nevertheless, they also lived long enough in various parts of Devon and Cornwall to think that the 'here and gone' railway essayist could not understand the West Country's history. Kingsley saluted Froude in *Westward Ho!* by describing Drake and his followers at Plymouth as 'England's forgotten worthies'. In 1871, addressing the Devonshire Association at Bideford, Kingsley had not changed his belief in the need for patriotic history to form national conscience and character:

I am not yet ashamed of England's forgotten worthies—not now forgotten; for there is one man [Froude?] at least in this room whose pen has recalled them to our memories once and for all, and whose history of them will endure, I trust, as long as the English language endures, to teach Englishmen what manner of men the fathers were, what manner of men their sons should be. . . . (Kingsley 1871: 378–79)

Kingsley's Elizabethans were not only heroes of the past: they were pioneers of the modern world in which 'commoners' with Devon accents could claim their place in society. Froude gave him historical authority for this view:

The Catholic faith was no longer able to furnish standing ground on which the English or any other nation could live a manly and godly life. Feudalism, as a social organisation, was not any more a system under which their energies could have scope to move. Thenceforward, not the Catholic Church, but any man to whom God had given a heart to feel and a voice to speak, was to be the teacher to whom men were to listen; and great actions were not to remain the privilege of the families of the Norman nobles, but were to be laid within the reach of the poorest plebeian who had the stuff in him to perform them . . . The England of the Catholic Hierarchy and the Norman Baron, was to cast its shell and to become the England of free thought and commerce and manufacture, which was to plough the ocean with its navies, and sow its colonies over the globe . . . (Froude 1894, Vol. 1: 455)

Following Froude, Kingsley presents Richard Grenville as 'one of those truly heroical personages whom Providence, fitting always the men to their age and their work, had sent upon the earth . . . wherever . . . great men and great deeds were needed to lift the medieval world into the modern'. Meeting the need for national myth, Kingsley was also teaching the arrogant nineteenth century to respect the sixteenth and the metropolitan know-it-alls to appreciate the regions: 'it is to the sea-life and labour of Bideford, and Dartmouth, and Topsham and Plymouth . . . and many another little western town, that England owes the foundation of her naval and commercial glory'. The novel's hero, Amyas Leigh, is presented as in some ways better educated than a Victorian, even though he believes in Devon folklore and talks 'like Ralegh, Grenvil, and other low persons, with a broad Devonshire accent . . .' (Chapter 1, Kingsley 1878a: 2, 7, 10). That ironically used phrase, 'low persons', can be elucidated in the context of Leslie Stephen's shrewd account of Charles Kingsley's political allegiances:

He hated medieval revivalism . . . He looked back to the sixteenth, not to the twelfth century . . . The Young England party seemed to him to desire the conversion of the modern labourer into a picturesque peasant, ready to receive doles at the castle-gate and bow before the priest with bland subservience. Kingsley wanted to make a man of him; to give him self-respect and independence, not in a sense which would imply the levelling of all social superiorities, but in the sense of assigning to him an honourable position in the social organisation. (Stephen 1909, Vol. 3: 44–46)

In an age that worshipped the Gothic and medieval in fiction, painting and architecture, Kingsley stands out as a Victorian Elizabethan. George Eliot found the Elizabethan setting of *Westward Ho!* 'unhackneyed, and . . . unsurpassed in the grandeur of its moral elements' (1855: 290). Rejecting the idealization of a feudal, aristocratic past, Kingsley had a little sympathy for the Chartist labourer and a lot of sympathy for the conscientious, middle-class professional. Although his Protestant hero, Amyas Leigh, is an unlettered Devon seaman, he is connected to families in the lower-middle ranks of society, yeoman farmers and landowners with pedigrees that rival the aristocracy and an entrée to the Queen's court. Despite his study of Hakluyt and other sources, Kingsley's Elizabethans are half-Victorian. His Queen Elizabeth is a prototype of Queen Victoria. His Elizabethan heroes are versions of the nineteenth-century middle classes gaining power from the landed interest after the Reform Act of 1832.

Kingsley's vision of a society uniting gentry and commoner had a particular resonance for readers during the period of the Crimean War. Britain's army in the Crimea was led by officers of wealthy, aristocratic background who bought their rank rather than earned it. Many of these officers faced public criticism when they returned home during the savage Crimean winter, leaving their men to endure cold, hunger and cholera without them. Moreover, the accurate war-reporting in *The Times* made Kingsley's readers aware of the bungling incompetence of British administration and the price paid for it by the front-line soldier. The French army, better led and organized for much of the war, made British aristocratic amateurism seem intolerable (Kerr 1997). Florence Nightingale and her lamp shone brightly as an example of what happened when male complacency was challenged by a woman gaining power not by means of birth but by professional competence. Tennyson had contrived to rescue glory from wrangling and misunderstanding amongst the officer-class. His 'Charge of the Light Brigade' only went so far as to say 'someone had blundered'. Kingsley's novel was more specific about who the blunderers were. The soldier in the field could not reason why; Kingsley did so for him in fiction. Those who were making up for government incompetence by knitting 'balaclavas' for the ill-equipped British and Irish foot soldiers, found Kingsley' s fictional Devon heroes to be a judgement on real-life aristocrats. Kingsley's Elizabethan Devonians, however, are part of a power structure that has been reformed rather than overthrown.

Kingsley did not want to replace aristocracy and plutocracy with anarchy or egalitarianism. He desired a meritocracy which united old tradition with present progress, hereditary monarchy with democratic Parliament. In the world of his novel, nobility is found in all classes and Elizabethan knighthoods are honestly earned, by contrast with the titles sold indiscriminately by King James. It is the lords and ladies rather than the minor gentry that are most subject to question. Don Guzman is the enemy not only because he is Spanish but also because he is a Don. The Spanish Empire is flawed because its aristocracy fails to lead its commoners. Don Guzman's plans are defeated by an English nation that unites gentry and commoner. Contrasting the Elizabethan and modern English navies at Plymouth, the narrator of the novel asks:

> Would our modern spectators, just come down by rail for a few hours, to see the cavalry embark, and return to-morrow in time for dinner, have looked down upon that petty fort, and petty fleet, with a contemptuous smile, and began some flippant speech about the progress of intellect, and the triumphs of science, and our benighted ancestors? They would have done so, doubt it not, if they belonged to the many who gaze on these very triumphs as on a raree-show to feed their silly wonder . . . But if any of them were of the class by whom those very triumphs have been achieved, the thinkers and the workers . . . then the smile of those men would not have been one of pity, but rather of filial love. For they would have seen in those outward paltry armaments the potential germ of that mightier one which now loads the Black Sea waves; they would have been aware, that to produce it, with such materials and knowledge as then existed, demanded an intellect, an energy, a spirit of progress and invention, equal, if not superior to those of which we now so loudly boast. (Chapter 30, Kingsley 1878a: 472)

Kingsley's thinkers and workers, the two groups so prominently included in 'Work' (1852–63), Madox Brown's famous painting of mid-Victorian society, are superior to the railway tourists with little understanding of the history of the West Country and its part in national destiny. The tourists returning in time for dinner are Kingsley's equivalent of the corrupt aristocracy to whom the common man's suffering is a game. (Such tourists not only went to Plymouth but actually visited the Crimean war zone for entertainment: see Kerr 1997: 30).

While Kingsley's heroes are all Protestant Devonians, the villains are Jesuits with Irish connections. George Eliot's review of the novel accused Kingsley of 'riding down' Jesuits and explained 'His view of history seems not essentially to differ from that we have all held in our childish days, when it seemed perfectly easy to divide mankind into the sheep and the goats, when we devoutly believed that . . . all the champions of the reformation were of unexceptionable private character, and all the adherents of Popery consciously vicious and base' (1855: 292). Kingsley responded defiantly to the accusation of bigotry: 'I can't withdraw what I said in "Westward Ho!" because it is true. Romanism under the Jesuits became a different thing from what it had been before . . . I love the old Catholic laity: I did full justice to their behaviour at the armada juncture . . .' (F. Kingsley 1891, Vol. 2: 81). It is true that while the English Catholic Eustace Leigh falls prey to Jesuit villainy in the novel, other members of the Leigh family and other Catholics are respected for remaining loyal to Elizabeth. The part played by Devonians in the brutal response to the attempted Spanish invasion of Ireland is justified in the novel in the same terms that Kingsley justified British use of force in the modern world: 'It was done; and it never needed to be done again' (Chapter 9, Kingsley 1878a: 176). The Imperialist in Kingsley argues that to spare the rod spoils the colonial child. On the other hand, as Kingsley struggled to put the best light on England's role in Ireland's past, he felt compelled to acknowledge the role of Irish Catholic soldiers in the Crimea. He wrote a pamphlet in 1855 to encourage morale amongst the troops there which began with the words 'I speak alike to Roman Catholic and Protestant' (Kingsley 1901: 199). He felt compelled to intervene in his fictional caricature of the Irish as childish and barbarous: his novel contains a footnote referring to the 'military brotherhood between Irish and English, which is the especial glory of the present war'. Free of Jesuit influence, Eustace might have become 'as brave and loyal a soldier as those Roman Catholics whose noble blood has stained every Crimean battlefield' (Chapters, 3, 5, Kingsley 1878a: 47, 98).

Despite its contradictions for a modern reader, Kingsley's novel was considered coherent by Victorians. Thackeray complained in

1854 that the wonders and horrors of the Crimean War had made novel-writing impossible: why should the public care about fiction when reality was so absorbing? (Thackeray 1946, Vol. 3: 403). Kingsley overcame the barrier recognized by Thackeray, creating a best-selling novel by weaving an ancient war against the Spanish together with the modern war against the Russians. Caroline Fox saw no contradiction in recommending the work as true to both the past and the present, 'a fine foe-exterminating book of Elizabeth's time . . . For Spaniards read Russians, and it is truly a tract for the times' (Fox 1882, Vol. 2: 239). A reviewer of the novel thanked Kingsley for reminding readers that modern Englishmen in the Crimea were made of the same heroic stuff as Elizabethan seamen and so were able 'after the lapse of centuries, grim and stalwart as ever' to scale 'the bristling heights of Alma' and roll back 'the overpowering columns of the Muscovite down the bloody valley of the Inkerman' (Anon. 1855b: 516). The process by which Kingsley turned history into myth that was then accepted as history is clearly present in Richard John King's account of his visit to Plymouth in 1859:

> No reader will have forgotten the life-like picture which has been drawn by Mr Kingsley in the concluding chapters of 'Westward Ho!'; and one of the first recollections occurring to the visitor who stands for the first time on the heights above Plymouth, will be of that eventful day when the news was brought to the English admiral, then, says the local tradition, playing at bowls on the Hoe, how the mighty crescent fleet, the horns of which were seven miles asunder, was slowly labouring up the channel. . . . (King 1874: 350)

The lack of evidence for Kingsley's Plymouth armada scenes does not matter to King; he can only see Plymouth sound through Charles Kingsley's spectacles, participating in a vision that has more to do with the present's need than the past's reality.

The continuing role of *Westward Ho!* in national mythology is still evident in 1870 when F.G. Stephens reviewed Millais' painting 'The Boyhood of Raleigh'. This romantic image shows young Walter and his half brother Humphrey Gilbert listening with rapt attention to a veteran seaman's tale. The toy boat and flotsam and jetsam beside them symbolize the heroic and dangerous nautical life that awaits the two youths. Stephens decides that this work 'glows in the warm light of a Devonshire sun' and that the mariner pointing out to sea is one of those 'half pirates, half heroes, such as Kingsley has delighted countless boys by describing' (Millais 1899, Vol. 2: 17–18). Such was Kingsley's success in imprinting Elizabethan Devon on the national consciousness, that Millais felt compelled to paint his image on the coast at Budleigh Salterton, near Hayes Barton, Walter Raleigh's Devon birthplace. He had to be present in the place that embodied the Elizabethan past just as his reviewer had to assume that the sunlight in the image had a Devonshire tint. History textbooks printed in thousands to educate English schoolchildren of the late Victorian and early Edwardian period also treated Kingsley's novel as history.

## The Art of Seeing

Despite its part in this national myth-making, *Westward Ho!* is more than a 'ripping yarn' to educate the children of Imperialists. George Eliot perceived that the 'perishable theorising and offensive objurgation' in the novel was made tolerable and preserved for posterity by the 'rich spices' of the local colour and the topographical descriptions. Kingsley, thought Eliot, had escaped from writing to a formula by the imaginative re-creation of direct contact with a locality. The novel contains 'close, vigorous painting of outdoor life' and 'genuine description of external nature, not done after the poet's or the novelist's recipe, but flowing from . . . spontaneous observation and enjoyment'. Eliot concludes that Kingsley 'knows and loves his Devonshire at first hand . . . in the conception of all that gives local colouring, he has his best gifts to aid him' (1855: 288–91). Eliot was responding to the novel's atmosphere of outdoor reality, of physical motion through a landscape, of contact with the seasons and with the cycle of night and day. Leslie Stephen described Charles Kingsley's passion for places in interesting language

> His delight in a fine landscape resembled the delight of an epicure in an exquisite vintage. It has the intensity and absorbing power of a sensual appetite. He enjoyed the sight of Atlantic rollers relieved against a stretch of purple heather as the conventional alderman enjoys turtle-soup. He gave himself up to the pure emotion as a luxurious nature abandons itself to physical gratification. His was not the contemplative mood

of the greater poets of nature, but an intense spasm of sympathy
which rather excluded all further reflection. (Stephen, 1909: 32)

Kingsley was familiar with the work of the Romantic poets
and claimed that Wordsworth had helped him to reflect on the
significance of Nature. Nevertheless, as Leslie Stephen suggests,
Kingsley's verbal love affair with places sometimes seems more
orgasmic than contemplative. His passion, however, was a passion to
understand as well as to feel, a passion derived from science as well
as poetry.

Kingsley loved the kind of book which seems to have been written
in the open air, with living creatures and solid rocks within the sight
and touch of an author on the move, walking or riding through a
changing landscape. He was as familiar with the work of geologists
and evolutionists as with novelists. The detailed observations of
Gilbert White's much re-printed A Natural History of Selborne (1788)
and the vivid colour plates of Philip Henry Gosse's A Naturalist's
Rambles on the Coasts of Devonshire (1853) were as exciting to Kingsley
as any fiction. He admired the Devonshire Squire and amateur
naturalist, Colonel Montague, for possessing 'the highest faculty
—The Art of Seeing', a faculty not derived from formal education
but from 'the camp and the ocean, the prairie and the forest; active,
self-helping life, which can grapple with Nature herself: not merely
with printed books about her'. Kingsley believed that the best way to
gain the naturalist's powers of observation was to work in the field as
a naturalist's assistant. One of Kingsley's most vivid childhood
memories was of his period at Clovelly in Devon assisting Dr Turton
of Bideford to prepare a book on shells: 'during an autumn's work of
dead-leaf-searching in the Devon woods . . . the present writer learnt
more of the art of observing than he would have learnt in three years'
desultory hunting on his own account . . .' (Kingsley 1890: 8–9,
42–43, 56–57).

This particular type of training made Kingsley sceptical of the
attempts at local colour in fashionable, urban fictions. In 1849
he criticized the enclosed spaces and limited social experience in
Harrison Ainsworth's novels from a rural and Christian, moral perspective: 'We are hurried from cabs to theatres, from theatres to
ball-rooms, from ball-rooms to Sybaritic saturnalia at Blackwall,
and at Elysian villas, and to all the pomps and vanities, one after
another.' Kingsley conceded that Ainsworth's attempts to 'cram-up'

knowledge of 'the dresses and customs of the times, local scenery and topography' were 'indigenous to our English, practical, historic, localising habits of mind'. On the other hand, he argued that local colour artificially acquired will only lead to 'substituting the guide book for poetry'. In Kingsley's shrewd estimation, Ainsworth 'writes of places he has evidently seen and studied carefully, not only in the county history, but, we should say, with his own honest eyes; he has brought away notions and names of every rock and ditch; and yet he cannot describe them' (Olmsted 1979: 636, 639). Although he obeys Kingsley's dictum of seeing nature directly as well as through books, Ainsworth merely transcribes detail from the place to the page, he does not use the Art of Seeing as the basis for imaginative *re-presentation* and *interpretation* of places in words. Kingsley argues that writers such as Walter Scott and Anne Brontë combine the 'historic, localising' habit of mind with vital powers of imagination and description. Kingsley admires those novelists who 'have imaged the scene to themselves, and, describing the pictures which they saw in their own minds, have therefore described well; arranging and graduating the masses and lights of the picture according to nature; presenting first to the mind those points which would in nature first catch the eye, and so leading us on to detail in a natural order. Mr Ainsworth's description, on the other hand, is a mere collection of facts and names *about* place, without order or chiaroscuro, top, or bottom, or middle—a tourist's guide, not a painter's sketch'. Scientific powers of observation need the Romantic poet's trans-muting imagination and the painter's sense of composition, if the writer is to internalize and then express a place rather than write 'about' it.

Kingsley poked fun at the Silver Fork novelists for peopling unreal places with unreal people, for always choosing aristocratic heroes with poetic, elegant names: 'Beckanhams, and Havilands and Vavasours: the very disyllables [sic] breathe the soul of music . . . for who can be noble with an ugly name? Let Newton henceforth be Villanova, and Rajah Brooke De Ruisselette! . . . "Vavasour," "De Courcy" and Co. are becoming ideal names, mythic symbols of heroism (of the fop species) . . .' (Olmsted 1979: 636, 640). The more radical side of Kingsley's personality rejects the notion that true nobility can only belong to an aristocrat with a trisyllabic Norman name: people of genius like Newton and men of action like Rajah Brooke of Sarawak may come from other ranks of society. In 1855, six years after writing this review, Kingsley dedicated his best-known novel *Westward Ho!* to Rajah Brooke and made his hero the Devon seaman Amyas Leigh; in 1857 he put a critical portrait of a poet in his novel *Two Years Ago* and named him Elsley Vavasour. Vavasour, like the real-life Ainsworth, only has limited ability to communicate with the genius of the place. He has deliberately to seek materials for a fictional seashore scene, since he is not:

> one of those men who live in quiet every day communication with nature, that they drink in her various aspects as unconsciously as the air they breathe; and so can reproduce them out of an inexhaustible stock of details, simply and accurately, and yet freshly too, tinged by the particular hue of the mind in which they have long been sleeping. He walked the world, either blind to the beauty round him . . . or else he was looking out consciously and spasmodically for views, effects, emotions, images . . .

Leslie Stephen's Kingsley has a 'spasmodic' relationship with nature: Kingsley's ideal differs from this. It is a person who does not have to work at collecting local colour since it is his permanent possession; a person who sees exactly what is before his eyes and reproduces that image faithfully yet combined with internal mental and emotional states. Accordingly, Kingsley describes a particular spot on the beach 'which would have made a poem of itself better than all Elsley ever wrote, had he . . . set down in black and white, just what he saw . . .'. He censures Vavasour for not paying attention to the territory under his feet: 'Why not let the blessed place tell him what it means instead of telling it what he thinks?' (1877: 153–55). In Kingsley's parsonical vision, 'blessed' is meant literally: God is in Nature and reverence for His work elevates you above those who seek to fictionalize Vanity Fair. It is, however, telling that the poem which Vavasour works up from studying local colour in the novel appears as Charles Kingsley's own work in his collected verse (see 'The Tide Rock'). There was a touch of aesthetic Vavasour in the moral parson, and a recognition of the difficulties involved in capturing the spirit of a place.

Kingsley applied his talent for reading places to many regions of the British Isles, including the Fens of Norfolk, the chalk streams of Hampshire and the mountains of North Wales. The West was the book that he loved to read the best. His own writing continually revolves around this theme. His education at Helston contributed to the portrait of Tregarva in *Yeast* (1848) and the Cornish scenes in *Hereward the Wake* (1866); his experiences as a traveller on the West Country moors led to a substantial 'prose idyll' entitled 'North Devon' (1849); his researches in Natural History on the coasts of North and South Devon led to the science of *Glaucus or the Wonders of the Shore* (1855) and to the fantasy of *The Water Babies* (1863); his interest in contemporary Devon landscapes inspired poems such as 'Dartside' (1849) and the novel *Two Years Ago* (1857). Despite the fact that his duties kept Kingsley away from the West, he was always an unwilling exile from his spiritual home. When the Squire of Clovelly died in 1860, Kingsley lamented that this was 'another link with the past and the West Country broken. I am afraid my lot in life will not take me thither again—and yet I love it more than all the world beside, and should like to crawl back thither to die, when my work is done' (Rogers n.d., Vol. 3: 82).

For Charles Kingsley the West Country was a region where romance could be found in reality. His moralizing theory of the relationship between topography and people originated partly in the novels of Walter Scott and partly in the Kingsley family's move from flat fen country to the hills and cliffs of Devon. Lowlanders occupied places that were desirable and fertile: they were regions 'the soonest conquered, the soonest civilised, and therefore the soonest taken out of the sphere of romance and wild adventure into that of order and law, hard work and common sense, as well as—too often—into the sphere of slavery, cowardice, luxury and ignoble greed . . .'. In such places, man was able to dominate nature and had no need of the superstition and the reverence that battling with a wilderness inculcates. Such a man, with nothing to teach him humility, might become a sensualist and an atheist. Highlanders, on the other hand, were taught reverence by nature: they had to resort to superstition and imagination in order to cope with the elements and landscapes that were beyond human control. Such people were interesting to parsons who deal with the unseen, spiritual world and to novelists who trade in imagination. Walter Scott's Scottish highlanders were not so much the product of the writer's imagination as realistic portraits of imaginative people, people who lived in a wilderness that nurtured imagination. Walter Scott did not create a theatrical backdrop for a costume drama. The landscape of mountains, lochs and glens 'was there as a fact; and the men of whom he wrote were conscious of it, were moulded by it, were not ashamed of its influence' (Kingsley 1892: 2–3). What Kingsley's Scott had discovered in his highlands, Kingsley found among the fishermen and labourers on the cruel coasts and moorlands of the West.

Kingsley put the minute particulars of his local knowledge to good use in *Westward Ho!* Parson Hawker was sceptical about the accuracy of the local colour in the novel, but it remains true to the spirit if not the letter of its area and its history. Anyone who has lived in North Devon will recognize the novel's litany of family names and their associated place-names. Readers unfamiliar with the territory may know the names from history or relate to them as word-music: there are the Bassets from 'beautiful Umberleigh', the Carys and Braunds from 'more beautiful' Clovelly, the Fortescues of Buckland, the St Legers from Annerly, the Copplestones from Eggesford, the Chichesters of Ralegh, the Grenvilles of Kilkhampton and Stow, the Coffins who have been at Portledge 'since Noah's flood' and Lucy Passmore the White Witch of Welcombe. Kingsley uses place-names with the air of one who knows how they are embedded in the landscape and in a local sense of the past. He conjures with the origins of 'Drake's Leat' on Dartmoor; he knows that 'Gallantry Bower' near Clovelly is called 'White Cliff' when at sea; he evokes a precise sense of location with 'Bideford East-the-Water' and a sense of both topography and time with 'Moorwinstow', the old version of the name later revised by Parson Hawker to suit his theories about Saint Morwenna. Like his fellow parson, Kingsley was willing to play with history in order to express a distinctive sense of place. Kingsley was fairly faithful to his local knowledge of Stow and its environs (probably gained partly from Parson Hawker), but he transferred the name of 'Chapel' from a house in Morwenstow to his fictional version of Tonacombe House, the home of the real-life counterparts of the Leighs in the novel (Byles 1906: 48–49).

Kingsley is at home amongst the distinctive but contiguous coasts, combes and moors of North Devon and Cornwall. His description of Marsland Mouth and its fellow combes has never been surpassed:

> Each is like the other, and each is like no other English scenery. Each has its upright walls, inland of rich oak-wood, nearer the sea of dark green furze, then of smooth turf, then of weird black

cliffs, which range out right and left far into the deep sea, in castles, spires, and wings of jagged iron-stone. Each has its narrow strip of fertile meadow, its crystal trout stream winding across and across from one hill-foot to the other; its grey stone mill, with the water sparkling and humming round the dripping wheel; its dark rock pools above the tide mark . . . its ridge of blown sand, bright with golden trefoil and crimson lady's finger; its grey bank of polished pebbles . . . Each has its black field of jagged shark's tooth rock which paves the cove from side to side, streaked with here and there a pink line of shell sand, and laced with white foam from the eternal surge, stretching in parallel lines out to the westward, in strata set upright on edge, or tilted towards each other at strange angles by primeval earthquakes;—such is the 'Mouth'—as these coves are called; and such the jaw of teeth which they display, one rasp of which would grind abroad the timbers of the stoutest ship. To landward, all richness, softness, and peace; to seaward, a waste and howling wilderness of rock and roller, barren to the fisherman, and hopeless to the shipwrecked mariner. (Chapter 6, Kingsley 1878a: 99)

The botanist and geologist are subsumed here in the observer physically present and emotionally engaged in the landscape, whose moving eyes trace the lineaments of the face of the land, seeing the cliffs ranging out to right and left and the river winding 'across and across'. 'Mouth', the place-name for such combes, is shown to be perfectly apt to its location; Kingsley's grim etymology takes us beyond sightseeing tourism to the realities of seafaring life.

The belief that romance had a reality in remote places was accompanied by a strong historical sense. Consider Kingsley's image of Lundy Island, combining geological fact with imaginative speculation and history as melodrama. In Kingsley's perspective, topography decoded makes the past present: a remote island can teach you about Sir Lewis Stukeley, the traitorous Devonian exiled by true Devonians for bringing about the downfall of Walter Raleigh:

Sixteen miles to the westward, like a blue cloud on the horizon, rises the Ultima Thule of Devon, the little isle of Lundy. There one outlying peak of granite, carrying up a shelf of slate upon its southern flank, has risen through the waves, and formed an

*5) Welcombe Mouth.*
Surf on the rocks at the border of North Cornwall and North Devon.
Charles Kingsley contextualises the place-name for the combes of this
coast: 'such is the "Mouth"—as these coves are called; and such the
jaw of teeth which they display, one rasp of which would grind
abroad the timbers of the stoutest ship'.

island some three miles long, desolate, flat-headed, fretted by
every frost and storm, walled all round with four hundred feet of
granite cliff, sacred only (then at least) to puffins and pirates.
Over the single landing place frowns from the cliff the keep of
an old ruin, 'Moresco Castle,' as they call it still, where some
bold rover, Sir John de Moresco, in the times of the old
Edwards, worked his works of darkness: a grey, weird, uncanny
pile of moorstone, through which all the winds of heaven howl
day and night. In a chamber of that ruin died Sir Lewis
Stukeley, Lord of Affton, cursing God and man. These things are
true. Said I not well that reality is stranger than romance?
(Kingsley Vol. 1, 1859: 106)

Kingsley's sense of human history recorded in distinctive landscapes helped him to escape from the crude nationalism of his novel.

*Westward Ho!* embodies contradictory feelings about Amyas' rival in love and war, Don Guzman, a figure representing the triple threat of Catholic, aristocrat and foreigner. After the death of Rose Salterne at the hands of the Inquisition, Amyas Leigh subsumes his love for Queen and Country in a personal vendetta against the Don. In a ship called 'The Vengeance', he pursues his enemy like a prototype of Melville's Captain Ahab destroying his own soul. In his re-creation of the Armada, Kingsley chose to put his Don aboard the historical 'Saint Catherine', a ship that actually took part in the fighting and was eventually wrecked off the coast near Aberdeen. Since this did not suit the needs of his Devon setting, Kingsley altered history to wreck 'The Catherine' on the granite fangs of Shutter Rock at Lundy Island. In a magnificent storm scene, as Amyas witnesses the drowning of all 'The Catherine's' crew, he is blinded by lightning. Once blinded by vengeance he is now blinded by God. As George Eliot realized, this is a symbolic punishment in the manner of the partial blinding of Rochester at the end of *Jane Eyre*. Like Rochester, Amyas has sinned too much to reach a happy ending lightly: he is allowed to marry Ayacanora only after due suffering. At this point the self-righteous Nationalist in Kingsley gives way to a wiser self: our English hero learns to respect and love a woman who is half-Spanish, and not only that, to gain a vision in his blindness of the true nobility of the Catholic enemy Don Guzman. In an extra-ordinary scene, Amyas not only sees the external character of Lundy, so well evoked by its place-names, but what is occurring beneath its waters:

> Then I saw the cliffs beneath me, and the Gull-rock, and the Shutter and the Ledge. I saw them . . . and the weeds beneath the merry blue sea. And I saw the grand old galleon . . .; she has righted with the sweeping of the tide. She lies in fifteen fathoms, at the edge of the rocks, upon the sand; and her men are all lying around her, asleep until the judgement day . . . And I saw him sitting in his cabin, like a valiant gentleman of Spain; and his officers were sitting round him, with their swords upon the table, at the wine. And the prawns and the crayfish and the rockling, they swam in and out above their heads . . . Then he spoke to me . . . and called me, right up through the oar-weed and the sea: . . . 'I sinned, and I am punished.' And I said, 'And, Señor, so am I.' Then he held out his hand to me . . . and I

97

stooped to take it, and awoke. (Chapter 32, Kingsley 1878a: 513–14)

Kingsley's Christianity was a potent force that could not be contained by Protestant Imperialism: it led him towards Christian Socialism in some of his activities and to a supra-national vision in a nationalistic novel.

The title of Kingsley's novel seems a little melodramatic and archaic today. It was possible to invent the American Wild West on television with the cry of 'wagons ho!' but such expressions seem out of place in the contemporary world. Kingsley's readers had different values. His local admirers were happy to market a coastal resort by naming it 'Westward Ho!' in 1863. It was the sound of the novel's title and its combination of regional, national and historical qualities that appealed to Kingsley in 1854 when he planned his writing: 'I intend to name my next work . . . "Westward Ho!" Does not the sound appeal to you—my dear brother?' (Colloms 1975: 185). Accordingly, the very last words of the novel refer to the 'cry' of 'Westward Ho!'. 'Ho!' is a performative speech act that demands an exclamation mark, a word of command and exhortation that requires to be spoken aloud and acted upon. Kingsley's novel, however, is thoughtful about what kind of action is required of us. Influenced by ancient Celtic myth, by Elizabethan science, and by the fact that the sun sets in the West, Amyas' intellectual brother Frank explains: 'All things move Westward-ho . . . the ocean follows the *primum mobile* of the heavens, and flows forever from East to West . . . Is not the West the land of peace, and the land of dreams . . . It is bound up in the heart of man, that longing for the west.' Amyas' response to this attractive yet deathly West is more realistic than the novel's literary reputation leads one to expect: 'I have lost the best friend and the noblest captain upon earth, not to mention all my little earnings, in that same confounded gulf of Westward-ho' (Kingsley 1878a 267–68).

Kingsley's fictional version of Adrian Gilbert also questions the logic of going west: 'strange how you women sit at home to love and suffer while we men rush forth to break our hearts and yours against rocks of our own seeking! Ah well! were it not for Scripture, I should have thought that Adam rather than Eve, had been the one that plucked the fruit of the forbidden tree' (Chapter 23, Kingsley 1878a: 230). Again and again, in narrative paintings, tracts and novels, the

Victorian stereotype of the Fallen Woman acts out the folly of Eve. It is exceptional to find this alternative reading of the myth, where Adam takes the blame. Kingsley did not only read comforting messages in Elizabethan texts and places. In his view, Humphrey Gilbert had 'gone west' like a devout Christian: the faithful man can welcome death as an opportunity to meet his maker, to return to Eden after the folly of life. On the other hand, Adrian Gilbert's image of male-invented folly forcing us out of Eden casts a shadow on the national propaganda in the novel. The forbidden fruit for male adventurers takes many forms: lust for gold, love of women, curiosity, vengeance, thirst for adventure. Earthly knowledge is impossible without eating the forbidden fruit, but it is not the knowledge that God sanctioned for us.

Amyas likes to 'wander on the quay and stare at the shipping, or go down to the pebble-ridge at Northam, and there sit, devouring with hungry eyes the great expanse of ocean, which seemed to woo him outward into boundless space . . .' (Chapter 2, Kingsley 1878a: 23). This 'boundless West' often referred to in the novel, takes us beyond the bounds of convention and narrow Victorian values. In the context of the novel as a whole, it refers not only to the Imperialist asserting his will across national bounds but to the scientist seeking to extend the bounds of knowledge, to the youth seeking the wisdom of adulthood. Although in the novel Kingsley tries to persuade himself that history is a record of God-guided progress, from Catholic piety to Protestant free enterprise, in private he admitted to a nightmare in which history is, in Wilfred Owen's expressive terms, a 'trek from progress', or in Victorian terms, a fall from Eden (I quote from Owen's poem 'Strange Meeting' and refer to F. Kingsley 1891, Vol. 1: 352). This contradiction too emerges in the novel, even to the point of admitting that the Crimean propaganda in the story is hollow. The narrator interrupts the final phase of the narrative to recommend that modern Victorians admit to doing less well than their Elizabethan ancestors: 'now that our late boasting is a little silenced by Crimean disasters' (Chapter 29, Kingsley 1878a: 461). When Millais' young Elizabethan Protestants looked westwards they saw, according to Stephens, the 'hated Spaniards'; Froude's and Kingsley's versions of the same youths also looked west with the image of Spanish atrocities in mind. If other empires were founded on violence, so much the better for a British Empire founded on ideals. Yet Kingsley was unable to sustain the motif of the hated Spaniard and the blessed Englishman. The sun was never supposed to set on the British Empire but when Kingsley looked west, his nation's imperial mission and Devon's part in it raised not only visions of glory but also dark doubts.

David Jones' poem 'The Tutelar of the Place' (1974) expresses the idea that the *genius loci* is a universal figure who will nevertheless only surrender her secrets to those who know her local ways and names. The interaction between people and locality is a universal experience that evolves in diverse forms. Writing 'about' place tends to be superficial and disengaged; writing 'from' place is actively attempting to protect and nurture the minute particulars of what David Jones thought-provokingly describes as a 'known' and 'differentiated' site. The best writing of Kingsley is 'from' the West. It involves more than an eye for landscape: it is a matter of allegiance to people and tradition, of appreciating in the long perspective of time how a site has become 'known' and evolved a 'differentiated' relationship between inhabitants and habitation. As Kingsley wrote the novel, the Tutelar of the Place vied with Britannia for his allegiance; the Tutelar did not provide the simple message that Britannia required. When Kingsley reconciled Amyas and the Don at Lundy Island his local knowledge of the minute particulars of place and people helped him to avoid the sweeping generalization and crude stereotypes that nationalist literature requires.

Kingsley re-created local colour in a regional fiction with national resonances. The landscapes, place-names, dialect, human manners and atmosphere in his writing are not transferable to another location, although they do enable a modern reader to see the connections between local knowledge and national/global problems. It is ironic that in celebrating Elizabethan facts and fantasies, Kingsley contributed to the process by which his wilderness and region of romance became a place of seaside resorts. He wrote to one of the founders of the place 'Westward Ho!' in 1864:

> How goes on the Northam Burrows scheme for spoiling that beautiful place with hotels and villas? I suppose it must be, but you will frighten away all the sea-pies and defile the Pebble Ridge with chicken bones and sandwich scraps. The universe is growing cockney, and men like me must look out for a new planet to live in, without fear of railways and villa projections. (Chitty 1976: 140)

Kingsley had to live with the knowledge that he had both worshipped the Tutelar of the Place and helped to destroy her.

## A Message from Clovelly

*Westward Ho!* formed the image of the West Country for many readers. Viewed from the modern world, it seems that with the assistance of romantic history (Macaulay and Froude) and stirring paintings (Seymour Lucas and Millais), Kingsley fathered a seaside resort, made Bideford permanently Elizabethan and Plymouth Sound perpetually associated with Drake and a mythical game of bowls. There is, however, one lesser known way in which Kingsley shaped the West Country in the national consciousness. This involves the story of Kingsley's contribution to the 'invention', or 'inventory' in art, of the remote cliffside village of Clovelly, just west of Bideford in North Devon. Clovelly had been painted on canvas by James Clark Hook before Kingsley painted it in words. Charles' brother and fellow novelist, Henry Kingsley, paid homage to the place and its artistic reputation in 1862 when describing the appearance of a fisher-boy from Clovelly in his novel *Ravenshoe*: 'You caught that face capitally, Mr Hook, if you will allow me to say so—best painter of the day!' (Kingsley 1894a: 127). Despite Hook's contribution, and the sketching of Clovelly by Charles Dickens and Wilkie Collins in stories of 1855 and 1860, the art critic James Stephens thought it was *Westward Ho!* which mainly 'directed all the world's eyes to the little cleft in the coast which looks upon the western sea and Lundy' (Ruskin 1903, Vol. 14: 346n.). In 1880 an article in *The Magazine of Art* guided its readers step by step down Clovelly's steep, cobbled streets, assisted by quotations from Dickens and from Kingsley's two West Country novels: *Westward Ho!* (1855) and *Two Years Ago* (1857). Kingsley, we are told, 'knew and loved every stone in the place'. To illustrate the point, Kingsley's description of Clovelly breakwater is quoted: 'thirty feet of grey and brown boulders, spotted aloft with bright yellow lichens and black drops of tar, polished lower down by the surge of centuries, and toward the foot of the wall roughened with crusts of barnacles, and mussel-nests in every crack and cranny, and festoons of coarse, dripping weed' (Fenn 1880: 87, 89). As the power of this description from Chapter 2 of *Two Years Ago* suggests, Kingsley had more than a tourist's knowledge of Clovelly: this place was a crucial part of his West Country childhood.

In 1831–32 Charles Kingsley's father moved from Barnack in the Fen country to become curate and then rector of Clovelly. Fanny Kingsley, wife of Charles, describes the Kingsleys' role at Clovelly as if they were at one with the place and its people. The parents, being of 'excitable natures and poetic feeling', shared their son Charles' enthusiasm for understanding their new locality; in David Jones' terms the Kingsley family had a poetic sensibility and a sensitivity to local colour which gave them access to the Tutelar of the Place. The fact that they were originally outsiders made them more aware of the distinctive nature of the region they had entered. In Fanny's words, they could learn from the contrast between 'the flat Eastern counties' and 'the rocky Devonshire coast with its rich vegetation, its new fauna and flora, and blue sea with long Atlantic swell . . .'. Charlotte Kingsley, Charles' sister, confirms Fanny's interpretation, contrasting the dramatic hills and cliffs of Devonshire with her former home: 'a country where all around nothing meets the eye but low fens, peaty dykes, and alder bushes, save where far away, the dim outline of a great cathedral rises against the sky, man's substitute for mountains'. This quotation is from *Ferny Combes*, Charlotte's travelogue about Devon introduced by a dedication thanking her parents on behalf of all the younger Kingsleys for 'awakening and fostering in their children a love of nature and beauty . . .' (Chanter 1856: 8). However, the Kingsleys' scientific and aesthetic fascination with the natural world did not exclude the world of humanity and work. According to Fanny, the Kingsleys not only appreciated the difference between the external character of eastern and western England but between 'sturdy Fen men and the sailors and fishermen of Clovelly'; the latter's dissenting tradition did not prevent them respecting their new Anglican rector for his ability to 'steer a boat, hoist and lower a sail, "shoot" a herring net, and haul a seine as one of themselves' (F. Kingsley 1891, Vol. 1: 9). Perhaps Fanny exaggerates but here is evidence that the Kingsleys not only thought of the West Country as a place to enjoy nostalgic history, picturesque sunsets and field sports on wild moors: they also saw the poverty and loss of life involved in earning a living from the sea.

Clovelly and its way of life was one of the experiences that Kingsley carried in his imagination, even after he had left the West Country to follow his vocation as preacher and social reformer in London. In June 1851, he was invited to give a sermon to working men in the capital. The radical in his nature made him eloquent. He daringly preached on the antithetical nature of Christian co-operation and the values of Victorian capitalism. At the end of the sermon, the incumbent of the Church publicly denounced Kingsley's words. John Martineau, one of Kingsley's pupils, left a record of the event that allows us to glimpse the public drama: 'It was a painful scene, which narrowly escaped ending in a riot' (F. Kingsley 1891, Vol. 1: 246). Kingsley was then temporarily banned from preaching in London but he found his voice in poetry. The 'outcome of it all' (to use Martineau's words), was a poem in which Kingsley responded to the attack on his Christian Socialism by sending the world a message from Clovelly. The poem is Kingsley's most eloquent tribute to the West Country as a place of work and danger. Charles Kingsley senior held quayside services for the Clovelly fishing community; Charles Kingsley junior honoured their work in 'The Three Fishers':

> Three fishers went sailing away to the West,
> Away to the West as the sun went down;
> Each thought of the woman who loved him best,
> And the children stood watching them out of the town;
> For men must work, and women must weep,
> And there's little to earn, and many to keep,
> Though the harbour bar be moaning.
>
> Three wives sat up in the lighthouse tower,
> And they trimmed the lamps as the sun went down;
> They looked at the squall, and they looked at the shower
> And the night-rack came rolling up ragged and brown.
> But men must work, and women must weep,
> Though storms be sudden, and waters deep,
> Though the harbour bar be moaning.
>
> Three corpses lay out on the shining sands
> In the morning gleam as the tide went down,
> And the women are weeping and wringing their hands
> For those who will never come home to the town;
> For men must work, and women must weep,
> And the sooner it's over, the sooner to sleep,
> And good-bye to the bar and its moaning.

The 'morning gleam' and 'shining sands', phrases which could have been part of a romance or tourist guide, are here part of a study in bleak beauty. Despite the Victorian assumptions about gender, the poem contrives to give an inclusive view of a whole community struggling to make a living from the sea. This poem combines literary craft with the accessible and quotable nature of the traditional, ballad form. It is not 'about' the West but 'from' it.

Kingsley was one of the pioneers of the West Country as a source both of artistic inspiration and of social comment. Just as he was in Clovelly long before its 'discovery', his poem put a theme of British coastal life into artistic form before it became the fashion among painters. Richard Redgrave had partially anticipated Kingsley in his painting 'Bad News from the Sea' of 1842 but most British artists explored this theme after Kingsley's work: consider C.J. Lewis' 'Break Break, Break' of 1862, Frank Holl's 'No Tidings from the Sea' of 1870 and Frank Bramley's 'A Hopeless Dawn' of 1886. These painters took some of their visual inspiration from the Belgian painter Jozef Israels, whose 'Fishermen carrying a Drowned Man' won acclaim at the Royal Academy Exhibition of 1862. Israels, however, like Kingsley, had gained his effects by living and working among the fishermen whose lives he portrayed. It was this example that was followed by the Birmingham artist, Walter Langley, who became a founder member of the Newlyn School in Cornwall in 1882. That year at Newlyn he painted a powerful image of an older and younger woman dreading bad news from the sea. The older woman has her head up and is gazing stoically seawards: she is old enough to have experienced the grief of bereavement before; the younger woman is bowed in grief and weeping, she is only just initiated in the cycle of suffering. Langley entitled the painting using the words given the world by Kingsley: 'But Men Must Work and Women Must Weep'. Langley had read Kingsley's poem on the night of a storm in Newlyn, and then seen signal rockets fired from Penzance as a warning to men at sea (Cross 1994: 30–31). The painting that results is part of a cultural tradition connected to a living reality. The Newlyn School's famous escape from the London studio to the West Country coast, from indoor society to outdoor work, provided a picture that is a more fitting vehicle for Kingsley's radical ideas than the name of a seaside resort.

Kingsley was, in Wendell Berry's terms, 'self-righteous' about the national mission and the West Country's part in it. He respected some ancestral knowledge but only at the price of accepting ancestral prejudices against 'foreign' races and religions. In his urge to defend the West against London snobbery, he became as nationalistic as those who felt, geographically and culturally, that they were at the centre of the nation's affairs. Kingsley's self-righteousness was, however, balanced by self-doubt. His doubts educated him, as did his gaze on the Western landscape and its people. He never made the mistake of becoming superior to the West Country territory of his childhood. This was the place which nourished his imagination and kept him in touch with life as it was lived by others. This territory under his feet, the territory that he loved to explore as walker and naturalist, helped him to hold his prejudices in check. Then he was able to escape from the region of nationalistic abstractions and stereotypes into the region of firm particulars.

# 4

# Territory and Community
## The Many Authors of Lorna Doone

*Many of those who journey 'down-along' to the West, would not think of doing so but for the friends they prize in the characters of . . .* Lorna Doone.

H. Snowden-Ward

*Those who follow Blackmore into Doone-land are apt to feel disappointed because the robbers' valley has not sufficiently steep and beetling sides, and because the fearsome water-slide is only a smiling summer stream.*

H. Snowden-Ward

*He used to say that 'Lorna Doone' drove him out of his favourite county, for he found himself the object of embarrassing attentions.*

DNB entry on R.D. Blackmore

### Lorna Doone before *Lorna Doone*

*Tales from the Telling House*, the title of R.D. Blackmore's collection of stories published in 1898, relates his literary work to the distinctive topography and oral traditions of Exmoor. His famous novel *Lorna Doone* (1869) contains a footnote providing a factual explanation of Telling Houses: they were 'rude cots where the shepherds meet, to "tell" their sheep at the end of the pasturing season'. Such cots, mainly made of turf, once existed at several sites on Exmoor (Blackmore 1994: 15; MacDermott 1973: 211–12). The preface to his lesser known stories explores the Telling House both as a physical location and as a metaphor. Re-creating a conversation with his grandfather, Rector of Oare and Combe Martin in North Devon and Somerset during the 1830s, Blackmore compares his four stories to four sheep that he has fetched 'by hook or by crook . . . out of the wilderness of the past'. The author is like a shepherd who uses the long crook of his imagination to rescue the narratives of outdoor existence that would otherwise be lost in the snowdrift of unrecorded history. While this gives the author authority, the numerous pirated editions of *Lorna Doone* made Blackmore aware of how this authority might be abused. He therefore plays with the analogy between branded sheep that might be stolen and copyrighted stories that might be plagiarized. Authors brand individual genius and style on their work; they also use, in T.S. Eliot's terms, *individual talent* to participate in a collective *tradition*. The difficulties of assigning tales to single authors is implied by Blackmore's fictional representative: 'You call this the *Telling-house* because people come here to tell their own sheep from their neighbours, when they fetch them home again'. But I should say it was because they tell such stories here' (Blackmore 1898: vii–x). Writers in neighbouring geographic and imaginative territory may have problems 'telling' their tales from those of others; on the other hand, meeting at the Telling House is a form of training in the art of narration, an opportunity for individual authors to participate in communal memory and invention.

R.D. Blackmore (1825–1900) was the main but not the only author of *Lorna Doone*. As this chapter will demonstrate, he shared authorship of the story with Wise Women, schoolgirls, reverend gentlemen, fisherfolk, doctors, travel writers and literary hacks. The numerous and diverse legends inspiring Blackmore's internationally known novel of 1869 are rooted in the English Civil War and the subsequent tensions between monarchs and Parliaments, Catholics and Protestants that erupted in 'King' Monmouth's ill-fated rebellion of 1685. The conflicts of the seventeenth century drew the remote territory and people of the West Country close to the centre of the nation's fate. Some of the place names of South and West England are the products of both Blackmore's romantic story and the bloody conflicts of the seventeenth century. Blackmore's novel gave us 'Doone Valley', 'Doone Country', the 'Doone Track' and 'Lorna's Bower'; history gave us 'Oliver's Battery' (Cromwell's artillery) and many references to the 1685 rebellion: 'Monmouth Ash Farm', 'Monmouth Beach', buildings named after Judge Jeffreys and Hardy's poetic reference, saying a lot in a little, to 'sad Sedgemoor'.

History and West Country legend started to brew together when Monmouth's officer, Major Wade, escaped after the battle of Sedgemoor only to be shot and captured on Exmoor by one John Babb, servant to the ancient Wichehalse family of Lynton.

Story-telling sometimes takes the form of the victim's revenge on the oppressor: the sharp swords used on the defeated rebels of 1685 were answered by sharp tongues promising that Monmouth was still alive and that those who betrayed him were cursed. Thomas Hardy was one of the inheritors of a Dorset tradition that the woman who betrayed the fugitive Monmouth to the King's troops was cursed by ill luck forever after.

A similar legend was attached to John Babb, who was blamed in a local Exmoor tradition for inciting Wichehalse to persecute Monmouth's followers and later for the demise of the herring industry at Lynmouth. Babb's granddaughter (Ursula Johnson 1738–1826), despite her long life near the limekilns at Lynmouth, was supposed to have inherited the family's capacity for bringing ill luck on themselves and others: her husband and son came to a sad end and she was credited with having the power of the evil eye. J.F. Chanter (vicar of Parracombe and son of J.R. Chanter of Barnstaple, one of the first collectors of the Doone legends), described Ursula Johnson in 1903 as a 'reputed witch . . . famous for her marvellous memory and extensive information on all matters of former generations'. The little we know of her is intriguing: she was an adept in the oral tradition but literate enough to sign her name during her marriage ceremony of 1765 (Chanter, 1903: 244). This is the character alleged to be the earliest recorded source of three interrelated Exmoor traditions that form the foundation of the novel *Lorna Doone*: the legend of Jennifred de Wichehalse, the legend of Tom Faggus the highwayman and the legend of those sinister outlaws, the Doones. Ursula was probably the chief but not the only link between 1685 and the Victorian interest in Exmoor legends. She died at the age of eighty-eight before the Reverend Matthew Mundy MA was appointed curate of Lynton in 1832, but he apparently heard similar tales from two other Wise Women: Ursula Fry, a Lynton laundress originally from Pinkworthy, who died in 1856 aged ninety, and Aggie Norman (the possible original of Mother Melldrum in *Lorna Doone*), who died in 1860, aged eighty-three. Some time in the 1830s and 1840s, Mundy had the legends copied out by local schoolgirls; it was also during this period that the Reverend J.R. Chanter had his clerk John Hearn record the stories. A glimpse of the circulation of the Doone legend in oral tradition *after* Blackmore's novel is provided by the Reverend Charles J. Cox who heard versions of it from many Exmoor residents, including Porlock fishermen and a parish clerk of Oare (Cox 1905). Apparently prior to the novel, the Reverend William Thornton, appointed assistant curate of Lynton in 1854, also heard of the Doones. He recalled that an old Exmoor farmer proudly showed him an 'antiquated fowling-piece with which an ancestor of his . . . had shot a Doone who was prowling about in his farmyard at night . . .' (Thornton 1899: 165). This is a reference to the long gun of Yenworthy, an impressive duck gun that later played a part in the tourist trade inspired by Blackmore's novel.

The historian is entitled to regard the detail of these stories with scepticism, especially bearing in mind that none of the original manuscript versions of the legends survive and Thornton was attempting to retell a story of 1848 in 1899. It is, however, indisput-able that the Exmoor legends collected by Mundy appeared in a guidebook, sixteen years before the publication of Blackmore's novel. Thomas Cooper, a Lynton doctor, wrote a guide-cum-history of Lynton and Lynmouth that contains many of the essentials of the story which Blackmore made famous (Chanter 1907: 83, 85, 100). Cooper's work is inspired both by the needs of the growing tourist trade in North Devon and a genuine interest in historical research. His work as a doctor seems to have put him in touch with the oral traditions of the region and his scientific training did not prevent him respecting tale-telling in local dialect: 'Much pains have been taken in preserving the Folk Lore of a district, where interesting local traditions, old stories and older superstitions, still survive.' Possibly referring specifically to the Doone legends in manuscript, Cooper explains that he has printed those stories that 'have not heretofore been published . . .'. Possibly referring to Ursula Johnson and her successors, Cooper explains with reference to Devon's tradition of pixie-lore: 'many is the tale told of them and their freaks, by the good old women of these parts'. Cooper gives details of the major Exmoor legends which appear again and again in later fictions and tourist publications. The de Wichehalse tale, involving the breaking of young Jennifred's heart by the fickle Lord Auberley, combines eighteenth-century diction, the Romantic Movement's interest in scenery and the moral tone of the mid-nineteenth-century literate, religious classes. When Jennifred's distraught father encounters

Auberley at the Battle of Lansdowne during the Civil War, the event is given the air of genuine history by details of the specific date (5 July 1642) and a passing reference to the death of Beville Grenville, the real-life descendant of the famous Grenvilles of Kilkhampton and Stow in North Devon. However, the history is presented in a style that is mannered and literary: 'Yes! the impious Auberley hesitated not to raise his hand against the man he had mortally and relentlessly injured. But the justice of heaven was now at hand . . .'. Matthew Mundy, one of the early collectors of this tale, is presented by his assistant Thornton as being a distinctly impractical, bookish person who would have found the wilderness of Exmoor most attractive from the safety of his study or pulpit (1899: 196–98). Perhaps Mundy's clergyman's voice is imposed here on the voice of the people. Note, however, a different tone, redolent of Wise Women, in the sentence immediately following the above quotation: 'The charm which had urged de Wichehalse to deeds of desperation was now broken . . .' (Cooper 1853: vi, 16, 30). J.F. Chanter imagined the Wichehalse tale not as a moral parable to be read but as a live performance by Ursula Johnson: 'the sad fate of "The Last of the Wichehalses," as she was called, over which old Ursula the Witch of Leymouth used to moan and babble to the cottagers on the beach, was the foundation of the Rev. Matthew Mundy's tale . . .' (1907: 85). The preface to the original manuscript of the Exmoor legends also apparently contextualized them as tales once told not by clergymen but by the cottagers of Lynmouth: 'the old house-wife, crouching over the smouldering turf, no longer enlivens the tedious winter evening with well-remembered tales of the desperate deeds of the outlaw, or the wonders wrought by the witches or wise men . . .' (Chanter 1884, Part 11: 221). The Wise Woman's voice is suppressed but not destroyed by the voices of the Reverend Mundy and Dr Cooper in what survives of these oral tales.

A place variously known as Bagworthy, Bagsworthy, Badgworthy, Badgerly or Badgery features in many tales relating to Exmoor and the Doones. Cooper introduces Bagworthy Forest with the air of one describing a place of known tradition and atmosphere: 'Situated among the extensive tracts of hills which surround Exmoor, far from the habitation of man, and until its enclosure in 1820, scarcely known to any but the half-barbarous shepherd, or the adventurous sportsman, stands the wood of Bagworthy . . . its boundaries half a century ago as pointed out by some of the olden shepherds, by far exceed its present dimension.' The Doones themselves are also presented as the topic of a traditional and collective conversation. 'Tradition relates' that the Doones were disturbed from their native territory in Scotland by the Civil War of the 1640s, and selected Bagworthy valley as a wild and remote place from which to assert their power uncontrolled by the law. 'The idea is prevalent that before their leaving home, they had been men of distinction and not common peasants.' Three tales of Doone outrages are then presented as historical facts: Thornton's 1848 story of the long gun of Yenworthy reappears with the addition that it was used by a woman to repel the Doones; the Doones robbed and killed a man called 'The Squire' who lived at a house called The Warren near Bagworthy; they entered a house at Exford and murdered a baby, reciting the couplet: 'If any one asks, who kill'd thee, Tell'm 'twas the Doones of Bagworthy.' (This couplet runs easier off the tongue if it is remembered that the local pronunciation of Bagworthy is 'Badgery'). Following this last outrage, the 'whole county' rose against the tyranny of the invading Doones, tracked them to their lair and arrested them (Cooper 1853: 63–65).

This second group of tales, like the Wichehalse legend, weaves together authentic history and invention, known topography and places in the mind. Each of the two groups of stories is set at the time of the Civil War and involves the breaking of taboos: in the Wichehalse tale, a vow to a pure maiden is broken with disastrous consequences, and a Lord, the leader expected to set a moral example, uses violence impiously against an injured father-figure. In the Doone stories, a woman is attacked, a helpless baby murdered and a 'Squire' or man of authority is robbed and killed. Once again, the crimes are not committed by those driven to desperation by poverty but by aristocratic figures who should know better, those expected to control crime not incite it. This makes the third related group of legends particularly interesting, for it is at this point in Cooper's book that we meet the highwayman Tom Faggus, an Exmoor anti-hero whose deeds and character owe a little to Dick Turpin and a lot to Robin Hood. The novelist John Fowles argues that the story of Robin Hood is the key to the psyche of a *dis*-united kingdom: the *English* are on Robin's side hiding in the green wood of imagination from the literal minded and imperialistic *British*, or followers of the Sheriff of Nottingham, the man who attempts to dispossess Robin of his lands and his Maid Marian (Fowles 1964). Robin appeals, in this topsy-turvy world, because he is a man who lives beyond the law in order to be just, who rebels against the evil Sheriff and usurping King John, because he is truly loyal to the real king, Richard. In law the sheriff hunts the outlaw; in justice the outlaw knows that the real criminal is the sheriff. Cooper's story of Tom concludes by specifically comparing him to the 'celebrated Robin Hood' but in Cooper's guide and R.D. Blackmore's later version of him, Tom is a 'Hood' with a Devonian character. He is a blacksmith of North Molton about to marry Betsy Paramore (Maid Marian) when the rich and powerful Sir Robert Bamfylde (the Sheriff) ruins him with a lawsuit. Ruined by the power of corrupt law, Faggus responds by living a life of violent justice. He ambushes Sir Robert, takes his possessions and then returns them, explaining that it is part of his code of honour never to rob a robber. Echoes of Wise Women are heard when Tom is given a horse with magical powers, a strawberry roan which helps him to escape the law when all seems lost. In Cooper's account, it is Faggus' Robin Hood tendencies that finally lead to his undoing: a detective disguised as a poor vagrant woman begging for charity lures the highwayman into a trap (1853: 65–67). The enduring power of Faggus and his integration with a landscape suitable for outlaws is suggested by the place-names associated with him. 'Robber's Bridge' near Bagworthy has been linked with both the Doones and Faggus. 'Faggus Mead' at Combe Sydenham and 'Faggus Stable' near Chargot Wood, Luxborough, were presumably the resting places of his enchanted horse. One story has it that an Exmoor farmer, attempting to sell his strawberry roan at Dulverton in the 1870s, described his horse proudly as 'Faggus colour' (Hurley 1973).

Despite their distortion in transmission from oral tales to literature, Cooper's three groups of legend preserve a tradition of popular rebellion, in reality at Sedgemoor and in myth within the minds of those who are only outlaws in their imaginations. Put together, the tales offer an intriguingly paradoxical world of difficult and limited choices: Lord Auberley embodies the law but is unjust. The Doones are former Auberleys whose true evil is unmasked; they become unjust outlaws, living not in a nourishing green wood but the dark and sinister wood of Bagworthy. Only Tom Faggus, the non-aristocrat, embodies the myth of the just outlaw. He may be regarded as even more a man of the people than Robin Hood: the well known version of Robin was a dispossessed landowner, while Faggus was more humbly a ruined artisan. Faggus does not defy the law as successfully or for as long as the dominant version of Robin. Faggus dies the victim of his own good nature: the generosity that makes him popular with the commoners also makes him prey to the humourless, devious and unscrupulous law. The tensions between oral tradition and moralising writing, between condemnation of crime and the imagined attractions of lawlessness are evident in Billing's *Directory of Devon* published just four years after Cooper's account: 'The district [the Forest of Exmoor] abounds with legends about robbers, called "The Doones of Bagsworthy"; "Faggus and his Strawberry Horse," and etc.—a sort of Dick Turpin, and compared by many to Robin Hood, for his kindness and generosity, though a most determined and noted robber' (Billing 1857: 353–54).

Cooper's version of the Exmoor legends reappeared in sporting literature, tourist guides and journalism. The popular novelist James Payn wrote a short article ironically entitled 'A Dull Day on Exmoor' which either invents new details of the Doone legend or preserves other aspects of the oral tradition. His Doones are rogue aristocrats living at 'Badgerly' who 'commit murder and eat human flesh habitually'. The Exford atrocity and its accompanying couplet re-appear with a few dramatic changes: the Doones not only murder the baby but eat it, saying: 'Child, if they asks thee who eat thee, Say thou 'twas the Doones of Badgerly.' This grim saying becomes their undoing: it is overheard and used to track them down by the 'local constabulary' (Payn 1856: 151–52). When the Reverend George Tugwell, curate of Ilfracombe from 1853 to 1867, retold the tale in his handbook of 1856 and in an article for *Fraser's Magazine* of 1857, the Doones are said to live in 'Badgeworthy' and their cannibalism is given more of a context: 'The Doones being hungry, and not over nice, and, moreover, not succeeding in their extempore forage in kitchen and storehouse, laid hands on the unfortunate infant, cooked him and eat him, with much unction and despatch . . .'. Murray's *Handbook*, an influential tourist guide often reprinted, had no qualms about advising travellers that these bloodthirsty freebooters once really existed: 'It is certain that for many years they were a terror to the neighbourhood of Lynton, and long succeeded in levying blackmail on the farmers . . .'. Condemning yet revelling in the sensational doings of the unjust outlaws, both Murray and Tugwell also recognized the importance of the just outlaw, Tom Faggus. Murray asserts that Exmoor is 'rich in stories' about Faggus while

Tugwell refers to the 'wonderful history' of the highwayman and his magic steed (Murray 1865: 179–80).

Tugwell adds significantly to the topography of Doone-land when he describes the Doones as living in a 'wild part of the moor, on the boundary line of Devon and Somerset'. The rich potentialities of this border-country are developed in Blackmore's famous novel. Tugwell's article for *Fraser's* may also have influenced the novel by presenting the Exmoor stories as being told by a local character, an Exmoor peat cutter called 'Jan', with raven black hair, piercing black eyes and a Herculean physique. He has a dark haired, beautiful and graceful daughter who 'like her father, was of the old British type of form—a strange beauty which still lingers in the Far West'. This is a simpler, embryonic version of Blackmore's 'girt Jan Ridd' and pretty Lorna Doone. There is also a glimpse in Tugwell's narrative of an element that may be true to the original oral narratives and is certainly found in the novel: an anarchic humour, too human to belong with urban sophistries and too subtle to be predictably rustic. When the Doones decide to attack the nurse and baby in the Exford farmhouse their cowardice and ruthlessness is all the more exposed by being presented ironically: they were 'aware, like the brave men as they were [sic], that the farmer and his servants were at work in distant fields'. The humour about Faggus is also barbed: 'like Robin Hood', Faggus was 'sufficiently generous to give freely what did not belong to him . . .' (Tugwell 1857: 489, 492).

The Telling House for these legends has so far included fishermen's cottages, the clergyman's study and the traveller's inn: the stories have migrated from the oral tradition to manuscripts and to printed publication of both a local and national circulation. The stories continued in both oral and written forms during the 1860s. One of the Telling Houses for them could be found in the dormitories of Blundell's School, Tiverton. J.F. Chanter stated: 'I can perfectly recall that when I first went to a boarding school in 1863, there was a boy there from the Exmoor neighbourhood who used to relate at night in the dormitories blood-curdling stories of the Doones . . .' (1903: 243). This may well have been J. Charles Cox of Luccombe, who wrote to *The Athenaeum* in 1905 explaining that he was familiar with Doone stories during his Exmoor boyhood in the 1840s and 1850s: 'I used to retail these blood-curdling stories of the Exmoor outlaws in a school dormitory, with the result that a clever room-mate of mine wove some of these together into a story called "The Doones of Exmoor" . . .' (Cox 1905). As Cox claims, and compatible with Chanter's date, 'The Doones of Exmoor', the fullest literary treatment of the Exmoor legends prior to Blackmore's novel, appeared in eight weekly instalments of *The Leisure Hour* (Anon. 1863). Each instalment is headed by a dramatic engraving of war and romance on Exmoor, and at the price of one penny per issue was attractive to a popular audience, even though this 'Family Journal of Instruction and Recreation' could not include the blood-curdling element without suitable moral and religious sentiment to counterbalance it. Many of the main aspects of the legends are repeated with variations: the period is set during the Civil War when Edward de Wichehalse and his only child Jennifred live a life of religious piety at Lee Abbey near Lynton while the Doones lead a life of crime in a remote glen called the Warren (the name usually given as the site of their murder of a 'Squire' near Bagworthy). There are only about twelve genuine, aristocratic Doones but they seem to live amongst a larger community of peat cutters and furze gatherers. The Exford outrage is presented in a more credible and less offensive way: the Doones do not engage in cannibalism and do not chant a gruesome couplet over their victim. They do, however, decide to murder a child witness of their crime to prevent information about it becoming known. Following tradition, the Doones are eventually attacked and defeated in their lair, but in this version the forces against them are given named leaders: Hugh de Wichehalse and Lord Auberley.

*The Leisure Hour* adds another aspect to the legends which makes it possible to weave the Wichehalses and Doones together in the way described by Cox: a new principal character enters the story. Prior to the main action, Lord Auberley has had a feud with another gentleman of respectable origins called Ferguson. As a result of Auberley's actions, Ferguson loses his true love and takes to a life of crime, eventually joining the Doones on Exmoor. He then attempts to take part in the abduction of Jennifred and her maid: this presumably continues or starts the tradition that the Doones stole women from the local population to continue the breeding of their clan. Ferguson's attempt is foiled due to the chance presence of his old enemy, Lord Auberley. After Auberley is injured during his conflict with Ferguson, he is nursed back to life at the Wichehalse household, even though they are upstanding Devon Puritans and he is a Royalist with suspect links in the world of a Catholic and foreign court. As a result of his quarrel with Ferguson and the Doones,

Auberley woos and then abandons Jennifred, an event that leads to the destruction of the last members of the ancient Wichehalse family. All this mechanically concatenates the Doone and the Jennifred legends, although the serial remains focused mainly on Jennifred and might be more accurately entitled 'The Wichehalses of Lynton' than the 'Doones of Exmoor'.

However, despite their limitations as credible fiction, *The Leisure Hour* tales remain true to the original Exmoor tradition by posing confusing and disturbing questions about masks and faces, right and wrong behaviour, local and national allegiance. At the outset of the serial, Auberley is an attractive if suspect character, while Ferguson is an out-and-out villain. When Ferguson warns Edward de Wichehalse that Auberley is the true villain and will break Jennifred's heart, the doting father is concerned but unable to trust this advice. In the event, Ferguson is unmasked as a reluctant Doone, and Auberley is unmasked as the unjust Lord who turns Ferguson to a life of crime and ruthlessly destroys Jennifred. In other words, Ferguson plays the part of Tom Faggus, the just outlaw, or at least the outlaw whose immoral behaviour has some justification, whose life might have turned out better if fate and society had been kinder to him. Tom Faggus himself appears briefly at the outset of the story. Adding to Cooper's account, Faggus is associated with the Exmoor Arms at Simonsbath where he disguises his true profession by coolly posing as a country gentleman. Following tradition, Faggus is shown to be kind to his magical horse and kind to the poor: after the usual sequence of amazing escapes with the aid of his supernatural steed, he is finally duped and hanged due to his kindness. He is linked to his landscape as the 'hero of the heath' and to the Robin Hood tradition by his 'audacity and benevolence' (1863, No. 610: 562). After Faggus leaves the narrative, Ferguson takes his role: he, like Faggus, resorts to crime partly as a result of the unjust law embodied by Lord Auberley, and he, like Faggus, is only allowed to defy the law and postpone the punishment of death for a temporary period. Murray's *Handbook* speculated that the unusual name of 'Faggus' might be an Exmoor version of 'Fergus': perhaps this is another link between Faggus the good highwayman and Ferguson, the reluctant Doone.

Although the handling of plot and character does not lead one to suspect that we are dealing with the prototype of a famous novel, there is one element of the story that retains life for a modern reader: the description of Exmoor topography. The lair of the Doones is described in a way that moves beyond the tourist's itinerary towards imaginative simulation and re-creation of a sense of place. The Scotland-England border territory with its 'mosses' or bogs, the country made famous by Walter Scott, is linked to Exmoor at the outset of the tale when Auberley explains the connection between the Doones and Doone-land: 'Lawless times make lawless men . . . but the nature of the country is enough to tempt such characters into existence.' It is impossible, he argues, to picture Exmoor 'destitute of *moss-troopers* [my italics]' (Anon. 1863, No. 610: 562). The Warren, a name suggestive of bewildering paths and hiding places, is given to the combe chosen as headquarters of the Doones. It is described as having 'rugged sides',

> covered with oaks and firs, intermingled with stripling trees of beech and blackthorn; and ever and anon huge projections of granite, flanked by variously formed masses of rocks, stood out in the declivity, defying an every-day intrusion and rendering a descent both difficult and dangerous. It was shaped like a horse shoe, the upper end being peculiarly steep, with a swampy flat below, shrouded by confused shrubs, and swollen during the winter season into a sombre tarn; whilst the lower and narrower end sloped gradually up towards the moor into a pleasant glade, which afforded an easy way of access into the whole dell. (1863, No. 612: 595)

After the execution of most of the Doones at Exeter Gaol, the Warren:

> resumed its ancient quietude. Never again was it the hiding-place of highwaymen. But though no longer a source of terror because of living predators, it became a spot intensely dreaded because of wandering spirits, who, according to the belief of the country-folk, assembled there at dead of night—the ghosts of the Doones—and flitted through the glen or amongst the ruins of their old habitations, perpetually restless and wretched, because their evil deeds followed them; nor would any venture near on any consideration after nightfall, lest they should chance to see or hear the tenants of the haunted dell. (1863, No. 613: 611)

This is a reference to the ruins, actually medieval in origin, of the Bagworthy Valley but it also takes us to the strange and supernatural land of Wise Women's tales. The Doones are dead but they have not gone away. These highwaymen and moss-troopers of the past, whether called Doone, Ferguson or Faggus, haunted the Victorian conception of Exmoor. The wild landscape with its eerie place names, windswept uplands, hidden combes and treacherous bogs, was read as a sign of the life of the outlaw. According to one local tradition, even the very architecture of Exmoor farmhouses owes its origin to the Doones: they are designed in a square so that their inhabitants can move from living rooms to stable without going out into the dark, the domain of outlaws (Snell 1903).

## R.D. Blackmore's *Lorna Doone*: A Confluence of Traditions

These Exmoor tales, spoken in the cottage, written in journals, were all available to R.D. Blackmore, a man who encountered the moor by means of family lore, rides through its landscape and knowledge of its literary image. It is clear that some of the surface details of his profound novel exist in previous written sources. Many of the evocative names of Blackmore's characters, such as John Ridd, Jasper Kebby and John Fry, can be found in Dr Cooper's guidebook. From *The Leisure Hour*, a source Blackmore acknowledged, he took the details of the Doones' abduction of local women, the dark tarn blocking the entrance to Doone Valley and the idea of the Doones signalling to each other within their echoing combe by means of whistling. However, Cox's description of Blackmore's response to *The Leisure Hour* is revealing: the serial gave Blackmore 'the clue for the weaving of the romance, and caused him to study the details on the spot'. In other words, the written source did not take Blackmore's gaze away from the topography of Exmoor and its associated legends: it sent him back to them, back to the land of his Exmoor boyhood, his own direct access to the atmosphere and characters underlying the printed serial. As Blackmore read the written versions of the tales, he recognized his own origins and landscape. *The Leisure Hour* serial is only an 1860's embroidery of the reality suggested by the Subsidy Roll of Charles I, which shows a Blackmore marrying a Wichehalse, or by the inscription of the Blackmore family on a house at Parracombe, dated 1638. While he was not born on Exmoor, Blackmore encountered this link with his ancient origins while still a boy. In 1835, he joined his father (1794–1842) at Ashford near Barnstaple, and his uncle (1798–1880) at Charles, while attending school at South Molton. He was living on the Western side of Exmoor, in the land of Tom Faggus, the North Molton highwayman. More importantly, he also spent much of his childhood with his grandfather (1764– 1842), rector at Combe Martin and Oare, the territory of Wise Women, Wichehalses and Doones. From 1837 to 1843, the period when the manuscript versions of the tales were being collected, Blackmore attended Blundell's School, the known Telling House of Doone legends in the 1860s and an important location in the novel. Cox's evidence suggests that after reading *The Leisure Hour* serial, Blackmore spent much time with Mrs Edith Ridler, an elderly shop-keeper of Porlock, 'asking all she knew and had heard of the Doones, and putting it down in a note-book . . .' (Cox 1905: 274–75). These references box the compass of Exmoor. The reputed locations for the writing of the novel (Malmsmead Farm, Withypool and Charles) support the idea of a writer wandering in reality and imagination over the varied locations of the moor.

The most revealing explanation of the genesis of the novel is given by Blackmore in the 1896 preface to his Exmoor short stories about the Doones and the Wichehalses. He conjures with his sense of place both in terms of geography and a unique family tradition:

> Sometimes of a night, when the spirit of a dream flits away for a waltz with the shadow of a pen, over dreary moors and dark waters, I behold an old man, with a keen profile, under a parson's shovel hat, riding a tall chestnut horse up the western slope of Exmoor, followed by his little grandson upon a shaggy and stuggy pony. (1898: vii)

This compresses much meaning: the parson's style of hat, the use of a Devon dialect word ('stuggy' means 'stout'), the sense of an outdoor world of 'dreary moors' and Exmoor ponies lead us to a specific region and time in the external world. Simultaneously, this word-picture images the landscape of memory and romance, the internal world coexisting with the outer world, the place of 'dark waters' encountered by Jan Ridd as he grows to manhood and the place where dreams waltz with the pen of the inventive writer. Blackmore was only one of the many authors of *Lorna Doone*, but he was the most successful at transmuting the power of the oral tradition into literary form.

The differences between Blackmore's novel and its sources are caused by a variety of factors. His understanding of the craft of novel writing prevents him slavishly following *The Leisure Hour*'s serialized novelette. The writer of the serial devoted most words to the tragic story of Jennifred Wichehalse and her father, fewer words to the Doones and even fewer to Tom Faggus. Blackmore devotes many of his words to the Doones and Faggus, and while including touches of the Wichehalse story, omits Jennifred's tale from the main action of his novel, leaving this for his 1898 short story 'Frida's Leap'. This means that he has no need of a Ferguson and a Lord Auberley to link the Doones and Jennifred and has more space to develop the characters that interest him and can be interrelated without resort to a mechanical plot. Blackmore also distances his work from some of the more sensational aspects of its oral origins. He maintains the magical elements of the original tales but uses them to serve the novelist's aim of verisimilitude: the tale of Wizard's Slough turns out to be a cover story concealing the digging of a mine; Counsellor Doone plays on rural superstitions as a means of stealing Lorna's necklace.

The idea that the Doones were cannibals, encouraged by Tugwell and others, is only believed in the novel by foreigners and the gullible. Jan Ridd explains 'For though it is said at the present day, and will doubtless be said hereafter, that the Doones had devoured a baby once, as they came up Porlock hill, after fighting hard in the market-place, I knew that the tale was utterly false: for cruel and brutal as they were, their taste was very correct and choice, and indeed one might say fastidious' (Chapter 56, Blackmore 1994: 484). Blackmore may have heard a Porlock version of the Exford incident, and he acknowledges here the status of the Doones, outside his novel, in oral tales of the past and present. However, Blackmore knew that the kernel of the Doone legend, the essence of their fascination as taboo-breakers, lay in their role as aristocrats gone to the bad, leaders setting an immoral example. This aspect of them was not invented by him and is present in Doone legends from Cooper's narrative onwards. Blackmore realized that this element could con-tribute to the black humour of his novel. Hence his Doones refrain from cannibalism not because it is wrong, but because they have been brought up to dine like gentlemen.

Part of the fascination of *Lorna Doone* is that it manages to assimilate oral tales within literary conventions while retaining the zest of popular culture. Where Blackmore adds to the origins of his work, he still does so in the spirit of the oral tradition. He creates a lot of activity in the reader's imagination by those brief but masterly touches, the expressive names of the leaders of the Doones. 'Ensor' stands for their ancient Scottish and aristocratic origins, the veneer of hallowed tradition on their profound corruption; 'Carver' stands for their brutality and bloody crimes, and 'Counsellor', blasphemously stolen from the description of the son of God made famous by Handel's *Messiah*, for their cunning and presumption. This unholy trinity of names, combined with physical characteristics such as white hair, long beards, massive size and pitiless eyes, raises the hairs on the back of the reader's neck more successfully than the tales of cannibalism in the sensational Doone journalism. Although Blackmore intervenes in the novel with authoritative footnotes to assert the real existence of the Doones, his creations actually dwell in a territory subsuming Exmoor in allegory and myth. *The Leisure Hour*'s dozen Doones become Blackmore's forty thieves, partly because it is credible for a group of that number to terrorize Exmoor and partly in deference to the expectations formed in the reader's mind by youthful reading of Ali Baba.

Jan Ridd, the novel's narrator and main character, also links the local and the mythical. Jan does not appear in the original Exmoor legends, although the names John Rydd and John Red appear in Cooper and a prototype of his character appears in Tugwell. His archetypal Christian name and exploits as a farmer and wrestler make him seem just as rooted in the West as the characters Blackmore developed from the early manuscripts. Ridd was accepted as having real-life counterparts by several West Country readers of *Lorna Doone*. Nevertheless, his life at Plover's Barrows Farm mingles Exmoor with the world of the literary idyll. (Blackmore prefaced his romance with a quotation from an idyll of Theocritus that he had published in translation in 1855; see Bibliography). Also, Jan's heroic physique and heroic acts suit a figure of mythical proportions. The 1869 preface to the novel referred to John Ridd's 'Herculean power' while one reviewer compared him to Tom Hickathrift, a character in traditional children's tales (Anon. 1869). An early Norfolk version of Jan, Tom is a poor but exceptionally strong labourer at the time of the Conquest; he kills a marsh-dwelling giant and is knighted for his valour. Similarly, John is a yeoman, inferior to the social status of Lorna and the Wichehalses, but superior for his virtue and strength. Like Tom, he kills the giant Doones and is knighted. In this context, John Ridd seems at home in the world of Wise Women's tales told to frighten children from doing wrong (the function of Doones) and set them an example of courage against the odds (the hero's growth to maturity).

The eponymous heroine of the novel benefits from Blackmore's assured handling of the literary and mythical. *The Leisure Hour* serial shows the Doones attempting to abduct a mature Jennifred and her maid, two lifelessly pure figures. More daring and more subtle, Blackmore lets his Doones abduct Lorna Dougal as a child and then provides her with a feisty Cornish maid: both of his women are substantial characters by comparison with their flimsy literary originals. Their role as female innocence trapped in the valley of male brutality is made credible. Blackmore is fairly explicit that the Carver element among the Doones would have forced their attentions on the growing Lorna, except that the Ensor/Counsellor element knows that she is a rich, high-born heiress: once respectably married to a Doone, she will enable them to take revenge on the man who dispossessed them of their Scottish inheritance. It is for devious reasons that her purity is safeguarded. Like Jan, Lorna has both local and mythic dimensions: she is less interesting for her character than for her situation, less vivid as a stereotype heiress than as a Persephone embodying an Exmoor springtime, trapped in the wintry land of the Doones until giant Hercules Ridd comes to her rescue. Young Hercules has to overcome respect for Ensor's old age and fear of Carver's ferocity, as well as see through Counsellor's cunning, before he can win his bride. Since his father was killed by the taboo-breaking Doones, and since he initially believes that Lorna is a Doone, Jan Ridd even has to violate his own family allegiance in order to win her.

Blackmore integrates his semi-mythical characters with the topography of his region. He links the place-names of Exmoor, many of them rooted in the landscape since the Domesday Book, both to his locations and his characters. Blackmore's 'Girt Jan' belongs in a region with actual names like 'Hollow Girt'; Betty Muxworthy, a more convincing name than the Betsy Paramore of the Faggus tales, takes her rural surname from a local place-name. Blackmore also exploits the atmospheric potential of pre-existing names such as

*6) Tarr Steps, Exmoor.*
This ancient bridge is associated with Mother Melldrum,
the Wise Woman of *Lorna Doone.*

Gibbet Moor and Black Barrow Down. Similarly, he makes good use
of names with legendary associations in Exmoor tradition: The
Warren (the scene of a Doone outrage), Tarr Steps (made by Satan
and the winter headquarters of Mother Melldrum) and Cloven Rocks
(the site of the final struggle between Jan and Carver). Blackmore
knows how to distinguish between names that belong and names that
have been imposed. Repeating Dr Cooper's guide, Jan Ridd informs
the reader that the romantic 'Valley of the Rocks' is only the tourist's

version of what insiders have always called 'the Danes', a word related to 'den' and suitable to describe the dwelling of his story's Wise Woman. When Blackmore's invents a name, such as 'Plover's Barrows Farm' and 'Wizards' Slough', he makes it true to the spirit of the landscape, its wildlife and its folk-tales. Blackmore accepts the tradition that the Doones live near Bagworthy and Oare on the borders of Devon and Somerset: the name 'Oare' is derived from 'hoar', a word meaning boundary and often attached to a landmark such as a prominent tree. 'Hoar Oak' appears on the map of Exmoor and in Blackmore's novel. The Reverend Tugwell drew attention to the fact that the Doones live not only in a wilderness but between two counties. Blackmore the novelist uses this to explain that the outrageous outlaws survive partly due to a lack of co-operation between the JPs and militia of two rival counties. Blackmore the myth-maker, however, develops his Doones to dwell between the boundaries of reality and nightmare.

Blackmore pays special attention to the topography surrounding Doone Valley. This begins in the distinctive qualities of Exmoor but reaches as far as the zones of the folk tale, the faery and the erotic. Approaching Doone-gate on Doone-track, the hero has to work out which one of three ways leads to a door rather than to an abyss. The Doones have a sliding door, which means that the answer to this riddle can vary. The hero who wishes to enter their lair travelling from the cultivated Plover's Barrows Farm must negotiate a hidden staircase carved in rock and a pit whose bottomless waters embody the mystery and fear of death: 'I heard the cold greedy wave go lapping, like a blind black dog, into the distance of arches, and hollow depths of darkness' (Chapter 8, Blackmore 1994: 71). There is also a waterslide, as powerful as a waterfall but with its own distinctive character: 'The water neither ran nor fell, nor leaped with any spouting, but made one even slope of it, as if it had been combed or planed, and looking like a plank of deal laid down a deep black staircase' (Chapter 7, Blackmore 1994: 61). Succeeding in clambering up this moving staircase with the aid of a stick shaped like Neptune's trident, the hero is faced with the allurements of Lorna's hidden bower and the threatening darkness of Bagworthy Forest. The bower is described with the aid of Virgil's *Aeneid*. Blackmore's ferns and spring owes a little to Exmoor's topography and a lot to erotic fantasy. Bagworthy Forest, contrasting with the womb-like bower, has a presence befitting the lair of giants and

7) *Plover's Barrows, Exmoor.*
Illustration from the 1883 edition of *Lorna Doone.*

evil-doers. The 'rounded heads and folded shadows' of these woods can be seen from afar; close to, they form the 'blackest and the loneliest place of all that keep the sun out'; within their bounds the trespasser feels the weight of the forest hanging on him 'like a cloak containing little comfort'. The reader is warned to avoid the Doone Valley in the language of biblical prophecy: 'Who maketh His sun to rise upon both the just and the unjust. And surely, but for the saving clause, Doone Glen had been in darkness' (Chapters 15, 33, Blackmore 1994: 122, 261).

Blackmore's success in making this semi-real landscape seem wholly real is proven by the droves of visitors trying to find the Doone Valley ever since the publication of the novel. In 1879 the master of the Devon and Somerset stag hounds noted that Blackmore's novel had imposed the 'new name' of 'Doone Valley' on the landscape (Fortescue 1887: 251). In 1893 one of Blackmore's converts explained 'Some of us have tramped for whole days on Exmoor, looking out for the homes and huts of the Doone family, and the curious waterway by which "girt Jan Ridd" first found by chance his secret and unexpected entrance into the Doone stronghold'. The same commentator thought that Blackmore had managed to entrance visitors as well as locals with his weaving of words and topography: 'Many an American and many an Australian, has gone to Exmoor mainly in the hope of tracing out the story for the brave, gigantic John Ridd, and exquisite Lorna Doone' (Rawle 1903: 28). Like Kingsley in the case of *Westward Ho!*, Blackmore had given the process of combining invention and landscape unstoppable momentum. In 1910 an influential 'topographical' edition of the novel was published with illustrative photographs to prove the existence of the sites alleged to be Blackmore's inspiration. This was not called the 'Exmoor' but the 'Dooneland edition'. The Ordnance Survey included 'Doone Valley' as a place-name and then changed its location, possibly due to the influence of a local enthusiast, Sir Atholl Oakeley. (Oakeley published a popular pamphlet claiming to establish the true site of the valley; see reference in bibliography.) Today, the question of whether to name Hoccombe or Lank Combe as Doone Valley remains too controversial to be confronted; instead, the name 'Doone Country' is placed near Bagworthy. James F. Muirhead, preparing Baedeker's *Handbook to Great Britain* in 1887, expected to find Blackmore's territory in reality but was disappointed by the 'discrepancy between the actual scenery of the Doone valley and the description of it in Lorna Doone'. Blackmore replied to him: 'I romanced therein . . . solely for the uses of my story. Disappointed tourists have reproached me . . .' (Dunn 1956: 139). It is true that some of Blackmore's vocabulary ('cliffs', 'crags' and even 'mountain gorge') exaggerate the true character of the Bagworthy Valley. Nevertheless, the combined effect of his place-names, characters and legends make Lorna Doone a romance that remains true to the spirit of its unique territory. The real location of the Doone Valley, combining Exmoor with the imagination, is in the minds of the readers of Lorna Doone.

The topography of warrens and sloughs, riddles and perils, is appropriate to a novel that remains true to its oral sources by posing complex questions about appearance and reality. The main characters participate in black, satirical, anarchic and richly ambivalent humour, the type of topsy-turvy comedy glimpsed in the early Exmoor tales. When Jan's mother explains that her son would not even steal an apple, Counsellor Doone comments: 'I greatly fear that his case is quite incurable. I have known such cases; violent prejudice, bred entirely of education, and anti-economical to the last degree. And when it is so, it is desperate: no man after imbibing ideas of that sort can in any way be useful' (Chapter 51, Blackmore 1994: 429). The joke here is multiform: the Counsellor is deadly serious while the reader cannot resist laughing; the honest man is being described in the way that most people would describe the Doones, but in the corrupt world which Blackmore describes, honesty is often less powerful than ruthless deceit. The Doones pervert language and challenge values in disturbing ways. When Jan's mother dares to complain to the Doones about their brutality, Jan the narrator comments: 'Now, after all, what right had she, a common farmer's widow, to take it amiss that men of birth thought fit to kill her husband?'. The haughty double talk of the Doones continues: the local law-abiding folk are just 'rustic people' or 'clods of Exmoor' who are 'apt to misconceive' the 'sufferings' of the Doones. Far from murdering Ridd, 'brave and noble' Carver Doone simply defended himself (Chapter 4, Blackmore 1994: 35–36, 40). The reader learns to translate these phrases into their opposites: it is the Doones' victims who suffer; the cowardly and ignoble murderer is Carver; he and his mighty clan are eventually killed or defeated by the local 'clods'.

However, even honest Jan Ridd is forced to note the hypocrisy and injustice of society: he too resorts to the language of paradox and ambiguity in order to describe the ways of the world. Sometimes his target is society and moralizers in general: 'the principal business of good Christians is, beyond all controversy, to fight with one another' (Chapter 2, Blackmore 1994: 15). Sometimes he satirizes unjust outlaws and sometimes the outlaws' apparently willing victims. After the failure to conquer the Doones, 'Offerings poured in at the Doone-gate faster than Doones could away with them; and the sympathy both of Devon and Somerset became almost oppressive' (Chapter 55, Blackmore 1994: 468). Sometimes his target is the just outlaw or criminal with a justification: Tom Faggus the highwayman, we are told tongue in cheek, 'was living a quiet and godly life; having retired almost from the trade (except when he needed excitement, or came across public officers), and having won the esteem of all whose purses were in his power' (Chapter 22, Blackmore 1994: 171). On another occasion, we are told that Tom has moved from Exmoor to Berkshire where there are 'richer yeomen than ours be, and better roads to rob them on'. Sometimes the target is London presumption: Jan dismisses the capital as: 'not worth seeing . . . a very hideous and dirty place, and not at all like Exmoor' (Chapters 12, 24, Blackmore 1994: 98, 185). On another occasion, however, Jan recognizes the advantage of London manners: 'Here there are quick ways and manners, and the rapid sense of knowledge, and the power of understanding, ere a word be spoken. Whereas at Oare, you may say a thing three times, very slowly, before it gets inside the skull of the good man you are addressing. And yet we are far more clever there than in any parish for fifteen miles'. Sometimes Jan's humour extends to the highest in the land. Lord Feversham, the commander of the King's forces at Sedgemoor, is described as having 'won this fight without seeing it, and who has returned to bed again, to have his breakfast more comfortably'. The dreaded Judge Jeffreys of the Bloody Assizes is summarized as 'The first man now in the kingdom . . . for his kindness in hanging five hundred people, without the mere grief of a trial' (Chapters 66, 72, Blackmore 1994: 578, 633). The energy of Jan's humour flows at his own expense and even at the expense of the King: 'Loyal, too, to the King am I . . . But after all, I could not see (until I grew much older, and came to have some property) why Tom Faggus, working hard, was called a robber, and felon as great; while the King, doing nothing at all (as became his dignity), was liege lord, and paramount owner; with everybody to thank him kindly, for accepting tribute' (Chapter 11, Blackmore 1994: 90). This is comedy undermining every position, a carnival of discrowning: Jan has no respect for property until he gains some, and is loyal to the King except when he thinks about it. Others are so unthinkingly loyal to the King that they thank him for robbing them. The highwayman is superior to a King insofar as he is a hard-working robber while the King is a lazy one.

This kind of humour is a verbal equivalent of the outrageous behaviour of the Doones; it robs society of its dignity and righteousness. Jan openly compares the Doones to kings, lords and parsons, and by implication to the respectable professions: 'according to our old saying, the three learned professions live by roguery on the three parts of a man. The doctor mauls our bodies; the parson starves our souls; but the lawyer must be the adroitest knave, for he has to ensnare our minds' (Chapter 39, Blackmore 1994: 312). The doctor is a Carver, the parson and the lawyer combine qualities of Counsellor and Ensor. Alan Brandir comments on his noble family's blood-tie with the Doones: 'what noble family, but springs from a captain among robbers? Trade alone can spoil our blood; robbery purifies it. The robbery of one age is the chivalry of the next' (Chapter 21, Blackmore 1994: 161). In this corrupt world where the just are unjust, the highwayman who has been dispossessed of his property and right to common land by the corrupt law has some right to redress.

Blackmore altered the period of the early Exmoor tales from the Civil War of the 1640s to the Monmouth rebellion of 1685. Nevertheless, the original tales were told by Ursula Johnson, whose renowned memory included records of her family's links with the aftermath of Sedgemoor. Ursula was only one of many who had reason to remember the horrors of 1685. In focusing on Sedgemoor, Blackmore remains true to the history and oral tradition of the West Country. He also read about the Monmouth episode in Macaulay's famous history and in the authentic primary sources about the Wade story reproduced in Cooper's guidebook. The historical Hugh de Wichehalse who died in 1653 has a fictional counterpart in *The Leisure Hour* serial that leads the attack on the Doones. Blackmore makes him live beyond 1653 to coexist with the real John Wichehalse of the Monmouth period, the JP instrumental in the capture of Major Wade after Sedgemoor. Hugh Wichehalse is the willing punisher of unjust outlaws in the serial: in the novel, he and his son Marwood collaborate with the Doones. This time-frame allows Blackmore to satirize corrupt justice and to let all his main characters, including the Doones, Tom Faggus and Jan Ridd (outlaws just and unjust, and the rare honest man), participate in the Monmouth rebellion. In other words, Blackmore's novel daringly makes legendary characters collide with authentic history viewed from a Western province. The many theories about the origins of the Doones include the Reverend Thornton's claim that his Exmoor friends regarded these outlaws as fugitives from Monmouth's defeated army. It is difficult to know how much the novel invented or copied this tradition: the plot certainly makes some half-heartedly Catholic Doones join the Protestant rebels. They do not, however, return to Exmoor since they are caught and hanged by a regiment whose brutality Blackmore drew from history: 'Kirke's Lambs'. Blackmore's Jeremy Stickles is a King's man, but he is willing to admit that the 'Lambs' are worse than the Doones: in this case reality was as horrific as legend. 'Kirke's Lambs' took their name from their regimental insignia; the ironic and chilling contrast between their title and their brutal behaviour is compatible with the double talk and Doone-names consistently used in the novel.

Unlike the Doones, Faggus and Ridd escape from Sedgemoor. Compared to the sketch of him in Cooper, the Faggus of the novel is a more human figure combining virtues with vices. Like his legendary version, he is the victim of injustice, generous-natured, and daring under fire. The novel makes him a master tale-teller with no Falstaffian cowardice but Falstaffian tendencies where lying, eating and drinking are concerned. In the legends his horse Winnie is the traditional means of his miraculous escapes; Winnie also is crucial to his escape at Sedgemoor but she can only perform her magic role with vital assistance from the human Jan Ridd. In this way, the novel qualifies the supernatural element of the original tales while remaining true to their spirit.

Since Faggus' role is to rob the rich and powerful on behalf of the poor, it does not seem incongruous for him to join a rebellion carried out in the name of the people. Jan is suspicious of Faggus until the rebellion. His decision to risk his own life saving the wounded Faggus during the battle shows that the just outlaw is worthy of the honest man's pity. In the legend, Faggus is caught and executed at Taunton. The novel ends differently: a reformed Faggus lives on happily married to Jan's sister, Annie, bringing up his children to be honest. The only surviving young Doone is parented by Jan, so the future belongs to those once outside the law but now inside justice. Jan's consistent inconsistency towards the real king, 'King' Monmouth, the Doones and Faggus finally resolves itself mainly in favour of the Robin Hood tradition. Legalized theft and illegal theft are both condemned: illegal but just stealing from the rich to help the poor is sanctioned during exceptional times. Jeremy Stickles explains provincial Exmoor from a London perspective:

> Now the neighbourhood itself is queer; and people have different ways of thinking from what we are used to in London. For instance now, among you folk, when any piece of news is told . . . the very first question that arises in your minds is this—'Was this action kind and good?' Long after that you say to yourselves, 'does the law enjoin or forbid this thing?' . . . It . . . explains your toleration of these outlaw Doones so long. (Chapter 53, Blackmore 1994: 443)

The denouement of the novel, exemplifying Jan's insistence that the Exmoor people love justice, reverses Jeremy's priorities. Like Tom Faggus and Jan Ridd, the reader is expected to reject the letter of the law in favour of the 'kind and good' spirit of justice.

While negotiating with literary conventions, the novel often shows an awareness of the arts of tale-tellers: this emerges in the portraits of Mother Melldrum, Tom Faggus and John Fry as story-tellers and, of course, in the ever-present voice of Jan Ridd. Blackmore was a writer who understood the power of speech and popular tradition. When Jan says the word 'Doone' out loud in the Valley of the Rocks it echoes as sombrely as 'doom'. In the very last written words of the novel Jan explains how, like a white wizard saying a spell, he resolves difficulties and doubts by saying out loud 'Lorna Doone'. This last utterance, where *the sound* of the male outlaw's doom is tamed by the female loving-kindness of 'Lorna', serves as a fitting ending to a work of individual literary genius which grows from a collective, oral tradition.

## Lorna Doone joins The Royal Family

By 1880 seventeen editions of *Lorna Doone*, each of 2,000 copies, had been published. By 1893 the book had reached its thirty-eighth edition. A twentieth-century commentator celebrated the lasting success of Blackmore's novel: 'No part of the country is so saturated with one modern book as is Exmoor . . . with *Lorna Doone*' (Garvin 1925). Yet the novel that has become a byword for literary romance, an inseparable part of Exmoor's tradition and the public perception of the West Country, began life as a commercial disaster. Five hundred copies of the first three-volume edition were printed and offered for sale at a price of one and a half guineas each. Two hundred unsold copies had to be sent in bulk to Australia. The second, cheaper, one-volume edition of the novel metamorphosed failure into success and permanently fixed a romanticized Exmoor on the national and international literary map. A reviewer commented in puzzlement that the novel 'had somehow managed to get through its first three volume stage without attracting any particular notice', but now, 'in a cheap edition, has mysteriously asserted itself and taken the world by storm' (Anon. 1871: 43). The availability of a cheaper edition made some difference to the book's fate but what really happened between the first and second publication of the novel to change its fortunes so radically?

Blackmore modestly liked to tell the story that his literary fortune was made by sheer luck. He had happened to make his heroine a relation of the minor aristocracy of Scotland, and a reviewer confused this aspect of the novel with the ancestry of the real-life Marquis of Lorne, then in the news as the bridegroom elect of Princess Louise, daughter of Queen Victoria. Blackmore refers to this indirectly in his preface to the twentieth edition of his novel, implying that the coincidental similarity between the names 'Lorna' and 'Lorne' drew attention to his novel: 'The literary public found your name akin to one which filled the air, and as graciously as royalty itself, endowed you with imaginary virtues.' The engagement of the Princess was announced in October 1870, the same month that the one volume cheap edition of *Lorna Doone* was published; the perception that the novel had 'taken the world by storm' is recorded in a review of January, 1871. The marriage between Lord Lorne and Princess Louise took place in March 1871, and a mainly commendatory review of the novel appeared in *The Saturday Review* of November that year. This chronology is compatible with the theory that the public's appetite for a royal romance also gave it a taste for Blackmore's literary and romantic brew of West Country legend and Scottish brigandry. According to this interpretation, just as 'The Marquis of Lorne' became a popular name for a public house from the 1870s onwards, for similar reasons Blackmore's novel became part of everyone's library. The review that Blackmore mentions has never been found but there is plenty of evidence of the popular interest in the Lorne romance and in perceived Highland tradition.

The marriage between the Lord and the Princess was a highly public affair, which exploited 'Scottishness' for dramatic effect. A monarchy with unpopular German connections was covering itself in tartan, the colours of a foreigner who was also a native. An account in *The Annual Register* is informative. The Marquis, described as a man with features 'which photography had made so familiar', wore the uniform of an Argyleshire regiment. His parents, the Duke and Duchess of Argyle, arrived in a carriage containing a 'brawny Highlander, kilted, and wearing a tall feather in his bonnet . . .' whose presence caused a 'chorus of murmurs' amongst the crowd. Members of the wedding party also wore highland costume, and when the newlyweds left the church, 'following an ancient Highland custom, a new broom was thrown after them as they got into the carriage'. The Highland imagery was sustained after the wedding: when the royal couple made their first visit to Inverary, the Princess wore a shawl of Clan Campbell tartan (Anon. 1872: 32, 37, 86).

The public orchestration of events increased the popularity of a queen recently criticized for her lack of participation in public life. When Victoria travelled to Buckingham Palace in March with Princess Louise and the Marquis, she noted 'Immense crowds at the station and quantities of people everywhere, who cheered tremendously. The loyalty towards me and friendliness to Louise very great' (Buckle 1926, Vol. 2: 125). Similarly, during the wedding, the large crowd outside the church were described as having 'wet eyes' and 'agitated hearts'. This description of Victoria's loyal subjects may also enable us to imagine the reactions of Blackmore's readership to the meetings and partings of Lorna Doone and Jan Ridd and to the brief but vivid appearance of Lorna's aristocratic cousin, Alan Brandir of Loch Awe, 'son of a worthy peer of Scotland', in the early part of the novel (Chapter 21, Blackmore 1994: 159). Lorna and Jan are much lower in the social hierarchy than the royal newlyweds, but both the real and fictional lovers symbolized the notion that romance and propriety could be reconciled, that a noble lady could sometimes be matched with a man of lower status but high virtues.

However, Blackmore's novel not only tapped reassuring national sentiment; it also touched on a nerve of political anxiety. The long and unfortunate history of monarchs with embarrassing marriages had resulted in convention and legislation designed to protect the State's concerns regarding the sovereign's personal life. While the marriage between a princess and a marquis was clearly not a misalliance between one class and another, it was a break with the convention that royalty could only marry royalty. Some contemporaries regarded the marriage as a love-match, symbolizing an old tradition making room for modern romance. An article in *The Gentleman's Magazine*, signed 'W.E.H.F.', welcomed the Princess' marriage, arguing that if the heir to the throne married one of 'inferior rank' it would be a 'public misfortune' but that the daughter of a Queen could be allowed to marry a person of lower status (WEHF 1871). The *Register* commented: 'thus, amid general expressions of sympathy and approval, was another old landmark of exclusiveness abolished and an ungracious rule gracefully broken'. The love-match did not, in fact, unite Queen and Country. While the House of Commons, guided by the monarchist Gladstone, granted Princess Louise a dowry of thirty thousand pounds by a majority of three hundred and fifty to one, the *Register* conceded: 'In the country . . . the feeling . . . was not quite so unanimous. At Nottingham the proposed grant had been condemned by a mass meeting, which separated with shouts for the English Republic.' At a meeting of working men in London, the Princess' personal popularity was acknowledged and her decision to marry a Scotchman approved; nevertheless, the granting of the dowry was condemned (Anon. 1872: 38).

While the workers objected to paying taxes for romance among those with suspect German connections, the respectable only wished to enjoy romance within the limits of social hierarchy. *The Saturday Review*'s account of *Lorna Doone* is illuminating: 'there was no more equality or likeness between John Ridd and Lorna Doone than there would be at this present time between an earl's daughter and a proprietor farmer whose education stopped when he was twelve years old'. In other words, while a princess and a marquis could be matched as an exceptional case, a real-life Jan and Lorna should still be kept apart. This reviewer then goes on to show how, nevertheless, Blackmore's romantic misalliance could be assimilated within the rules of class: 'These things, however, must not be taken realistically. They are meant to be typical rather than actual, and to symbolise constancy on the one hand, and the natural union of grace with strength on the other, love binding all together; and so we take it here.' Here romantic allegory is only the dressing on a system of values that actually privileges the accident of birth and the inherited possession of land and wealth. The reviewer defends marrying for love but adds 'there must be some kind of harmony between the lover and the beloved', implying that a harmony between pedigrees and bank balances remains important (Anon. 1870: 603–4). Nevertheless, the history of the unpopular royalty of the Regency was proof that unhappy personal relationships make for bad politics: romance had its uses in the aims of the State. Royal personages could marry a little outside their social class, if that meant their marriages would last.

It was also necessary to balance hierarchy with the prospect of improvement and progress for all. In the aftermath of Chartist unrest, the period combining Victoria's popularity and social consensus inaugurated at the Great Exhibition of 1851 had depended on the theory of 'removable inequalities': everyone should know their place but also know how to improve their lot; if you worked as hard and remained as true as Jan Ridd, you could better yourself. English society was imagined as a tall house with upper floors but a broad stairway to the top. Whether from Scotland or the West Country, from the lower or higher classes, armed with religious faith and Samuel Smiles' hugely popular manual of self-help, all could climb to success and happiness. Blackmore's own views on race, empire, class and trade unionism were compatible with this ideology. His best book, however, as this chapter shows, is an extraordinarily vital combination of the literary and respectable with an oral, popular and anarchic, comic tradition. *Lorna Doone* gives a satirical view of London values and English justice that would speak to the republicans and reluctant royalists of the day. While Alan Brandir shares in the glamour and romance of the Victorian perception of the Highlands, Blackmore makes him a helpless victim of the Doones. Counter to the public image of Victorian Balmoral, the Doones associate the Scottish and aristocratic with savagery and ruthless hypocrisy; the portraits of Judge Jeffreys and Kirke's Lambs are no kinder to English tradition. The Robin Hood/Tom Faggus element in the novel is also antithetical to the values presented in *The Saturday Review*. Read carefully, Blackmore's romance is in tension with realism; read at the time of the royal marriage, the romance was enlarged and the realism minimized in what amounts to a rewriting of his story.

The particular circumstances of the novel's sudden rise to fame show how it could be assimilated within the contradictory values of its time. It had not lost the power to engage with popular perceptions at the close of Victoria's reign. While Blackmore openly signalled that his novel was a romance and not historical, he also included footnotes in this story that presented the Doone legends as factual. For many of Blackmore's readers his romance *was* reality. One of the many adaptations of his novel for the stage was advertised in 1903 as benefiting from the advice of a 'Miss Ridd, a descendant of the hero of the story'. This was in the tradition of earlier events of 1901 when one Ida M. Browne, writing under the name of Audrie Doone, claimed that the Doones had really existed and that she was their descendant. Most of the alleged evidence for her theory was destroyed in a convenient fire and her cause was further damaged by the historian E.J. Rawle, who published a work in 1903 systematically disproving her claims and arguing that the Doones owed more to Blackmore's imagination and Exmoor tale-telling than to history.

The reactions to this type of controversy in the popular press of the day are a tribute to Blackmore's ability to make romance seem real. Intellectually, the commentators respected Rawle's scholarship; emotionally, they wanted their imaginative identification with the figures of the novel to be accorded the status of truth. The *West Somerset Free Press* referred to Rawle's 'ruthless extermination of cherished beliefs' while *To-Day*'s reviewer commented bitterly: 'Another cherished illusion of mine is in a fair way to be killed'. The *Bristol Times and Mirror* was regretful but stoic: 'It is a painful thing to knock down popular beliefs . . . but it is better that the truth should prevail'. These 1903 reactions were anticipated by the response to Rawle's *Annals of Exmoor Forest*, a work that deflated Doone legends about Bagworthy valley in 1893. *The Daily News* responded by insisting that mere research should not get in the way of wish-fulfilment: 'we insist that he shall not abolish the Doone settlement at a stroke of his too well-informed pen. We proclaim that the story of John Ridd, and Lorna Doone, shall forever be a living part of the history of Exmoor' (Rawle 1903: 23, 26).

Both the romantics and anti-romantics in this debate made the mistake of assessing a novel by the criteria applied to history.

*8) Church of St Mary, Oare, Exmoor.*
The 'exact spot' where Lorna Doone was shot by Carver Doone.

Thomas Hardy responded to *Lorna Doone* more subtly, in a way that acknowledged both its fictional status and its claim to a kind of truth. Hardy ignored what might be called 'the Wild Doone Chase' and the sentiment surrounding the story of Lorna and Jan. Instead he focused on the novel as an evocation of Exmoor and West Country life. Owing to his own priorities, Hardy was able to appreciate in

Blackmore those skills required by a regional, rural writer defending a way of life against the rise of urban culture and central control. Writing to Blackmore after reading *Lorna Doone* in 1875, Hardy saluted Blackmore's use of his West Country heritage and powers of observation: 'Little phases of nature that I thought nobody had noticed but myself were continually turning up in your book . . .' (Purdy 1978, Vol. 1: 38). This chapter has traced the long evolution of some related West Country legends originating in the capture of Monmouth rebels on Exmoor in 1685. Preserved in Wise Women's tales, these legends were resuscitated in mid-Victorian journalism and assimilated within national concerns from 1875 to 1903. It would simplify the complex evidence to argue that one of the most famous contributions to the creations of the literary West Country owed more to national ideology than regional differences. Such was not Hardy's judgement; he implied that the regional realism of Blackmore's story, its links with a collective tradition rooted on Exmoor, did survive alongside its literary romance.

Blackmore can be located within the structure of territories introduced at the outset of this book. Like Hawker and Kingsley, he avoids abstractions and generalities. Like them, he writes *from* not *about* his place; like them, he shows affection for local foibles and respect for local knowledge. Like them, he succeeds in capturing the flavour of his district by the artful use of place names, dialect and topographical knowledge. Blackmore is in some ways more searching than Hawker and Kingsley in his exploration of the relations between Londoners and rural 'clods', between workers and their 'betters'. In this he anticipates the still greater achievements of his successor: Thomas Hardy. Blackmore goes further than Hawker and Kingsley in suggesting the presence of a community, both when it behaves with cowardice and courage. This sense of community is due, as this chapter has shown, to the unusually collective activity underlying the genesis of the novel. It is also due to Blackmore's skill as a recorder of communal life, his creation of a voice that represents many voices. It is possible to say, as Wendell Berry says of Huckleberry Finn, that Jan Ridd, whose rural voice is a continual presence in the novel, speaks 'of and for and as his place'.

# 5

# Territory and Tragedy
## Hardy at King Lear's Heath

*Nature is played out as a Beauty, but not as a Mystery . . . I want to see the
deeper reality underlying the scenic . . . The exact truth as to material fact ceases
to be of importance in art—it is a student's style—the style of a period when the
mind is serene and unawakened to the tragical mysteries of life.*

Thomas Hardy

*No man can understand Hardy who has not been lost on the heath at night.*

Ralph Wightman referring to the
heath near Hardy's birthplace

## The Origins of Wessex

The Wessex that Hardy (1840–1928) disinterred from the ancient
past and restored to life now has a pervasive presence, not only in the
South and West of England but in the minds of a global readership.
It is a territory on the map and in the imagination that has been
much explored by tourists, historians, geographers, biographers and
literary critics. It is a brave critic who thinks he can add to the
investigations of so many predecessors; it is a complacent critic who
thinks that nothing more can be said about Hardy's rich and complex
world.

The many commentators on Wessex tend to adopt opposite ends of
the spectrum of interpretation. The first generation of critics, from
Hardy's contemporary Herman Lea onwards, tend to see his work as a
fairly literal transcription of the South Western counties (see, for

example, Kay-Robinson 1972). A later generation of critics have stressed the artificial and invented nature of Hardy's territory: they show how Hardy revised his texts to increase the presence of a Wessex that was not so present in the first editions of his work; how he was reluctantly influenced by literary pilgrims eager to find exact locations for his novels (Gattrell 1988; Keith 1969). One critic argues that Wessex, minus its darker side, became conflated with an idea of a rural and quintessential 'England' during the early twentieth century (Widdowson 1989). The purpose of this chapter is to examine what lies in the gap between the first and later critics of Wessex: the place where the territory of the mind and the territory underfoot are kept in balance, are recognized as separate but linked. This is the way that Hardy asked his readers to consider his collected works in 1912. He warned 'keen hunters of the real' to recognize the imaginative element in his writing. On the other hand, for those who might forget the territory underfoot, he explained that he had striven against 'tricks of memory' and the 'temptations to exaggerate' in order to record a region faithfully. He holds the differing elements in his work in a state of creative tension when he explains that his Wessex is 'done from the real—that is to say, has something real for its basis, however illusively treated' (Orel 1967: 46).

Some of Hardy's first readers thought of him in the context of popular West Country writers. Hardy himself encouraged this in his first published novel (*A Pair of Blue Eyes*, 1873) when he referred to the inhabitants of his literary version of Cornwall as 'West-country folk'. In 1877 a reviewer singled out Hardy and Blackmore as the two contemporary writers with the specialist knowledge necessary to show us the world of the rural labourer (Anon. 1877: 211–12). In 1890 a critic found no contradiction in treating Hardy's Wessex as a place where a 'Westcountryman' lives (Gosse: 1890: 295). In 1892 another critic placed Hardy on the literary and regional map as follows: 'Only Charles Kingsley and Mr Blackmore have rivalled . . . him in bringing that beautiful West Country home to us' (Morris: 1892: 219).

Although Hardy combined 'that beautiful West Country' with a disturbing and tragic Wessex, he did share sources of inspiration with Kingsley and Blackmore. Like them, he had access to a particular combination of county and regional lore, a body of knowledge encompassing many things including topography, local history, habits of speech and attitudes of mind. Like his fellow West

Country writers, he loved and defended the region's dialects, folklore and oral traditions. Like Blackmore he was conscious of the long shadows cast by the Monmouth rebellion and the Napoleonic era, those phases in history bringing the West Country into contact with the wider world. Hardy's possessions included a set of seventeenth-century playing cards which recorded scenes of the Monmouth rising: this was a tangible equivalent to the oral tradition connecting his mother's ancestors with the battle of Sedgemoor. These are the kind of details Hardy may have had in mind when he wrote to Blackmore in 1875: 'A kindred sentiment between us in so many things is, I suppose, partly because we both spring from the West of England' (Purdy 1978, Vol. 1: 38).

Gerald Manley Hopkins claimed that the music of regional dialect could be transmitted in print when he referred to the 'Westcountry instress' of William Barnes' poetry (Motion 1994: 143). Part of Hardy's mind was willing to accept the notion that thinking on the scale of the region and the county could be a key to understanding literature. It is intriguing to discover him acknowledging Henry Fielding as an influence and claiming him as a fellow writer because his 'scenes and characters are Dorset and Somerset'. Nevertheless, Hardy was sensitive to the Arnoldian idea that the provincial tone was a mark of an inferior mind. He worried that his 'Wessex Poems' would suffer from an 'unspoken disqualification in being "local"—as if humanity could not be sampled as readily in a western county as in, say, a Fleet Street office' (Purdy 1978, Vol. 2: 210; Vol. 6: 156). Hardy was a literary giant rooted in a county and a region but too big to be contained by them. He was interested in the West Country not only as distinctive but as typical; he was interested not only in celebrating the West but in showing it *to* the world and showing it *in* the world. In novels and verse he succeeded in covering the map of the West Country with Wessex, a place that lives alongside and even instead of reality. Despite his admiration for William Barnes, Hardy presented him as a man whose 'place-attachment was strong almost to a fault', whose achievement could only be appreciated by those willing to look through the 'veil' of his dialect (Orel 1967: 82, 105). Hardy's fictional Wessex grows from but outgrows Barnes' Dorset, engaging with urban worlds and the Europe embroiled in wars from Napoleon to the twentieth century.

Hardy's account of his literary territory suggests that 'Wessex' as used to mean a part of the nineteenth-century world did not come into common usage until after 1874, when he introduced it in Chapter 50 of *Far from the Madding Crowd* (Orel 1967: 8–9). His claim to be the primary inventor of the word in this context is justified: it was only after Hardy's famous novel that the term passed into the work of George Eliot, newspaper articles and everyday use, culminating eventually in the 'Wessex edition' of Hardy's novels and the numerous place-names in Dorset inspired by these fictions. However, Hardy also conceded that he did not invent 'Wessex' so much as 'disinter' it. The Heptarchy or seven kingdoms to which Hardy draws attention in *The Return of the Native* was a Saxon region of shifting borders and names during the period from the sixth to the ninth centuries. The seven kingdoms were Kent, East Anglia, Mercia, Northumbria and three territories with related names: Essex (the East Saxons), Sussex (the South Saxons) and Wessex (the West Saxons). While Essex and Sussex survived as county names, Wessex became covered under a newer toponymy. As early as 1832, before Hardy's birth, Barnes began uncovering this ancient Wessex in ways which Hardy was to adapt for his purposes as a novelist and poet. Barnes was beginning his campaign to prove that a gentleman's education in Latin and Greek led him to neglect Saxon English and therefore to look down on its descendant, the speech of Dorset. This, according to Barnes, was not a bastardized version of Standard English but a pure throwback to the original form of a national language (Barnes 1832: 590). Wessex, for Barnes, was a place defined both by language and topography. Dorset dialect was once spoken 'with little variation' in 'most of the western parts of England which were included in the kingdom of the West Saxons . . .' (Barnes 1840: 31). This, as Barnes understood it, covered a wide southern and western region: '—the counties of Surrey, Hants, Berks, Wilts, and Dorset, and parts of Somerset and Devon . . .' (Barnes 1848: 1). For Barnes, the West Country's topography is linked with the speech habits of its inhabitants. The River Parrett, for example, marks a boundary between victorious Saxon and defeated Celt: hence the difference in dialects on the east and west sides of the river (Barnes 1886: 6). Terrain combines with cultural tradition to resist the power of transport, communication and even the Norman Conquest: 'while the land-owning Norman families . . . retained their Latin-French tongue, the wood-girt and hill-sheltered tuns of the West were still vocal with the purest Saxon . . .' Barnes' Wessex, insofar as it survived in speech and culture, was not closed in the past. It survived in ways that offered a superior alternative to what Barnes called the 'tart and smart' speaking and thinking of the modern centre. Barnes used his antiquarian researches and experience as a Blackmore Vale man to question the modern notion that 'every change from the plough towards the desk, or from the desk towards the couch of empty-handed idleness, is an onward step towards happiness and intellectual and moral excellence' (1848: 16, 49).

It is not generally known that Barnes' idea of a new/old Wessex, existing as a language and a region, began to circulate *before* Hardy's famous contribution to its rebirth. In 1858, long before the beginning of Hardy's writing career, Charles Kingsley published an account of a fishing trip to Newbury in Berkshire, presenting it as part of Barnes' wide-ranging, still-existing Wessex. Kingsley not only quotes the local dialect with approval, referring to the manner of speech as 'good Wessex', but also presents himself as one of the locals, referring to 'us Wessex chalk-fishers' (C. Kingsley 1891: 44, 56, 58). In the following year, the travel writer Richard John King accepted Barnes' notion that Wessex could include Devonshire when he linked the 'ancient' and still surviving dialect of that county to 'the genuine Saxon of Wessex' (King 1874: 361). By 1868, Barnes was prefacing an edition of his poems in a way that suggested ancient Wessex and modern Dorset were now inseparable: 'As I think that some people, beyond the bounds of Wessex, would allow me the pleasure of believing that they have deemed the matter of my homely poems in our Dorset mother-speech to be worthy of their reading . . .' (Barnes 1868). The re-creation of Wessex was gathering pace. By 1876, it was possible to speak of the 'Wessex labourer' as a contemporary reality accurately reflected in Hardy's 'Wessex novels' (C. Kegan Paul 1876: 793). In 1889 a critic presented Hardy not as the inventor of a semi-real territory called Wessex, but as the 'historian' of a real geographical entity whose borders and presence could be taken for granted (Barrie 1889: 58–59). In 1905 an interviewer of Hardy presented his findings under the newspaper headline: 'A Talk with the Wessex Novelist at Casterbridge': Hardy had successfully played the leading role in turning several modern counties into Wessex and melting Dorchester into Casterbridge (Smithard 1905: 4).

While Hardy's fictional world owed more to the collective interest in Wessex than he admitted or remembered, there were other important sources for his invention. In 1911 Hardy wrote to his publishers suggesting that his own efforts to create a map of Wessex for inclusion with his novels could be improved by an artist adding 'ships & fishes in the sea, & trees and animals in the forests & moors, as in old maps by Speed &c' (Purdy 1978, Vol. 4: 185). This reference to the work of the famous cartographer John Speed (1552?–1629) suggests that Hardy wanted his Wessex map to serve differing functions. It was to exude historical pedigree and authenticity at the same time as demonstrating respect for county boundaries and compass bearings. On the other hand, it was to use inventive illustrations in order to convey the South West's topography and maritime tradition, and its interaction with the human imagination. A copy of Hardy's own version of the map can be viewed in *The Countryman* (Volume 13, July, 1936: 488–89). The map that was finally produced to illustrate his novels, and which now has canonical status with the texts, combines history and imagination more or less as Hardy prescribed (see, for example, Pinion 1984). Real place-names in orthodox lettering lie next to Hardy's invented place names in italics, actual coastline lies near to cameos of 'monsters from the deep': this is a visual equivalent to the pull between reality and fantasy in Hardy's verbal version of Wessex.

## Egdon Heath and King Lear's Heath

'Nobody "guided him into Wessex". He had always been there', responded Hardy indignantly, to a critic's suggestion that he owed his invention of fictional territory to R.D. Blackmore's example (Purdy 1978, Vol. 6: 155). The place he had always been was, literally speaking, the remote hamlet of Higher Bockhampton, near the heathlands of Dorset. Hardy combined several of these heaths to create one mighty Egdon Heath situated at the centre of his own map of Wessex: it is also at the centre of the imaginative source of his world. Hardy's early poem 'Domicilium', written some time between 1857 and 1860, recreates his birthplace at Higher Bockhampton as it once was in 1800, not surrounded by the trees and cultivated fields of later times but by wild heathland. In this particular place and time, made vivid to Hardy by his grandmother's stories of smuggling and the Napoleonic wars, humans shared existence with snakes, bats, ravens and 'heath-croppers' or wild ponies. Hardy's childhood territory was part of a network of heathy areas west of the river Avon, estimated to be 100,000 acres in extent during the mid-eighteenth century, 55,000 acres at the close of the nineteenth century and 15,000 acres during the 1980s (Hawkins 1986: 27, 34–37). Hardy ensures that modern readers can still simulate the experience of wandering in this now dwindling wilderness, which to him was part of a 'vast tract of unenclosed wild'. Hardy sustains his readers contact with this unique place and builds up its specificity: it appears in many of his poems, short stories and novels. He creates a place name for it, characteristically rooted in his landscape and yet imaginatively transformed. Moving 'Eggardon', the name of a hill fort in West Dorset, eastwards, he coins 'haggard Egdon', a description whose alliterative sound expresses bleakness. He also provides an aural image of an Egdon wind that gains its distinctive note from blowing through hundreds of 'heath-bells'. Complementing sounds with visual impressions, he suggests that this 'dark sweep of country' seems like an 'instalment of the night' on the earth before the night has appeared in the sky. He contrasts the apparent monotony of Egdon's slopes seen from a distance with the extraordinary and colourful world that it contains when examined microscopically. He finds ways of providing a textual counterpart to the evidence of the long human occupation (Celtic barrows, Roman roads and beacon fires) hidden in the palimpsest of the heath's wild landscape. He touches in the ancient history of this region within a region, quoting Leland and the reference in the Domesday Book to a 'Bruaria' or 'heathy, furzy, briary, wilderness'. (Book 1, Chapter 1, Hardy 1979: 43, 55).

This is the territory without that Hardy found to be the perfect symbol for a territory within. The work of Freud and Jung shows how creative writers and myth-makers anticipated the discovery of the unconscious mind. Without the language of fiction, these two influential if controversial thinkers could not have mapped the hidden territory of the mind. Hardy's Egdon needs to be understood in this context. Like the concept of the unconscious, the heath is continually present but not always noticed; the heath's allies are darkness, dreams and phantoms; it does not obey the normal rules of time; its nature cannot be controlled or predicted. It is the 'enemy of civilisation': agricultural improvers try to cultivate it just as the conscious attempts to control an unruly Id. Ignored, this force of Egdon is liable to rise up and kill you; understood, as Clym understood it, and it can be a source of wisdom and happiness.

Who is in charge of Hardy's Wessex? Is it those doomsters, Time and Chance, blind from birth, pictured in Hardy's remorselessly argued sonnet, 'Hap'? Is it a God behaving like one of the 'wanton boys' from the world of Shakespeare's Lear? Is it an angry 'President of the Immortals'? And if so, does this Zeus preside in the recesses of the mind? Is it Hardy's Immanent Will, evolving like Shaw's Life Force, from blindness through human agency towards consciousness and morality? Or, far from being under conscious control, are Wessex and its inhabitants the slave of irrational passion and unconscious drives? Understanding the nature of Egdon helps us to answer these questions.

Hardy knew by experience of the tragedies that arise when people become the slaves rather than the masters of their own misunderstood passions. He describes Egdon in one poem as a 'tract of pain' ('A Meeting with Despair'). In his novel, Egdon's face expresses 'tragical possibilities'. The territory before Hardy's eyes combined in his mind's eye with the disturbing zone of Shakespearean tragedy. Barnes' excavation of the past included reference to one Ina, who became King of the West Saxons in 688. Camden and Polydore Vergil in the sixteenth century contributed to a process whereby the story of the historical King Ina became combined with the ancient legend of King Leir or Lear, the tragic figure made famous in the work of Geoffrey of Monmouth and Shakespeare. The heath where Lear battles with the storms without and within his mind first appears in a stage direction added to Shakespeare's story by Nicholas Rowe, although its presence is established in the bard's lines. When Hardy reread *Lear* in 1895 it was the 'grand scale of the tragedy, scenically' which struck him (F. Hardy 1986: 282). The scenic properties of Shakespeare helped him to make sense of his own reactions to his native heathland.

Hardy put together Shakespeare's verse, Rowe's stage direction and Camden's Ina-Lear during a short story of 1888, speculating that Egdon Heath had 'not improbably . . . witnessed the agony of the Wessex King Ina' ('The Withered Arm', included in *Wessex Tales*). When Andrew Lang attacked the pessimism of *Tess of the d'Urbervilles* in 1892, Hardy defended himself by giving his Wessex a Shakespearean pedigree. Protesting against the gods, argued Hardy, was not his personal foible. Although his protest may have 'some local originality' deriving from his Wessex upbringing, Wessex as the site of Ina-Lear's heath is a place where the local and the universal meet (Orel 1967: 28). In 1895 Hardy continued to display his

Shakespearean Egdon before the public: 'It is pleasant to dream that some spot in the extensive tract whose south-western quarter is here described, may be the heath of the traditionary King of Wessex —Lear' (Preface to *The Return of the Native*). In 1903 a scholarly monograph was published undermining Hardy's historical speculation about a Wessex Lear: 'the anecdote in Camden's *Remaines* . . . will prove—though this involves the destruction of a favourite fancy of Thomas Hardy's—to have been transferred to King Ina from Polydore Vergil's account of Leir' (Perrett 1903: 8). Hardy took the criticism in his stride, responding to Perrett: 'The wish, was, of course, father to the thought when I associated Lear with Wessex, & I think I shall stick to Camden . . . for the pleasure of the dream' (Purdy 1978, Vol. 3: 177). Hardy's dream was the polite Victorian reader's nightmare. The man from the heath was posing heathen questions for the orthodoxly religious. In 1896, responding to the publication of *Jude the Obscure*, Edmund Gosse challenged Hardy to justify sending a tragic and rebellious message from his fortunate position in the 'arable land of Wessex' (Lerner 1968: 121). In fact, Hardy's Wessex was not an arable land of rural idylls. His Wessex derived from the reality of rural poverty, from Swing riots and Tolpuddle martyrdom. It was a world including the barren reality of 'Flintcomb Ash' and the troublesome shades of Egdon. The pretty Wessex marketed for tourists was actually conceived by Hardy as part of a world of Shakespearean tragedy in which humanity are flies and the gods are no more responsible than 'wanton boys'.

How did Hardy understand the world of Lear? We know that he took some scholarly notes on the details of Shakespeare's play and questioned whether Shakespeare had damaged the intensity of the tragic action by splitting our interest between the King and Gloucester; we can speculate that the scenic qualities of the play were Hardy's special interest. King Lear's heath is a place where elemental forces strip away the accidentals of costume and rank to reveal human failings and aspirations. It is a place where both the individual body and the body politic are judged, where the king has to listen to the poor fool and find what he shares in common with 'poor naked wretches'. It is a place, as Freud pointed out, where outer and inner topography meet. In Lear's world, a place made by Shakespeare and other writers, people are driven by forces that they cannot understand or control. In the conventions of fairy-tale, humans are compelled to do what they do not wish, or find that their wishes come true in a way that horrifies them. There are echoes of *Lear* in many parts of Hardy's work, including his tragedy of Tess who is described as 'more sinned against than sinning' and his treatment of the tragic rise and fall of Michael Henchard who ends his life Lear-like on the heath attended by his Wessex fool, Abel Whittle. Here I am concerned with some lesser known applications of Lear's world to Hardy's.

## 'Blue Jimmy' and the Tramp Woman's Tragedy

The word tragedy makes several appearance in the arresting titles of Hardy's works: consider 'A Sunday Morning Tragedy', 'A Tragedy of Two Ambitions', 'The Tragedy of a Pure Woman', 'The Famous Tragedy of the Queen of Cornwall'. Hardy did not use the term 'tragedy' lightly when he signposted his literary territory for his readers. His fiction and critical writings make it clear that he was familiar with the long literary and dramatic tradition of tragedy from Sophocles to Shakespeare. He knew of the aesthetics of tragedy as conceived by Aristotle and elaborated by Renaissance critics. He was familiar with the unities of time, place and action, the role of the chorus, the structure of exposition, climax, turning point and denouement that characterize tragic drama. He also knew of the deeper questions of character, environment and fate raised by tragedy: the notion of irreconcilable conflict, the idea of a good character marred by a fatal flaw, the significance of moments of blindness and recognition in the tragic protagonist's rise and fall. The appearance of omens, ghosts, witches and supernatural agencies in tragedies were of special interest to him and influenced his attitude to place. He could link this ancient tradition with a modern reality: the fatalism and superstition bred amongst the poverty of rural labourers in Dorset.

The supernatural in tragedy may also be understood as an early symbol of the unconscious mind or, in Hardy's terms, of the will that is immanent but not fully controlled or understood. The ancient tragedy of the human battle with the blind forces of Nature contains within it the more modern tragedy where humanity battles with inner forces. Freud's study of 'The Three Caskets' uncovers the ancient roots of the story of King Lear's choice amongst three daughters. The Goddesses of the Weather were known as Horae; the Horae evolved into the Morae, the Three Female Fates, with one eye between them, who weave, measure and cut the thread of human life.

Lear's elemental heath is the place where Horae and Morae meet (Freud 1986a). In his own way, Hardy visited Freud's heath. Nature, thought Hardy, was exhausted as an inspiration for pretty landscapes but not as a 'deeper reality', in which could be read the 'tragical mysteries of life' (F. Hardy 1986: 120, 185). The modern, thinking observer would seek those places that possess a 'negative beauty of tragic tone' such as Egdon Heath or the mysterious stone pillar high on Batcombe Down in North Dorset, known as the 'Cross-in-hand' (see Chapter 45 of *Tess of the d'Urbervilles* and the poem 'The Lost Pyx'). These are places where mysteries without express mysteries within. Hardy creates a territory where the narrative drive enables one to encounter the mysterious, unconscious drive of human behaviour.

Hardy described himself in the poem 'Afterwards' as a person who used to notice things. Where some saw an innocent-looking green field at Ilchester in Somerset, Hardy looked through the externals of the site and re-created in his mind's eye the prison that had once stood there. It was once a place much feared and hated by local people, where men were hanged for crimes such as horse-stealing. One of the ghosts appearing at this site for Hardy was that of James Clace, known as 'Blue Jimmy', hanged at Ilchester as a horse-thief in 1827. He was part of Somerset and Dorset's past; Hardy spoke of him as an inhabitant of Wessex. Blue Jimmy plays a significant role in the work that Hardy thought to be his best poem, 'A Tramp Woman's Tragedy'. This poem teases us about its relationship to history and place: it is headed '182—' and thinly disguises Ilchester as 'Ivelchester'. The insistent tetrameters of this ballad evoke the outdoor, walking, wandering life of the tramp woman and her companions: her fancy-man, Jeering Johnny and Mother Lee. Their wanderings can be traced in detail on a map of the south and west. They are first pictured tramping from west to east: starting at Winyard's Gap on the border of Dorset and Somerset, going past 'sad Sedgemoor', scene of Monmouth's defeat, and reaching the Poldon Hills overlooking the Somerset levels. They are also pictured as far East as the New Forest in Hampshire, before returning west through Somerset and Dorset: crossing Blackmore Vale, travelling along the Mendip Hills and into Marshwood Vale in South-west Dorset. They move via inns that are not known to the polite traveller. Invisible to society, they are not overlooked by Hardy who is looking for the tragic consequences that the reader anticipates when considering the situation of the foursome and the 'Jeering' qualities of Johnny. The tragic climax of this Wessex odyssey occurs at a place called Marshall's Elm on 'Poldon top'. The tramp woman begins by teasing her lover and flirting with Jeering Johnny. Having begun the process, she cannot stop it. She is actually carrying her lover's child but chooses to falsely tell her lover that the baby is Johnny's. She metaphorically twists the knife in her lover; he literally knifes Johnny to death. As in *King Lear*, suffering is piled on suffering. The murderer is hanged at Ivel-chester and his child is stillborn. The tramp woman has to live with the knowledge that her actions have resulted in the death of two men and an innocent baby. After the tragic climax and *Hamlet*-like number of deaths (Mother Lee has also died of unexplained causes), Hardy uses the conventional ghost to help his denouement. The reader is left to speculate whether the ghost is real or whether it is a sign of the tramp woman's Lear-like loss of sanity under the stress of grief and remorse. The ghost of her lover appears to the tramp woman, asking again whose child it was: she tells the ghost the truth that she should have told the living man. Like other tragic protagonists, she repents too late, when it is impossible to make reparation for her action. She ends the poem alone, haunted by her guilt, wandering the Western Moor (Exmoor). The poem gives us little overt evidence of the reasons for her fatal and apparently inexplicable actions. All we know is that she is motivated by a desire to tease and by 'wanton idleness'.

The real secret of her actions appears in an article on Blue Jimmy that appeared long after the poem was first published. This article is signed by Florence Dugdale, Hardy's second wife, but it bears the marks of Hardy's distinctive style and vocabulary. (*The Life* of Hardy published under Florence's name was also mainly written by Thomas.) The article considers the conundrum that although a horse-stealer stood to gain relatively little financially from his crime, he stood to lose his life if caught. The so-called deterrent of capital punishment had no effect on people like Jimmy. Specifically, the article describes Blue Jimmy's continual thefts (he was said to have stolen over a hundred horses) as demonstrating 'a mechanical persistence in a series of actions as if by no will or necessity of the actor, but as if under some external or internal compulsion against which reason and a foresight of sure disaster were powerless to argue' (Dugdale 1911: 225). Hardy's poem transfers the compulsive actions of Blue Jimmy to the tramp woman. Her tragedy is the product of an unconscious drive that she cannot control until after it has been fulfilled. Lear-like and Michael Henchard-like, she ends her life wandering in a lonely wilderness of regrets, a wasteland that reflects the senseless waste of her life.

## The Milkmaid's Tragedy: In an Uncanny Place

Visitors to modern Dorchester can see a thatched cottage by the River Frome that is pretty enough for a conventional postcard. For Hardy this site had different associations: it was the cottage of the hangman who plays a significant role in his story of 'The Withered Arm'. The topography of this Wessex Tale, mainly based east of Dorchester amongst the Dorset heathland, has been mapped in detail by Denys Kay Robinson. I am less concerned here with identifying the story's setting than the relationship between it and the internal world of its characters. A summary of the story only hints at its complexities. The tale begins and ends in the mind of a 'lorn milk-maid' Rhoda Brook. Rhoda has borne a child to Farmer Lodge and then been abandoned by him; he later marries the young and pretty Gertrude. Rhoda hears reports of Gertrude's beauty from her son who appears to play a very minor role at the start of the tragic tale. Dwelling on the image of her rival in her imagination, Rhoda has a dream in which Gertrude sits astride her, taunting her with the symbol of her triumph: a wedding ring. In her dream, Rhoda grips the spectre by the arm and casts her off. From this moment, the dream becomes reality: the real Gertrude's arm begins to wither as does her happiness and her marriage with Farmer Lodge. The desperate Gertrude, guided ironically by her rival Rhoda, seeks advice from Conjurer Trendle, a 'cunning man' who lives on Egdon Heath. The conjurer explains that the only cure for Gertrude's affliction is to touch the body of a man recently hanged. Years pass and Gertrude continues to decline until news of a young man due to be hung at Casterbridge gaol gives her hope. The young man concerned was an innocent observer of a rick-burning but condemned to die as an example to others. When Gertrude enters the room where the corpse is lying she discovers it to be none other than the son of Rhoda and Farmer Lodge. The final twist in the tragic tale is that Rhoda and Farmer Lodge are also present: they have come to bury their child. Seeking a secret cure Gertrude encounters the very people she most wants to avoid; seeking only to be healed she ends up causing harm to her predecessor in her husband's life. This is the tragic climax. In the denouement, Gertrude dies from the shock of her experience and the chastened Farmer Lodge leads a better life. His will shows his recognition of his sin: he leaves his money to a home for orphaned boys as a way of atoning for the abandonment of his son. He also leaves an annuity for Rhoda but despite her poverty she refuses to take it: she will never forgive him for his actions.

The relationship of this tale to the form and content of tragedy is clear. The story also conforms with Freud's definitions of the uncanny. According to Freud, the uncanny is something once known, made unknown and then known again. It is alien yet familiar. The etymology of the term 'uncanny' in German and English reflects its contradictory qualities, its place at the bridge between conscious and unconscious. A 'canny' person may be able to come to terms with the uncanny but for some it will remain beyond their 'ken'. The experience of the uncanny is the conflict that occurs when a superstition that we think we have outgrown seems to have validity. The uncanny happens in life but not necessarily in fiction. A fairy tale, gruesome though it might be, cannot be uncanny because, says Freud, the convention of such a tale is that it is not true. A realist tale, such as Hardy creates, with a careful simulation of topography and related occupation, is sufficiently like life to give us the sense of the uncanny. Freud picks out the following as having the power of the uncanny: the dead body, the double, repetition and the evil eye. These phenomena seem both strange and familiar because they take us back to the forgotten foundations of the mind's fears and wishes. A dead body evokes both our fears of the dead and our refusal to accept the fact of death; the double disturbingly reminds us of the unfulfilled but possible futures that circumstance now denies us; repetition in life is an echo of our instinctual demands which reason cannot control and the evil eye returns us to a state of childhood where thoughts are omnipotent, and the wish is as good as the deed (Freud 1986b).

Hardy's Wessex Tale has all these phenomena. Gertrude is the double of Rhoda: she is the young and successful wife that Rhoda the mistress wanted to be. Repetition against all the efforts of morality and conscious intention is provided both by Rhoda's actions and Gertrude's. Rhoda cannot stop putting the evil eye on her rival: Gertrude cannot stop causing harm to the Brooks. All the characters in the story are in the grip of uncanny forces which they wish to control but cannot. Conjurer Trendle ambivalently denies his own psychic powers, Farmer Lodge is made furious by village superstitions because he 'half entertained them himself'. Rhoda declares about her curse on Gertrude: 'could it be that I exercise a malignant power over people against my own will?'. Gertrude, instead of praying for Christian goals, finds that her affliction makes her desperate for the corpse supposed to heal her: 'her unconscious prayer was, "O Lord, hang some guilty or innocent person soon" '. In fact, her wish is fulfilled in a way she did not wish: an innocent hanged man causes a shock that leads to her death. All of the major figures participate in the tragedy: Lodge causes the suffering but only recognizes it after the deaths of his son and wife; Rhoda suffers the tragedy without the benefit of atonement and recognition as her rejection of Lodge's money at the conclusion of the story implies. As Rhoda ages, her abundant hair becomes white and worn away at the forehead, 'perhaps' because of the pressure on it as she leans against the cows to milk them. The 'perhaps' allows for the possibility that Hardy has created an outer sign for her internal grief, a Wessex equivalent for her Lear-like suffering. The story relates Egdon Heath to the agony of Lear and reproduces something of the ancient King's suffering in the life of a milkmaid.

## Ravished by Music: A Tragicomedy

Lear is accompanied on the heath by a Fool who tells him the truth in riddles. Hardy's Wessex is also a place of dark comedy or tragicomedy. The story entitled 'The Fiddler of the Reels' makes a tragicomedy out of a world caught between the ancient forces of Egdon Heath and the modern forces of the Great Exhibition of 1851. This event is described in the tale as the equivalent in time of a geological fault line that divides ancient and modern worlds. Rather than viewing this national event from a national perspective, Hardy focuses on its implications for three Wessex characters, 'Mop' Ollamoor the itinerant fiddler, Car'line Arspent a young woman of 'fragile and responsive organisation' and decent Ned Hopcraft the mechanic. Hardy adds to the power of his story by letting his scene draw on the energies of the wider Wessex already known to his readers. The action takes place near his fictional version of Lower and Higher Bockhampton where he was born (called Mellstock as in *Under the Greenwood Tree*) and the heath country of East Dorset (called Egdon Heath as in *The Return of the Native* and 'The Withered

Arm'). Mop's devilishly clever fiddling is contrasted with the more respectable musicianship of the Mellstock village choir. Car'line is too fascinated by the seductive and rascally Mop to take much interest in an honourable proposal of marriage from Ned Hopcraft. Having been rejected by Car'line, Ned leaves Wessex to work on the construction of the huge glasshouse designed to house the Exhibition. He then receives an artful letter from Car'line indicating that Mop has vanished from her life and that she is willing to consider marriage to him. Ned invites her to join him but when he greets her stepping off one of the excursion trains especially arranged for the Exhibition, he soon discovers that she is accompanied by Mop Ollamoor's daughter. Ned agrees to marry her and take responsibility for the child. When the work made available by the Exhibition ends, the country couple decide to return to their native Wessex. Car'line goes on ahead priding herself on her status as a London wife, only to fall under the spell of Mop again when she hears him play at the Quiet Woman Inn on Egdon. She dances until overcome by exhaustion and collapses. A tragic denouement seems likely when Ned arrives and threatens to do violence to his rival. The tragedy becomes comedy when it becomes clear that the villain cannot be found, and that instead of abandoning his child and running off with another man's wife, he has run away with his own daughter. More paradoxically, Ned is apparently more distressed by the loss of his adopted daughter than gladdened by the fact that Car'line remains with him. Ned is now disgusted by his native landscape and returns to London. Ollamoor and his daughter are never found but are rumoured to be working together in America.

The reader can recognize Hardy's familiar pattern: the compulsive repetition of folly, the failure of conscious control, the 'uncanny way' in which Car'line meets her seducer again, the fact that the movements of characters to London and back are as determined by human passion as economic necessity or interest in the Exhibition. The symbol for unconscious, instinctual, sexual power is the fiddle-bowing of Mop. Like the sword-play in *Far From the Madding Crowd*, Mop's music enables Hardy to describe surrender to sensuality without causing offence to his readers. Mop is described as having 'weird and wizardly' power over impressionable young women. Whereas good-hearted Ned is impotent where music and passion are concerned, Mop knows how to play on the fiddle and the heart strings. His music causes Car'line 'excruciating spasms' and 'blissful torture'.

His fiddle emits an 'elfin shriek of finality' as Car'line falls to the floor in a dancer's equivalent of erotic exhaustion.

Two incidents in particular mark Mop's sensual yet other-worldly power. One incident occurs after Mop's second musical 'seduction' of Car'line. Ned seeks him outside the Inn but 'a mass of dark heathland rose sullenly upward to its not easily accessible interior, a ravined plateau, whereon jutted into the sky . . . the fir woods of Mistover backed by the Yalbury coppices—a place of Dantesque gloom at this hour, which would have afforded secure hiding for a battery of artillery' let alone 'a man and child'. Hardy's invented place-names link this to a specific location near Bockhampton but he is also describing an infernal region of the mind. Mop is as hidden, mysterious and wizardly as the human unconscious. Another incident occurs during Car'line's visit with Ned to the London Exhibition. While standing amid an exhibition of furniture, Car'line suddenly glimpses a person reflected in a mirror, a person 'uncannily' like Mop Ollamoor. When she seeks the real counterpart of the image, he cannot be found. The reader is left to speculate on whether Mop was really present or whether this symbolizes the hold which he retains over Car'line's unconscious self, even though she is married to another. Hardy the man noted the destruction of the South West's culture by the new mobility of the railways. Hardy the writer makes a powerful and disturbing Wessex temporarily invade London.

## The Tragedy of War

The folly of Lear results in the folly of war; war also invades Hardy's territory. His Egdon Heath is as old as Lear but it is also the site where beacon keepers watch anxiously for news of Napoleon's feared invasion of England. Viewed at twilight or lit at night by beacon fires, the heath has sinister aspects. In Hardy's tragic Napoleonic drama, *The Dynasts* (1904–1908), the hollows of the heath's surface are compared to the eye sockets of a skull (1920: 53). Egdon is linked to the dark forces that cause the senseless, irrational destruction of war. Many other parts of Wessex are also touched by war-madness. Even the Cornwall that Hardy romanticized as Lyonesse was not immune. In 1870 Hardy was walking with his fiancée Emma in the garden of Saint Juliot rectory in North Cornwall; they were reading Tennyson together. This image seems appropriate for a romantic Lyonesse. In fact, however, Hardy's gaze was roving outside the garden, looking from the local to the world. Out of the corner of his eye, he noticed a ploughman at work in the nearby Valency valley; in one corner of his mind, while sharing poetry with Emma, he was assimilating the latest news about the bloody battle of Gravelotte that brought France's second Empire to an end. This Cornish image, like other Cornish memories combining topography and emotion, gestated in his mind for many years before emerging in a poem. In 1916, when another more bloody war was in progress, Hardy revived his memory of 1870 to create 'In Time of "The Breaking of Nations" ' (F. Hardy 1986: 378). In this poem the breaking of the clods of Cornish soil is compared but contrasted with the breaking up of nations and frail human bodies. Hardy was keenly aware that wars inspired by Dynasts were fought by ploughmen. He also questioned the way in which historians record war. For him, history was less the result of conscious intention than of blind chance and unconscious forces.

Hardy saw the ghosts of both the great and the humble when he looked at landscape in the context of his particular sense of history. He read Weymouth, for example, as evidence of the links between King George III and his many subjects during the period 1796–1805 when England expected Napoleon's forces to invade. According to tradition, the imposing chalk figure of King George cut in the downs above Sutton Poyntz near Weymouth is shown travelling eastward because the King's courtiers wanted him to leave the provincial bathing place and return to the sophistication of the capital (Powys 1937: 49). Hardy's Napoleonic fiction asks us to travel from city to province and to see the city from the provincial's view. He makes a place in his fiction not only for the king and his courtiers but also for the soldiers and sailors from the provinces who gave their lives in the King's wars. Like R.D. Blackmore, his ear was attuned to catch oral traditions preserving the common man's views. Through oral tradition, Hardy knew descendants of the local people who had cut the figure of the King in the turf; he knew the particular spot on a path over Bincombe Down where two deserters from King George's German legion had been shot; he knew from his own grandparents how the guardians of beacon fires on the high places of Dorset and 'Bang-Up Locals' or militia men guarding the coasts had panicked when the dreaded 'Boney' was thought to have landed. His local knowledge was later complemented by some painstaking research into the period at the British Museum, by his interviews with soldiers who could still remember the Napoleonic wars and by his visits to relevant battlefields in Europe.

In 1916, the year of the Battle of the Somme, Hardy was still partly living in the Napoleonic past. Florence Emily, his second wife, records in a letter of 17 September how Hardy deciphered the meaning of a bracken covered track on a Dorset heath. Hardy had found the remains of the old coach road that passed close to his remote birthplace, linking Dorset and London, the province and the world. This inspired in Hardy's historical imagination a series of visions of the coaches and their occupants who had once travelled the abandoned way. He saw in his mind's eye: George III, Pitt, Nelson, Captain Hardy and finally his own mother as a child (Millgate 1996: 120–21). It is characteristic of Hardy's vision that there is an unbroken connection between the landscape and humanity, between the past and the present. It is also typical of his Wessex values that this series of images starts with King George and ends with the country child Jemima Hardy, one who had known the reality of rural poverty and passed on a sense of its horrors to her son. When, in 1903, Hardy ascribed the inspiration of his ten-year struggle to write his epic Napoleonic drama, *The Dynasts*, to 'accidents of locality' or the coincidental connection between his childhood territory and the impact of the Napoleonic threat on England, he had in mind a landscape as packed with information as any history book (Hardy 1920: i).

There is no more tangible evidence of Hardy's encounter with the Napoleonic past than the macabre caricature of Napoleon which he saw on the wall of a cottage at Sutton Poyntz (Overcombe in *The Trumpet Major*, 1880). The history of the print seen by Hardy begins in 1806 when a Hanoverian artist named Dahling drew a sketch of Napoleon on parade after he had made a victorious entrance into Berlin. Tinted in sepia by F. Arnold, this sketch became a popular print, depicting Napoleon in profile to the left, wearing a small hat and a dark coat with epaulettes, the cross and ribbon of the Legion of Honour prominent on his breast. In one version, the head and shoulders of the sketch were engraved in colours by Lehmann of Berlin. It was this that became the origin of one of the most famous and influential caricatures of Napoleon by J.M. Voltz (1784–1858), a German painter and engraver. In 1813 the victorious Napoleon of 1806 was now the man who had suffered defeat at the bloody battle of Leipzig. Voltz produced a gruesome and fascinating print ironically

9) *The 'Hieroglyphic Napoleon'.*
Compare Hardy's description in *The Trumpet Major.*

entitled 'True Picture of the Conqueror, Triumph of the Year 1813'. At first sight and from a distance, the print seems like a flattering sketch of Napoleon. On closer inspection, however, the 'true picture' of the conqueror reveals a very different message. Everything in Dahling's original image is transmuted into visual propaganda at Boney's expense: his hat becomes a Prussian Eagle which has seized him in its claws, his coat now contains the names of all his defeats in battle, his Legion of Honour is turned into a sinister spider, and his epaulette becomes the Hand of God which tears asunder the web of evil being spun from Napoleon's evil heart. Most gruesome and sinister of all is Napoleon's face: handsome in profile by Dahling, it is now made up of a series of interlocking, writhing corpses. The visual message is clear: the man who appears handsome from afar is the cause of mass slaughter throughout Europe. It was claimed that twenty thousand copies of the 'corpse-head' or 'hieroglyphic head' were sold in Berlin within a week. It is certainly true that the caricature was reproduced in seven other countries. A.M. Broadley, historian of the Napoleonic era and an acquaintance of Thomas Hardy, explains that the Hieroglyphic Head was popular with all those Germans, Russians, Spaniards and Frenchmen determined to stop the slaughter that Napoleon's ambitions caused (Broadley 1911, Vol. 2: 256–57).

Voltz's influential print was used as the heading for an English broadside against Napoleon printed by Rudolph Ackermann, and it is a version of this that Hardy must have seen in Dorset (versions of this broadside and print are in the reserve collection of Devon County Library and the Dorset County Museum). Hardy's gaze on this print in Sutton Poyntz was at the end of a long and influential relay of gazes at Napoleon, from the admiring to the condemnatory, and the European to the English. Secluded in a nineteenth-century cottage, this *objet trouvé* spoke volumes to Hardy about the war and human suffering; in its hieroglyphs Hardy could see how Wessex innocents were tangled in a web of national and international folly. Adapting the 1813 caricature to fit the needs of a novel mostly set in the time *before* Trafalgar in 1805, Hardy makes his fictional Bob Loveday describe an English version of the print in *The Trumpet Major* (1880):

> It was a hieroglyphic profile of Napoleon. The hat represented a maimed French eagle; the face was ingeniously made up of human carcasses, knotted and writhing together in such directions as to form a physiognomy; a band, or stock, shaped to resemble the English channel, encircled his throat, and seemed to choke him; his epaulette was a hand tearing a cobweb that represented the treaty of peace with England; and his ear was a woman crouching over a dying child. (Chapter 25, Hardy 1986: 244)

Bob Loveday finds the print patriotic and stirring but Hardy's heroine, Anne Garland, is repulsed by the thought of the costs of patriotism: 'It is dreadful! . . . I don't like to see it'. Perhaps Anne senses that her fate is similar to that of the woman pictured crouching over a dying child.

Hardy ensures that the powerful presence of Napoleonic history in Dorset is faithfully represented in his fictional Wessex. He picks up and dusts off for our inspection some of the innumerable mosaic pieces of the Napoleonic past that would otherwise be forgotten. Various poems systematically map the various parts of Napoleonic terrain in the South West: in 'San Sebastian' he makes us encounter a wanderer on the road from Hintock (Melbury Osmund in North Dorset) to Ivel (Yeovil in Somerset) who is haunted by his participation in the siege and atrocities of San Sebastian; in 'Leipzig' he takes us into the Ship Inn of Casterbridge (Dorchester) where one Norbert records a combined German and Dorset contribution to the defeat of Napoleon; in 'The Alarm' Hardy recalls the fear of Napoleon's invasion, deciphering the remnants of beacon keepers' huts on Egdon (Puddletown) Heath and other high places. *The Trumpet Major* and the Wessex scenes of *The Dynasts* give us a comprehensive picture of a distinctive landscape in time of war, including evocations of the ridgeway from Dorchester to Weymouth, the cliffs of Saint Aldhelm's Head and 'White Nothe' or 'Nose', the back sea and the front sea divided by Chesil beach, Captain Hardy's house at Portesham, and HMS *Victory* imagined as viewed from the Dorset coast on its way to battle.

Hardy sustains the presence of the Napoleonic past in his fictions by using the same characters and topography in several works, enabling the reader gradually to accumulate a sense of a map which combines terrain, time and human emotion. Private Cantle, the young beacon keeper in *The Dynasts*, is aged 'Granfer' Cantle in *The Return of the Native*; the story of Corporal Tullidge's deafness is told both in *The Trumpet Major* and in the ballad 'Valenciennes'; Sergeant Stanner in the first published version of *The Trumpet Major* sings two verses of a satire on Boney and English society that Hardy later expanded and published as 'The Sergeant's Song' within his collected verse; Solomon Longways appears in *The Mayor of Casterbridge* and attends the burning of the effigy of Napoleon at Casterbridge in *The Dynasts*.

Hardy weaves together fiction with fiction but also weaves fiction with history: in his short stories, novels and verse he continually draws his readers' attention to his claim to be shadowing actual events, real people and places. *The Trumpet Major* is introduced as more founded on oral and written testimony than any other Wessex novel. Hardy was told that the place where two German deserters were shot during the Wars was unmarked: he 'marked' the place on Bincombe Down by writing his story 'The Melancholy Hussar of the German Legion'. His poems are a long record of encounters with witnesses of history and participants in it. 'A Peasant's Confession', a poem about the turning point in the Battle of Waterloo, is prefaced with a quotation from a French historian to suggest the veracity of the tale. Hardy's Napoleonic ballads are the poetic equivalent of gravestones erected to give dignity and individuality to otherwise anonymous and forgotten soldiers. 'The Alarm', a story passed on in the Hardy family, is headed with the word 'Traditional' and the date 1803, suggesting both the specific truth of the story and the collective memory of it. The tale 'Valenciennes' is headed 'In Memory of S.C. (Pensioner) died 184—' and is loosely based on one Samuel Clark, an officer's servant at Waterloo buried at West Stafford in Dorset near Hardy's birthplace; 'San Sebastian' is introduced with the heading 'with thoughts of Sergeant M— (Pensioner) who died 185—', a figure possibly partly derived from Sergeant Matthews of the Dorset Regiment who was awarded the Waterloo Medal. The fact that the fine detail of his 'facts' is sometimes questionable is less important to Hardy than that the reader should take the general point of the genuine connection between landscape, people and human history. He gives us the sense of being archaeologists digging up buried truths, uncovering a past that has helped to make our present. The sense of a living connection between past and present is one of the finest achievements of his writing. In 'One We Knew' he recreates his maternal grandmother Mary Head recalling the French Revolution and its Napoleonic aftermath 'not as one who remembers but as one who *sees*'. This sense of the immediacy and pervasiveness of history is shared by Hardy's readers: he gives us a sense of being able to reach out and touch the past in objects such as the Sutton Poyntz caricature, in buildings such as Gloucester Lodge at Weymouth, in landscapes such as Puddletown Heath. Enchanted by his words (spellbound or 'spela' bound), readers do not so much 'learn about' history as *see* it.

One of the culminations of this tendency in Hardy's work may be seen in the short story 'A Tradition of 1804'. This 'tradition' synthesizes both fact and invention, the actual nature of possible landing places on the Dorset coast and Hardy's insertion of his imagination into this landscape. His story daringly takes history one step further than truth by making Napoleon actually land near

Lulworth Cove on a reconnaissance mission for his planned invasion. Leslie Stephen had advised Hardy about the difficulties of incorporating historical celebrities in fiction, suggesting that the artist could not rival or interfere with their pre-existing presence. Ignoring this advice, Hardy dares to describe Boney's famous features *seen* through the eyes of a Dorset shepherd on a Dorset beach. Having invented the legend Hardy was surprised to find that after the publication of his story, it became locally accepted as fact (Orel 1967: 24)! In an important sense, however, he was not distorting history but finding a fictional counterpart for it. Napoleon really did invade Dorset in terms of the memories, fears and imaginations of Hardy's ancestors and their descendants. Boney's presence was so invasive that he became assimilated in the local, pre-Napoleonic culture of folk tales and mummers' plays. Hardy's fictional history was true to the inner life of his fellow inhabitants of the south coast. In *The Dynasts* it therefore seems appropriate that the bogey-man Bonaparte is linked with the pagan and ancient figure of the Cerne Abbas giant, a presence in the Dorset landscape before Napoleon was known. These two larger than life figures, one etched in the landscape and one etched in the mind, are inextricably linked with Dorset-Wessex not only due to history but also due to Hardy's role as creator and witness.

The epic tale of *The Dynasts* is framed by dialogue between 'phantasmal intelligences', Hardy's version of the gods and choruses which motivate and comment on dramatic action in Greek, Elizabethan and Jacobean drama. Hardy's Intelligences consist of a Semi-Chorus of Rumours bearing news of the real and imagined events, the Shade of the Earth commenting passively on human violation of the planet, and the Spirits Ironic and Sinister showing us the dark reality and black comedy of man's inhumanity to man. In addition, the Spirit of the Years provides the 'passionless Insight of the Ages' or records human action viewed in a long comparative perspective but without accepting the responsibility or the necessity for moral judgement. Amongst these Intelligences, only the Spirit and Chorus of the Pities offer moral judgement, hope and sympathetic identification with suffering. These various spirits brood in the background of all Hardy's Napoleonic work and over his Napoleonic landscape. The Rumours control the action of *The Trumpet Major* when citizens panic at the report that Napoleon has landed. The Shade of the Earth presides over Hardy's magnificent evocation of

Waterloo in *The Dynasts* as viewed by the helpless little creatures that dwell on the battlefield. The Spirits Ironic and Sinister are present when the speaker of 'San Sebastian' acknowledges that his daughter constantly reminds him of a young girl that he raped in time of war. These Spirits are also present when a Peasant confesses, privately to his priest but publicly to us overhearing him, that he was partly responsible for the downfall of Napoleon ('The Peasant's Confession'). The Spirit of the Years (the passionless insight of the ages) alternates with the Spirit of the Pities more or less constantly in these stories: Hardy's narrators bear witness to history both in the sense of attempting to record the facts without being judgmental and in the sense of giving moral vision.

Assisted by these various Intelligences or points of view in tension, Hardy's Napoleonic fictions consistently explore the conflict but connection between private and public loyalties, the personal and the wider world. Often the personal and private emerges to rival the world of drum and trumpet history. In *The Dynasts* Hardy presents the nationally commemorated death of Nelson in his own off-centre, idiosyncratic way. His namesake Captain Hardy is imagined below deck, explaining his reverie to the dying Nelson:

> Thoughts all confused, my lord:—their needs on deck,
> Your own sad state, and your unrivalled past;
> Mixed up with flashes of old things afar—
> Old childish things at home, down Wessex way,
> In the snug village under Blackdon Hill
> Where I was born. The tumbling stream, the garden,
> The placid look of the grey dial there,
> Marking unconsciously this bloody hour,
> And the red apples on my father's trees,
> Just now full ripe.
> (Hardy 1920, Part I, Act V, Scene IV: 97)

Captain Hardy's grey stone house at Portesham under Blackdown Hill still stands to this day and visitors can recognize that the above words fit the actual location like a glove. On the other hand, Hardy plays with history and topography to create the atmosphere he requires: his namesake was actually born at Kingston Russell, still in Dorset but some miles from Portesham. The literary and philosophical truth here, a subject for the passionless Spirit of the Years and the compassionate Pities, is that the shadow on the apparently peaceful and placid sundial marks the death of Nelson and many others at Trafalgar. As apples ripen (notes the Shade of the Earth), men's plans for slaughter mature (so say the Spirits Ironic and Sinister).

It is a daring anachronism to make such famous historical figures discuss the Wessex that was actually only revived by Kingsley, Barnes and Hardy long after the Napoleonic period. In this sense, Hardy's work both accepts the power of history and resists it, asserting the rights and reality of the writer's imagination among real things, facts and events. When the locals gather on Puddletown Heath to watch for Boney, Hardy cannot refrain from including a reference to his own personal location in the landscape, in history and in the scheme of moral values. An anonymous young man on the high vantage point notes 'the lantern at Max turnpike is shining quite plain' (Hardy 1920, Part I, Act II, Scene V: 52). This is a reference to Hardy's chosen location near Dorchester, Max Gate, a place whose name commemorates the existence of an otherwise forgotten gatekeeper called Mack. Hardy is deliberately putting himself in the epic picture and not only as a descendant of those who actually fought in the Wars: he hopes that his modern fiction throws light on the darkness of past human behaviour, that it opens a gate on the past that helps us to understand the present. Hardy resists the history of war, the seductive qualities of its apparent glamour and heroism, by judging it with the aid of the Compassionate Pities. In 'The Bridge of Lodi', the narrator visits the site of an early victory by Napoleon and is astonished to find that its modern inhabitants have no interest in this part of their history. The narrator considers adopting their attitude and then decides that recording this past is vital, although he leaves the reader to speculate on the reasons for his decision. In *The Dynasts*, the Spirit Sinister has a cynical explanation for the activities of military historians and romancers: 'My argument is that War makes rattling good history; but Peace is poor reading. So I back Bonaparte for the reason that he will give pleasure to posterity' (Hardy 1920, Part I, Act II, Scene V: 54). Hardy was not immune from the romance of the Napoleonic past, but he also subjects this romance to a merciless, moral gaze, like the gaze of the caricaturist who turned Napoleon into a corpse head.

In 'Leipzig' the narrator mentions that the fifty thousand men who died in the battle were ' 'lotted their shares in a quarrel not theirs' and quotes the old people of Leipzig bitterly asking the men of the church: 'O so-called Christian time!/When will men's swords to ploughshares turn?'. They are accusing the clergy of failing to live up to their own scriptures : 'and he shall judge among the nations . . . and they shall beat the swords into ploughshares . . . nation shall not lift up sword against nation, neither shall they learn war any more' (Isaiah 2: 4). Hardy's Spirit of Pities does not lose sight of this theme. In 'The Peasant's Confession' we are told in terms reminiscent of the Sutton Poyntz print, about 'Great Napoleon, who for years had strewn,/Men's bones all Europe through'. The Peasant goes on to confess his remorse for allowing his loyalty to Napoleon to be overcome by his desire to protect his property from devastation, although the modern reader blames the armies who wreck peasants' lives as much as the peasant who resorts to murder in pursuit of survival. In *The Trumpet Major* the omniscient Spirit of the Years continually intervenes in the present narrative to place it in the sobering perspective of the future. The veteran Corporal Tullidge is pictured singing his irreverent and satirical song, unaware that he will die at the 'bloody battle of Albuera' in Spain. The narrator vividly re-creates the life of a candlelit party at Overcombe Mill, only to throw on it the shadow of death: 'There is not one among them who would attach any meaning to "Vittoria", or gather from the syllables "Waterloo" the remotest idea of his own glory or death' (Chapter 5, Hardy 1986: 92). In this long perspective, the past is first made present and then covered in the shadow of the future.

The novel concludes conjuring with time. Anne Garland wishes a prosperous voyage, an easy conquest and a speedy return to a group of admirers. The omniscient narrator, a Spirit of the Years, knows that none of these wishes will come true for the majority: 'Of the seven upon whom these wishes were bestowed, five, including the trumpet major, were dead men within the few following years, and their bones left to moulder in the land of their campaigns' (Chapter 41, Hardy 1986: 377). The grassy downs above Weymouth still preserve their character but the King and fifteen thousand armed men who once paraded upon them are now 'lying scattered about the world as military and other dust, some at Talavera, Albuera, Salamanca, Vittoria, Toulouse, and Waterloo; some in home churchyards, and a few small handfuls in royal vaults' (Chapter 12, Hardy 1986: 150). Death the leveller mocks the pretensions of the great and turns all into the same dust, notes the dispassionate Spirit of the Years. The Spirit Ironic notes, however, that the living deal with the rite of death in differing ways, according to the rules of man-made status. When the list of killed and wounded at Trafalgar is finally published it does not contain the names that are of most interest to Miller Loveday and his family: 'To their great pain it contained no names but those of officers, the friends of ordinary seamen and mariners being in those good old days left to discover their losses as best they might' (Chapter 35, Hardy 1986: 328). Hardy leaves the reader with no alternative but to read 'good old days' in an ironic and bitter voice with regard to the lives of the majority.

Hardy succeeds in creating a perfect visual image for the way that the small were trapped within the lives of the great during this period. Towards the close of his novel he includes a scene of the cutting of the turf to create the giant image of George III that still towers over the Weymouth coast today. John Loveday, the trumpet major, explains that from the low-lying perspective of his family's mill at Overcombe/Sutton Poyntz: 'The king's head is to be as big as our mill-pond and his body as big as this garden; he and the horse will cover more than an acre.' Later Anne and John walk up to the downs and witness forty navvies labouring to imprint a permanent image of the King in the landscape. Anne walks from the horse's head down his breast to his hoof, and then returns via the King's bridle arm, past the bridge of his nose and into his cocked hat. John meanwhile, conscious of his duty to step aside and let his inferior brother claim Anne, stands 'in a melancholy attitude within the rowel of his Majesty's right spur'. For the Lovedays, personal romance is at least as important as national and international destiny. Nevertheless, it is the King's war that makes hopes of romance and life futile. The Garlands and Lovedays are important to Hardy but are pygmies within the profile of giant King George (Chapters 37, 38, Hardy 1986: 346, 348).

Hardy referred to the Napoleonic Wars in 1903 as 'the Great Historical Calamity, or Clash of Peoples, artificially brought about' (Hardy 1920: i). His analysis was that the artificially manufactured enmity between the working classes of differing nations was largely brought about by the selfish interests of Dynasts. Hardy was sceptical of all those, regardless of nationality, who wanted either to maintain or found dynasties of rulers. He therefore shared in the fascination yet horror which many felt at the career of Napoleon: this low-born stranger brought dynasties based on the right of birth crashing down and appeared by his military prowess to prove the possibility of an era of meritocracy. In fact, Napoleon only replaced the old dynastic system with a new one, other people's family and friends with his own. *The Dynasts* draws attention to this theme. After Napoleon's defeat at Leipzig, a chorus of Ironic Spirits records how the 'old dynastic routine' is being reimposed at a time when Napoleon's 'new dynastic structure' is 'unsustained'. When Napoleon has finally been defeated, the Spirit of the Years notes that 'Europe's wormy dynasties rerobe/Themselves in their old gilt, to dazzle anew the globe!' (Hardy 1920: 393, 518). The sham theatre of monarchy has been destroyed, replaced with a Napoleonic sham, and then refurbished, and all at an unimaginable cost in human life. In spite of this, Hardy manages to wring some hope from the black farce of history, the nightmare from which humanity tries to awake. Influenced by Schopenhauer, Hardy developed a theory of an Immanent Will that has some similarities with the 'Elan Vital' of Henri Bergson and the 'Life Force' of Bernard Shaw (the latter concept was expounded in *Man and Superman* in 1901, before the main writing of *The Dynasts*). In such theories a Christian god is replaced by an imperfectly conscious force that can only enact its will through humans who are in turn only semi-conscious of the Will that moves them. In this theory, evil is explained as a mistake made by a fallible Will. As Life Force and human puppets learn through a painful, bloody process of trial and error, so the Will that is immanent in us all grows to full and more humane consciousness. Great Men such as Napoleon and King George cannot be solely blamed for the suffering of their followers: all are caught, whether French or Wessex labourers, in a tangled web spun by a Will which does not know its own mind. By implication, however, individuals can be brought to account for the extent to which they blind the Will to suffering or make it grow morally. In 1908 Hardy lets the Chorus of the Pities have the last word on the future of the Immanent Will: the wars or 'rages of the ages' and the blindness of the Will is to be overcome in a 'genial, germing purpose', 'Consciousness the Will informing, till It fashion all things fair'. The advent of twentieth-century warfare was to change Hardy's mind: henceforth the Spirits Ironic and Sinister take charge of Wessex.

## Scientific Slaughter

Hardy created Wessex with a keen eye on nineteenth-century realities. His Wessex responds to the relentless pace of change. Unlike many of his readers, he resisted the temptation to create a rural golden age from which to escape modernity. He remained rooted in his landscape but able to relate that landscape to the wider world. *The Dynasts* contains scenes that anticipate the aerial and cinematic perspectives available to modern filmgoers and travellers; the reader is taken soaring above Wessex to view it in relation to the whole of Europe. During the Boer War he let his imagination include even more distant parts of the globe that were nevertheless connected in the huge web of British Imperial ambitions. Hardy was aware that many of the West County labourers stereotyped under the name 'Hodge' were dying for their nation. True to his comments on the humanity underlying the name 'Hodge' in *Tess* and his essay on the Dorsetshire labourer (1883), he individualized and commemorated 'Drummer Hodge' in a poem. The Drummer is violently displaced by war: he belongs in a 'Wessex' chalk landscape but ends his life on the veldt, viewed by 'strange-eyed constellations'.

Hardy imagines Wessex in the world and the world reaching Wessex. In 'The Souls of the Slain', a dialogue amongst the dead of the Boer War precisely set during a wintry December of 1899, he is careful to show the links between far and near, tracing the particular lineaments of the Dorset coast but suggesting how the sea it touches leads to many shores. When the poem was first published in 1900 in *The Cornhill Magazine*, Hardy prefaced it as follows: 'The spot indicated in the following poem is the Bill of Portland, which stands, roughly, on a line drawn from South Africa to the middle of the United Kingdom; in other words, the flight of a bird along a "great circle" of the earth, cutting through South Africa and the British Isles, might land him at Portland Bill' (Purdy 1954: 109). The poem is a detailed verbal evocation of the sights and sounds ('sea-mutterings') of Portland, a unique place that combines the qualities of a peninsula, an island and a high place. Its distinctive curving profile is high enough in altitude to appear unexpectedly in the background of many views in Dorset. Hardy describes its lighthouse ('turreted lantern'), and makes us aware of its near-encirclement by powerful seas. The sermon-like quality of the ghostly General's speech is perhaps inspired by the local place-name 'Pulpit Rock'. The voices of the dead are appropriately heard in a location overlooking 'Deadman's Bay', where many sailors have met their end. Hutchins' *History of Dorset*, one of Hardy's sources for the creation of Wessex, explains how the turbulent waters of Portland Race have sent many ships to their doom (1973, Vol. 2: 827). In this extraordinary location, Hardy expresses some unusual thoughts on how to mourn the war dead. The souls of the dead, returning from South Africa like strange night moths drawn to the Race, expect to hear how their martial valour is celebrated. In Wessex a different kind of mourning takes place: the men are not admired for their heroic and bloody deeds on the battle field but for all their contributions in peace time to the loving kindness of day to day family life. At the conclusion of the poem, only the ghosts of those who accept this scale of values return homeward: those that choose the glory of war and drum and trumpet history vanish into the annihilating whirlpool of the raging sea. The clashing waters of the Race become an equivalent for Dante's circles of hell.

This nightmare vision allows some hope that past slaughter will make present wisdom, since it is the peace-loving ghosts that haunt the land. Hardy could not be so hopeful when grappling with the clash between his Victorian mind-set (thought to be pessimistic but including the possibility of human progress), and the cataclysm of twentieth-century, world-wide, mechanized slaughter on a scale never before seen. Hardy confessed that he would never have ended *The Dynasts* on a note of hope, had he known of the world war to come (F. Hardy 1986: 368). In 'Channel Firing', a remarkably prescient poem of 1913, he anticipated the horrors of the 1914–18 conflict. As in the 'Souls of the Slain', Hardy is interested in what the dead can teach the living. The roar of gunnery practice near Portland in 1913 was so powerful that it seemed to wake the living and the dead. In the poem, the dead are the typical, familiar members of Hardy's rural Wessex, including kindly Parson Thirdly of *Far from the Madding Crowd*. These dead men comment on the past and present. The nineteenth century is 'indifferent', unaware of its contribution to future disaster; the modern world by implication is just as bad but armed with worse means of destruction 'striving strong to make/Red war yet redder'. The skeletons of Victorian Wessex consider whether the world will ever be saner but decide not. Parson Thirdly decides his forty years of Christian teaching has been wasted. Is it Hardy's humane speech or the guns that have the last word?

This is the final stanza, well worth committing to memory for the purposes of meditation on Wessex and war:

> Again the guns disturbed the hour,
> Roaring their readiness to avenge,
> As far inland as Stourton Tower,
> And Camelot, and starlit Stonehenge.

Hardy compresses many historical, legendary and topographical associations in this image of ancient place-names and modern warfare. His imagination roves over political and poetic territory. His chosen landmarks and marks of history are Stourton Tower near Stourhead, Wiltshire, an eighteenth-century tribute to King Alfred as the founder of English justice; King Arthur's Camelot, the place of right not might associated with Glastonbury and South Cadbury in Somerset; and Stonehenge, also associated with Arthur and his magician Merlin, the famous and ancient monument that has symbolized national dreams from Geoffrey of Monmouth through William Stukeley to the present. It was regarded by some as a war memorial to Arthur and his righteous warriors. The image leaves those who know Hardy's region to speculate on the palimpsest of propaganda and actual history that surrounds us in the landscape. Hardy summons chivalric ideals, whether Celtic or Saxon, to protect England in a world of unchivalrous naval guns. The Arthurian ideal is the antithesis of vengeance and might being right: but Hardy's poem makes us continually aware that his speech embodying ideals is in danger of being drowned by gunfire.

Hardy can be located within the structure of territories introduced in the preface and preliminary chapter of this book. Like other regional writers debated here, he avoids the abstract, eludes self-righteousness, grasps the detail and preserves a link between the mind and the surface of the earth. He is also unique among his fellow regional writers in many ways. He excels as poet, short story writer and novelist; he sets an image of a changing region within a panoramic view of ideas and moral issues. He combines his profound knowledge of his territory, not with the conventions of romance, like Blackmore and Kingsley, but with those of tragedy. His sense of tragedy, however, is one combined with a sense of community. The modern playwrights Bertholt Brecht and Arthur Miller have criticized the tradition of tragedy for excluding the common man and encouraging the passive and pessimistic acceptance of suffering. Hardy cannot be accused of confining his tragedy to the lives of the great and famous. He has been perceived as a pessimist but described himself neither as a pessimist nor an optimist. He called himself a meliorist: one who believes that progress is possible but not inevitable (Archer 1901: 313). Behind his fear of disaster, he provides a glimpse of a community that learns from its mistakes and takes responsibility for its actions. His tragic Wessex places responsibility on the community of his readers: will they blind the Immanent Will or help it see, will they be at the mercy of instinctual and unconscious drives or will they learn both to respect and control them?

# 6

# Sabine Baring-Gould's Territory
## Where the Squarson meets the Labourers

*There is an old grandmother on Dartmoor from whom I have had songs . . . She cannot be induced to sit down and sing—then her memory fails, but she will sing whilst engaged in kneading bread, washing, driving the geese out of the room, feeding the pig; naturally, this makes it a matter of difficulty to note her melodies. One has to run after her, from the kitchen to the pig-sty, or to the well-head and back, pencil and music-book in hand.*

Sabine Baring-Gould

*Motorists rushing over Lew Down on the road from Okehampton to Launceston would not suspect that the Baring-Gould kingdom lay within a few yards of them.*

John Betjeman

## Baring-Gould's place on the map and in society

Some people remember Baring-Gould (1834–1924) as the writer of 'Onward Christian Soldiers'; a few remember him as the recorder of 'Widdicombe Fair', the Devon folk-song that immortalizes 'Uncle Tom Cobley and all'; very few remember him as a writer who made a significant contribution to regional writing in the form of over thirty novels, numerous short stories, articles and topographical accounts. Since he is a relatively unfamiliar figure, this chapter begins with a semi-biographical introduction putting Baring-Gould in his place.

As a child Baring-Gould lived north and south of Lew Trenchard at Bratton Clovelly and Tavistock: his childhood territory was at the heart of the West Country peninsula, on the western side of Devon's Dartmoor but within sight of Cornwall. He was a descendant of a long line of landowning Goulds and Baring-Goulds associated with Lew since 1626. Owing to Sabine's efforts as a restorer and adapter of the past, it is still possible to visit Lew and see the place as he wanted it to be seen. Stand at the centre of Sabine's Lew Trenchard and look around: here is the church of Saint Peter (founded in the sixth century and formerly dedicated to Saint Petroc) with its rood screen, benches and memorials to several generations of Baring-Goulds; there is a vast manor with grounds originating in the reign of Henry III but adapted by Sabine with touches of Rhenish style reflecting his European travels as a child (his grandson called the impressive but eccentric result 'Baring-Gould Tudor'). Walk from here to discover a dower house dating from at least the seventeenth century with an even older structure in front of it: a towering Menhir that Baring-Gould restored. All around you is solid proof that he carried out at least two of the purposes that he set himself at the age of seventeen: 'I formed my purposes, and from their accomplishment I have never deviated. My first was the moral and spiritual improvement of Lew Parish . . . My second purpose was the restoration of the parish church . . . The third purpose I had in my mind . . . was the restoration and reconstruction of the manor-house' (1925a: vii–viii).

Many years later in 1876, having become both parson and squire (or 'squarson') of Lew in succession to his uncle and father, Baring-Gould had the power to carry out his plans. They were acts of homage to the past and of conformity with aristocratic and Christian ideals; they were also acts of rebellion against his father, Edward Baring-Gould (1804–72). Edward wanted his son to be a mathematician and a squire: Sabine remained innumerate and wanted to enter the church. Edward detested rural isolation and seized every opportunity to travel abroad; he preferred the scenery of Switzerland to Dartmoor. Sabine, although he shared his father's enthusiasm for European travel, rejected the role of absentee landlord and fell in love with the moor. Edward replaced the oak pews in Lew church with deal pews in 1832: Sabine reconstructed the oak pews in 1877. Edward removed the original rood screen in 1832; Sabine saved fragments of it and used them to reconstruct and re-install the screen between 1889 and 1915. Edward turned the long gallery within Lew House into three bedrooms: Sabine restored the gallery. Edward threw away the village stocks; Sabine rescued them. Edward, according to one story, buried the ancient standing stone near the Dower House because it encouraged superstition; Sabine had the stone dug up and re-erected (Monk 1961).

Saving fragments of the past and reconstructing it: these are also the terms within which Baring-Gould's many fictions work. He was both inventing stories and making an *inventory* of past experience and achievement. However, his fictions also engage with the process of social and technological change in the nineteenth century. This unusual scion of the aristocracy had links with both the ancient past and the modern world: he combined a lofty and patrician outlook with an ambivalent recognition of the values of democracy. While his father had married Sophia Bond, daughter of Admiral Francis Godolphin Bond, Sabine married a Yorkshire mill girl named Grace Taylor. Nevertheless, anticipating Shaw's Professor Higgins, he took the precaution of giving Grace a genteel education before introducing her to Lew parish as the squarson's lady.

Baring-Gould's landscape was haunted by a White Lady. She was associated with the long gallery and avenue at Lew House, with a white owl that flew in its grounds, with a local apple orchard, with an ancient oak at Lew Slate quarry, and with a stream by the road from Lew to Bratton. A local guide book explained that the Goulds were 'an ancient race which is honoured by the attendance of a true "White Lady." This is held to be the spirit of a certain Madam Gould; but she appears always in white, with long hair, and sparkling as if covered with water drops.' The reference here is to Margaret Gould (1711–95). This forceful personality, who once sat for a portrait by Joshua Reynolds, was known as 'Old Madame'. The Reynolds portrait has disappeared but tales of Madame's strong character lived on amongst the local people. The young Baring-Gould heard such tales in 1839 from elderly family servants who still remembered her. He passed on the stories to his readers during the 1920s, explaining that they were tales he had 'picked up as a boy' and that their authenticity was guaranteed by the fact that they were 'happily written down' by him 'as received' (1925a: 157–64). The aristocratic Baring-Gould began his writing career as an amanuensis for servants detailing the reality of a ghost.

This is how Baring-Gould tells one Madame story, supposed to have happened in 1795. A young man was riding from Tavistock to Lew on a clear moonlit night:

as he rode through Lew valley, he looked into a newly ploughed field, in which a plough had been left. On this was seated a lady in white satin, with long hair floating over her shoulders. Her face was uplifted and her eyes directed towards the moon . . . He recognised her at once as Madame Gould, and taking off his hat called out, 'I wish you a very good night, Madame.' She bowed in return and waved her hand. The man noticed the sparkle of her diamond rings as she did so.

He reached his relatives' house and told them of the incident, only to discover that Madame had died seven days previously. This tale worthy of M.R. James is matched by Baring-Gould's casual reference to the Madame Gould legends at the end of his reminiscences: seven parsons once met 'under an ancient oak by the slate quarry' to lay the ghost of the White Lady. Unfortunately, one of them was too drunk to remember the words of exorcism: consequently, they only succeeded in turning the lady from a white ghost into a white owl. In this instance, the power of Christian faith is mocked at the expense of an older world of animals and spirits. In his book on folklore, Baring-Gould explained the vision of the White Lady seated on a plough, not in terms of Gould family tradition, but as a folk memory of Frija, the Norse White Goddess of fertility and tillage. Being rational about events of 1795 was easier than dealing with more modern manifestations of the Lady. According to tradition, a local carpenter disturbed Madame Gould during the restoration of the church in 1832. Madame rose out of her coffin, emitting a spectral light, and chased the carpenter back to his house. In 1864, Baring-Gould and his wife were invited to high tea with the rector of Bratton Clovelly: when they arrived the cook refused to serve them. Her brother had been so frightened by a vision of the White Lady that he had fallen over and broken his leg. Baring-Gould was being made to suffer for the behaviour of the family ghost (1925a: 160–61; 1925b: 272–73; 1993: 48–49).

The ghost of the White Lady represents Baring-Gould's relationship with history: the past was constantly returning to haunt him, staring out of family portraits, speaking to him through local topography and the tales of local people. History, rural folklore and the arts of the oral tradition were Baring-Gould's family heirlooms.

## The Pursuit of Seity

Baring-Gould respected those who measured books in terms of local knowledge: 'Nothing offends a reader more than to find the local colouring of a story untrue to nature' (Anon. 1895a: 601). As a writer, he took care to make his local colour genuine. When he turned his Devon novel *Red Spider* into an opera, it was not enough that the libretto should retain a Devonian character: the music too was expected to express locality. Accordingly, he took his composer, Learmont Drysdale, to visit the novel's territory and to meet the original of Mrs Veale, the White Witch of his story (Wright 1898: 383). Responding to Duns Scotus' notion that every individual has a 'seity', something 'peculiar to himself, which makes him different from all other persons in the world', Baring-Gould commented: 'What the learned Scotus said of individuals may as truly be said of localities' (1981: 242). This 'seity' could take the form of houses made from local building materials. 'The houses the people inhabit are different in one county from another, differ in one district from those in another ten miles away. Here [Lew Trenchard] where I write the cottages are of stone . . . Five miles off, all is different. The farms and cottages are of clay, kneaded with straw . . .' (1892b: 240). Seity could take the form of costumes: Baring-Gould noted the Yorkshire mill girls' pink head-dress and white apron; the East Mersea fen-lander's second-hand, scarlet army coat. Seity could take the form of landscape: in his various regional novels, Baring-Gould sketched the fens of Essex, the salt district of Cheshire, the chalk cliffs of Devon, the rocky coasts and high moors of Cornwall. Above all, seity could take the form of the manners, dialect, external appearance and internal character of the working people whose lives and occupations were shaped by the particular identity of a given region. Baring-Gould argued that it was pointless to look for local colour amongst the upper or middle classes.

> The ladies and gentlemen in the hall at one end of England are like the ladies and gentlemen at the other end of England; and it is the same with the sweet girls and the honest, frank boys of the rectory and vicarage . . . But it is not so with the peasantry. They have their type in Northumberland, which is not the type in Devon, and the type in Yorkshire is not the type of Sussex.

Accordingly, his ambitious aim was 'to write a set of novels that shall illustrate the different types of character among the common people in different parts of the country' (1892b: 239–40; Dolman 1894: 18). True to his word, he set *Through Flood and Flame* (1868) and *Pennycomequicks* (1889) amongst Yorkshire mill hands, *The Frobishers* (1901) amongst the workers in the Potteries, *The Broom Square* (1896) amongst furze collectors on the Surrey downs, *In the Roar of the Sea* (1892) amongst the smugglers of the North Cornwall coast.

Baring-Gould's sense of place not only influenced the background of his novels but the characters and action as well. Writing of his Cheshire novel, *The Queen of Love* (1894), he explained that the specific topography of the salt district 'seemed as if it could produce in my mind only one kind of story' (1892b: 241). It is perhaps difficult for a modern reader to think like Baring-Gould: 'seity' is much diminished in a period of ceaseless mobility, when building materials are uniform, landscape can be artificially created and occupation is less related to region. Even in Baring-Gould's era, the end of regional identity was thought to be imminent. Baring-Gould justified *Red Spider* as a novel preserving 'Old customs, modes of thought, of speech, quaint sayings, weird superstitions' that were 'disappearing out of the country, utterly and for ever' (1888a: v). He shared with Thomas Hardy a concept of the fiction writer as an archivist with a limited opportunity to record in print what was disappearing in reality. Baring-Gould commented to an interviewer: 'The distinctive local peculiarities, the remarkable individualities of some of the villagers which have been so to speak, my meat and drink as a novelist, are fast dying out. With free education and cheap railway travelling I doubt if anywhere they will outlive the next thirty years' (Anon. 1895b: 291). The education and mobility which some regarded as liberating were regarded as partially destructive, dehumanizing forces by Baring-Gould: 'characters were far more common in past times than they are at present, when education has ground down all asperities and angles, and made men and women as much alike as marbles' (1925b: 137). Both Baring-Gould and Thomas Hardy challenge the assumption that happiness, culture and life itself are distributed in accordance with social and financial status. For both writers, the exuberance and eccentricity of life exists among the poor not the respectable. Despite their very different class origins, both writers found the source of their imaginative energy in the life of the Michael Henchards of their world.

Baring-Gould's interest in regional seity conceals a tension between two factors: nostalgia for an idealized past, when everyone knew their place, both socially and geographically, and a Dickensian, Christian sense that the workers were not just 'hands' but human individuals with heads and hearts, living in a world unhealthily hidden from genteel society, a world that deserved mapping. Baring-Gould drew the line at Christian Socialism but his faith was sincere enough to make him challenge the class system in which he had a privileged place. His empathy with a place and its people sometimes led him into dangerous territory. He describes the genesis of *The Queen of Love* (1894) his novel of the salt district of Cheshire, in a way that shows place partly from a worker's point of view:

> When engaged on a novel, I live in that world about which I am writing. Whilst writing a Cheshire novel, I have tasted the salt crystallising on my lips, smelt the smoke from the chimneys, walked warily among the subsidences, and have had the factory before my eyes . . . It has been so real to me, that if I wake for a moment at night I have found myself in Cheshire, my mind there. When I am at my meals, I am eating in Cheshire, though at the other end of England; when in conversation with friends, directly there is a pause, my mind reverts to Cheshire; and, alas, I am sorry to own it, too often, in church, at my prayers—I find my mind drifting to Cheshire. (1892b: 242)

Even Baring-Gould's parsonical duties could not suppress his writing mind, and this mind led him to places *and* their workers. His novel about the Potteries, predating Arnold Bennett's discovery of the literary possibilities of the area, contains the following analysis, placing Baring-Gould as a man whose conservatism made him a radical: 'A new and grinding tyranny has to be fought; it is no longer royal despotism, or feudalism, but it is the pressure of modern civilization. That which the public demands is cheap fabrics and cheap ware of every kind; and cheap fabrication means the oppression of the worker . . .' (Anon. 1901: 429).

J.M. Barrie considered Baring-Gould's genuine potential as a novelist to be unrealized because of his inability to sympathize with the sufferings of his characters, particularly his working-class figures

(Barrie 1890). Betjeman, on the other hand, inherited a West Country image of a Baring-Gould who treated all his parishioners as equals (Betjeman 1997: 167). In fact, Baring-Gould was a writer with contradictory qualities. When he speaks of a factory girl as a 'specimen', the chilling tone of the aristocrat is evident. Nevertheless, the squire who married a mill-girl, the parson with a sincere faith, does not always speak as one apart from and above the poor. He summed up his varied experience of regions and people as follows:

> I have been in many parts of England, twelve years in Yorkshire, ten in Essex, eight in Sussex, and in Devon as child and boy and later for over forty years a resident. And wherever I have been, I have seen many God-fearing and God-loving souls . . . And these have been in all classes: mill-hands in factories, colliers in the pits, agricultural labourers at the plough, clerks at their desks, shop-girls behind counters, employed and employers. . . .

While this attempts to be above class conflict, there were moments when Baring-Gould found virtue among the poor rather than the rich. As a preacher, he recalled a poor Yorkshire girl who had suffered disfigurement in order to save her brother from a fire and then been abandoned to die in the workhouse. Baring-Gould contrasted her with the society lady 'who has lived in luxury and adulation, and to Self and Self only'. At Judgement Day, he argued, earthly hierarchy will be turned upside down, and the lady will beg to 'take a place at the footstool of the poor factory girl . . .' (1924: 13–14, 24). Baring-Gould tells this parable in a passionate voice that cannot be dismissed as mere lip-service to piety.

Baring-Gould pursued regional seity in numerous novels, although he regarded the role of the novelist as hedged with difficulties:

> The historian dreads the play of his [the novelist's] imagination, altering facts; the religious man fears irreverence in handling them; and the critic disputes his acumen in investigation . . . But this is due to a misconception of what a novelist really is, or should be. He is not properly an enchanter, calling up fantastic visions, a creator of startling situations, and an elaborator of ingenious plots; least of all is he a mechanical reproducer of moving photographs. He is rather one who seeks to sound the depths of human nature, to probe the very heart of man, to stand

patiently at his side with finger on pulse. He seeks to discover
the principles that direct man's action, to watch the development of his character, and to note the influence the
surroundings have on the genesis of his ideas, and the formation
of his convictions. (1897: viii–ix)

Baring-Gould's ideal novelist is neither critic nor fantasist, neither
historian nor photographer; he reaches past both literal-minded
realism and the fantasies of the privileged to touch the realistic
imagination of the people. Although Baring-Gould was a parson, his
ideal novelist is not pious and squeamish; he is a doctor of the soul in
touch with the experience of humanity. Baring-Gould's own novels
aspire to this ideal but seldom achieve it. His contempt for the
ingenuity of plot often leads him to create 'startling' and improbable
situations, even by the standards of Victorian melodrama. Nevertheless, his fictions come alive when he focuses on the seity of a place
and its people.

## On Dangerous Ground: A Story of the Chalk Cliffs

Baring-Gould set out to map his West Country as systematically as
Hardy mapped his Wessex. Few of his fictions rival Hardy's. It is,
however, worthwhile exploring a representative example of his many
regional novels. *Winefred: A Story of the Chalk Cliffs* (1900a) is set
among the fisherman and smugglers on the border between East
Devon and Dorset. Baring-Gould's subtitle suggests his aim: to
explore the interaction between humanity and environment in a
distinctive region.

A synopsis of *Winefred* conveys more of its weaknesses than its
strengths. The story begins with a dramatic storm sequence on the
cliffs between Axmouth and Lyme Regis. Jane Marley, driven to
despair by poverty and the disapproval of society, attempts to kill
herself and her child Winefred. We learn that rustic Jane has been
seduced and abandoned by the effete, urban gentleman, Joseph
Holwood. The Marleys are rescued from death by the intervention of
Job Rattenbury, a tough but kindly local man who offers them
shelter in his cliffside cottage. As his name implies to those with
local knowledge, Rattenbury has made a fortune from smuggling.
The creative possibilities of this opening section are marred by the
dominant role in the plot played by a ferryman from Axmouth, a

sub-Dickensian villain called Olver Dench. Olver's deceits set Jane against her new-found protector and prevent her receiving the money paid to her by Holwood to salve his conscience. After the death of Rattenbury, Jane has the power to pass on his illegally gained money to his son Jack. Instead she uses it to buy Job's house and to pay for her daughter to be transformed into a lady in genteel Bath. The story ends unbelievably happily with Dench unmasked and destroyed, Jane reunited with Joseph and Winefred plighted to Jack. He rejects his father's occupation of smuggling for a more respectable profession at Beer's stone quarry and Winefred rejects hollow gentility for West Country life.

The novel's setting is much more convincing than its plot. Baring-Gould focuses his novel within the coastal area from Beer on the eastern side of Devon to Lyme Regis on the western side of Dorset, especially featuring Seaton, Axmouth, Bindon Manor, Rousdon and the Undercliff. Although inland centres like Exeter, Honiton, Colyton, Axminster and Dorchester appear briefly in the background, the action of the story seldom goes far from the sea and the cliffs. When he demonstrates his knowledge that Colyton may appear to be a village but has the status of a town, we can see that his romantic tale is very firmly set in an historical place. His sense of scale is precise: 'Beer was a hamlet, Seaton and Axmouth small villages'; his sense of distance likewise: Jack explains that Winefred 'lives on one side of the Axe . . . and there exists a ferry between the Axmouth and the Seaton side. I am at Beer, two miles distant from Seaton, and Seaton lies a quarter of a mile from the landing-stage of the ferry' (Baring-Gould 1900a: 148, 217). Those unfamiliar with this territory can still gain a sense of distance and location from the specificity of Baring-Gould's writing.

Baring-Gould also makes his readers, local or not, see the red earth and white cliffs of East Devon and West Dorset. His topography, history, place-names and geology are thoroughly researched, although not adroitly interrelated. He does not allow the reader to observe his landscape at a safe distance from the realities of weather and terrain. For instance, when Joseph attempts to escape from the chesil (shingle) bank at Seaton, he 'walked hastily away, that is to say as hastily as it is possible to walk over a beach of sliding rounded cobble stones'. Baring-Gould is also sensitive to the relationship between place and class. When a resident of genteel Bath hears rumours about Winefred's dubious Axmouth past from a person in Axminster, the following exchange takes place: ' "Axminster is not Axmouth." "It is on the same river." "So are Pangbourne and Tilbury. You do not inquire at one place relative to persons at the other." ' Baring-Gould's Axminster is not far from the mouth of the Axe in terms of miles but a long way in terms of social distance, as far as Thames-side gentility and leisure from Tilbury docks. If Axminster can look down on Axmouth, there are nuances even within the centre of Bath. Winefred is regarded with suspicion by the Tomkin-Jones family of Bath, but these superior beings are not as high up the social ladder as they would like to be. They live in a house 'opening into the street, but pretending to belong to the square . . .' (Baring-Gould 1900a: 60, 185, 278).

Baring-Gould sees his place in an historical perspective. The light and dark in his landscape of the past are not the same as they had become by 1900:

> It took long in those days, before the phosphorus match had been invented, to light a candle. Flint and steel had to be struck till sparks falling ignited tinder. Then a sulphur match had to be applied to the smouldering fire, and when the match blazed then only could the wick be ignited. It was for this reason that usually a rush-light was kept burning in every house.

The novel's time and space take an early nineteenth century form. Like the Hardy who wrote *A Pair of Blue Eyes*, Baring-Gould contrives to differentiate poor man's rural time from rich man's urban time: 'At the beginning of this century watches were not in such general use as they are now; they were costly, and possessed by the rich alone. The farmer had to content himself with the clock, the labourer with the sun, and at night with the cockcrow' (Baring-Gould 1900a: 61, 89–90). Time for travellers is also perceived differently in the period before the railway. When Joseph Holwood misses the coach from Seaton, he knows that he will have to wait until the following day before it is possible to make the connections necessary for an escape from a remote coast.

## Falling

Three actions in *Winefred* take us from the landscape to its people: they can be designated as falling, rising or polishing, and smuggling.

The Undercliff between Lyme and Axmouth is known to some as the setting for the film of John Fowles' *The French Lieutenant's Woman*. Baring-Gould knew of this unique coast through the records of its formation during a massive landslip in 1839. Contemporary newspaper reports spoke of an earthquake, a mysterious stench and sounds heard as far away as Lyme (Roberts 1840). As an historian-romancer, Baring-Gould assimilated the facts of this extraordinary event. Although he continually reminds the reader that he has set his scene in the early nineteenth century, he has no compunction about moving the landslip back in time to suit the needs of his story. John Fowles was told by a local farmer that on this stretch of coast the land is in love with the sea. Baring-Gould links this geological love affair with the love affair of his fictional Jane and Joseph. The fallen land is related to his version of a stereotype well known in Victorian narrative paintings, verse and novels: the Fallen Woman.

In its most typical form, this stereotype involves the story of a seduced and abandoned woman, whose fatal error with a man leads to an irreversible decline into poverty, despair and suicide. Augustus Leopold Egg's triptych of paintings known as 'Past and Present' (1858) is a typical visual representation. Hardy's *Tess of the d'Urbervilles* (1892) is the best known combination of the tale with a regional novel, and may well have influenced the creation of *Winefred*, despite the fact that Baring-Gould only admitted to a knowledge of Hardy's verse. The fictional Fallen Woman had potentially disturbing associations for contemporary readers, since it reminded them of the seduced women who became prostitutes and formed the visible presence on city streets of what was known as the Great Social Evil. This was not a problem exclusive to the major cities: well-meaning citizens of nineteenth-century Exeter founded a female penitentiary dedicated to rescuing young Fallen Women.

In fiction, the Fallen Woman was more often killed than rescued. Her sin was often considered so great that she could not be allowed to survive. Baring-Gould copies yet changes the story. He panders to his sensitive contemporary readers by making Jane simultaneously a deserted *and* a married woman. In fact, Joseph married her before abandoning her but Olver Dench makes her believe that the marriage was not legal. During the period when she believes this story, Jane is guilty of sin out of wedlock from her own point of view. This is certainly the assumption made by her neighbours. This plot means that Jane can suffer the ostracism of the typical fallen woman without shocking a reader who likes his heroines to be single or respectably married. It also enables Baring-Gould to show the respectable on both sides of the river Axe rejecting her on a false assumption: 'Seaton says, Away, across the water! you do not belong to us. And Axmouth, says Away!, you were not born here, and we are not responsible for you' (Baring-Gould 1900: 11).

Jane's story relates to but departs from its literary parents in other ways. Her seducer Joseph is a fool rather than a villain; instead of dying in grief and misery she is eventually reunited with her lover in a happy ending; most interestingly, rather than being a passive victim of male wiles, she is a very strong-willed, defiant woman. Death, her expected end in fiction, is only considered by her in terms of an act of defiance. Even after her rescue from her attempted suicide and murder of her child, she explains to her daughter 'I would throw you over the cliffs rather than that should happen to you which was my lot'. Jane is bent on social success or destruction: no compromise for her. Baring-Gould makes the reader see the picturesque, local scenery in a different context when describing Jane's efforts to kill herself and her daughter: 'it was to Winefred as though she heard the sea in louder tone, multiplied five-fold, laugh and smack its lips, conscious that living things with human souls were to be given to it to tumble and mumble, to pound on the pebbles and hack on the reefs. It was as though she saw through the darkness the cruel ocean throw up spray-draped arms to catch and clutch her as she fell' (Baring-Gould 1900a: 13, 169).

As a squarson, Baring-Gould had limited sympathy with social protest. In this case, however, he made every effort to see the regions of respectability through Jane's eyes: 'It is a hard thing for one who has land and a home, an income and kindred, to enter into the feeling of desolation and hopelessness that possesses the heart of one who is absolutely adrift in life, without a single attachment, without a single point in the outlook, on which to fix the eye and to which aim. Jane Marley's life had been broken at an early period—made purposeless by no fault of her own'. Baring-Gould combines the distinctive geological history of his region with a national issue when he asserts of Jane's moral character: 'If she staggered, it was not that her head was light, but that the ground gave way under her feet' (Baring-Gould 1900a: 116). Just as Jane has two homes destroyed by the landslip, her social being has been undermined by the immoral behaviour of her partner and the inhuman moralizing of her fellows.

The novel implies that we can no more blame Jane for her problems than blame the victims of the 1839 landslip. The contemporary notion that such an upheaval must represent a divine judgement is partly presented in a comic light in the novel: 'It may be the Last Day coming on us in Axmouth and going on next to Seaton, and destroy [sic] it by instalments. If so, I wish it had begun t'other end of England' (Baring-Gould 1900a: 301). Nevertheless, as a parson-novelist, Baring-Gould contrives to make Providence play its part in his plot. The novel reaches a climax when the landslip destroys the evil Olver Dench together with the illegally gained money he is attempting to steal. His death enables the mainly decent but misguided Jane and Joseph to communicate again. As the cliff falls, the Fallen Woman rises back into society.

## Rising and Polishing

Baring-Gould also integrates regional details with wider issues in his fictional manipulation of the chesil beach at the mouth of the Axe. Winefred philosophizes about her home territory as follows: 'polish is a great deal. I suppose we are all of us rolled up by the great sea of time, alike on the beach, but some are smoothed and shaped—and those are the ladies and gentlemen, and some are left in the rough, and those are such as mother and me' (Baring-Gould 1900a: 56). In this innocent explanation of the nineteenth-century class system, ladies and lower class women are created as naturally and inevitably as stones are made by the ceaseless action of the sea. The dangers of defying this given, natural order are clearly presented in the novel in a language of local wit and associations: 'a caravan came to Colyton last summer with wild beasts. They went in procession through the town; there was a zebra striped like a tiger. But a thunder shower came on just as the procession moved, and after it all the stripes had been washed from the beast, and out of the rain stepped a plain Neddy' (Baring-Gould 1900a: 273). Human beings, the narrative implies, can also suffer if they attempt to move out of their class.

However, the novel also examines the possibility of class mobility. Winefred and her mother make a precarious living partly by finding chalcedony which they then polish with a grinding wheel and sell to a lapidary in Seaton. The stones that they have collected are then sold as mementos to gentlemen-tourists. In the context of the novel as a whole, the reader knows that Jane plays the part of a pebble picked up, admired and discarded by the tourist Joseph. However, when Jane stumbles on the money which makes her independent of such a lowly trade, she uses it to polish her daughter into the lady her mother could never be. 'Only a little grindstone and shammy leather wanted, perhaps' says Joseph about the possibility of turning a humble girl into a lady. Winefred explains 'They are to roll me up and down, forward and backward, till all my roughness is rubbed away.' Later she is less hopeful about this human attempt to emulate the might of the sea and polish away her rough edges: 'I am harder than a chalcedony' (Baring-Gould 1900a: 59, 177, 208).

It is notable in this context that Joseph abandons Jane not because of her lack of upper-class connections, but because of her lack of education. This implies that a man of Joseph's status can marry beneath his rank, provided that his partner is given the polish that her environment did not provide. Baring-Gould said little in public about his own marriage to Grace Taylor, a Yorkshire mill girl. However, some of his novels explore this dangerous territory in disguised forms. As the story of Winefred reflects, Grace was required to attend two years of education prior to her entry into parsonical, gentrified existence at Lew Trenchard. Despite this apparent act of faith in the power of education to overcome class barriers, some local tradition suggests that Grace was not happy in her public role as the squarson's wife.

The novel reflects ambivalence and tensions in this area. Jane is made unconsciously to suggest the limits of being lady-like when she describes her plans for improvement: 'All Seaton, all Axmouth, every one shall perceive that we are not as we were; that my Winnie has no more occasion to go along the beach picking up chalcedonies, nor I to trudge the lanes, hawking pins and needles; but that Winefred is a lady, a real lady, with money to spend, dressing like a lady, doing nothing—like a lady' (Baring-Gould 1900a: 132). This seems a false choice between poverty-wages and living at the expense of others. The providential ending of the story suggests that both class misalliance (Joseph and Jane) and marriage within a class (Winefred and Jack) can be defended. One sub-plot in particular suggests that local sympathies are more important than social veneer. In Baring-Gould's version of the city of Bath, choughs are obscure birds that only exist on a coat of arms, a badge of class. In Baring-Gould's version of the village called Beer, choughs are rare but still existing creatures, creatures captured through the manly heroism of Jack and given to Winefred as a sign that local can be best. This uneasy play with class and emotional allegiance to local people is made more complex by that fact that the money which makes social mobility possible has been gained by smuggling.

## Smuggling

Writing as a parson, Baring-Gould dismissed the memoirs of Jack Rattenbury, Beer's most infamous smuggler, as being 'not of conspicuous interest' (Baring-Gould 1900b: 67). In his novel, protected by the licence of the fiction writer, Baring-Gould gave his hero the name of Rattenbury and a life history clearly based on the memoirs of his real-life counterpart. He chose to resurrect a figure whom the Commissioners of Customs were anxious to pronounce dead as early as 1857: 'smuggling has greatly diminished, and public sentiments with regard to it have undergone a very considerable change. The smuggler is no longer an object of general sympathy or a hero of romance . . .' (Jamieson 1992: 250). The numerous portrayals of the smuggler in paintings, prints and ballads suggest that he lived in the popular imagination long after he ceased to be active in reality. In his novel of 1900, Baring-Gould impersonates an early-nineteenth-century preventive officer speaking of local smugglers:

> We have watched Lyme so closely that there has been no chance of them to run a cargo there. It all goes into that d—d hole of Beer, which is next to impossible to keep in your eye day and night. And with its freestone quarries and burrows into every hillside, there is a veritable underground labyrinth, in which could be stowed liquor enough to supply the toping squires and merchants of the west for a dozen years. There is no tracking them there, they are in one rat hole and out at another, and verily, the Creator seems to have had smugglers in view when this coast was called up . . . They purpose bringing the kegs and bales to Heathfield Cross on Thursday night, and wagons will be in waiting to load them for Honiton, Lyme and Dorchester. They will cross the creek over against Hawkes-down, slip through Axmouth, then up the hollow way, and so to the Cross. (Baring-Gould 1900a: 61–62)

Baring-Gould also introduced his heroine Jane Marley as follows, linking smuggling and romance in spite of the efforts of the Customs Service: 'An atmosphere of romance surrounded her. Her father who was dead, had been a smuggler. Her brother had been quite recently shot in an encounter with a preventive officer . . .' (Baring-Gould 1900a: 49). There were some violent encounters between smugglers and preventive men on the Devon-Dorset coasts. In 1836, Jack Rattenbury's son came before Exeter Assizes for assaulting a customs officer at Budleigh Salterton (Jamieson 1992: 250). Since Baring-Gould's novel was set at the turn of the century, he was able to combine such matter with earlier details when smuggling was more prevalent.

*Winefred* does not simply present a landscape to be viewed but a place where hard work or dangerous, illegal activity is necessary for survival. How did nineteenth-century Devon appear, not to a tourist but to a poor man without employment? This is how the novel explores young Jack's search for work:

> He had been to Lyme, where he had endeavoured to obtain a place in a lawyer's office, but the vacancy was filled. He tried a bank, no clerk was needed. He visited Colyton, he went to Axminster, to Honiton, but found no vacancy anywhere. Business was stagnant, trade depressed; clerks of some standing were receiving their discharge, no young hands were being taken on.

When he lowers his sights to manual (but still skilled) labour, this is how the dialogue proceeds between Jack and a local farmer:

> 'Can you thatch?'
> 'I have not learned.'
> 'Then you cannot do it. Thatching a rick is not an acquirement that comes by the light of nature. What do you say about hedging? . . . Tate Wetherell was set to hedge after Dickon's death, last fall, and they are down already that he set up. You must know the sort of stones to use, and which end to drive in, how to wedge them tight, and how to fill in behind. It is an art.'
> 'I will endeavour to learn.'
> 'Thank you kindly, try on someone else's hedges, if you please. How about ditching?'

'Any one can dig.'

'I beg your pardon. Any one cannot so as to lay a drain. There are drains and drains. I have known many a hundred pounds thrown away as completely as if chucked into the Axe mud by setting men to drain as did not know the trade. It is sad misfortune, young man, that all the time and money that were spent on your education in what is of no profit to man or beast, were not employed in setting you to learn from an old farm labourer what is useful. You cannot mow—you would cut your leg off with the scythe. You cannot plough a straight furrow—you would be upset at once. You cannot shear a sheep—you would cut off the flesh and kill the poor beast. You could not milk a cow dry—but would spoil its udder. No scholars for me, thank you.' (Baring-Gould 1900a: 149–50)

Contradictory tendencies are present here. This is partly an excuse for Baring-Gould to air his personal views on education, to criticize the process which might put some oil in the rusty machine of class. On the other hand, there is a genuine respect for skilled, rural labour that the urban admirer of rural views might not possess. Also, the novelist makes it clear how men of good will might easily be turned towards smuggling in desperation when all the respectable alternatives were denied them. The real Jack Rattenbury apparently made efforts to earn a living within the law, but again and again returned to smuggling as the best of a limited choice.

Baring-Gould remains ambivalent in his judgement of smuggling throughout the novel. He insists, without comment, on his characters' lack of moral feelings about the subject. We learn that Jack 'had not an atom' of 'moral scruple' about it and that 'moral objection' did not 'enter into the composition of Winefred's dislike to the trade'. On another occasion, the narrator explains: 'Winefred had no decided opinions relative to the morality of smuggling. The atmosphere on that coast was charged with it. Her grandfather had been engaged in the contraband trade all his days, and her mother's brother had lost his life in an affray with the preventive men. On this account her sympathies were ranged with those who broke the law . . .' (Baring-Gould 1900a: 49, 63, 80). *Winefred* ends more conventionally than this, with Jack rejecting his father's smuggler's treasure for respectable employment in Beer Quarry. Nevertheless, the novel illustrates how this same quarry is related to storage for smuggling, and the book remains primarily sympathetic to moon-rakers.

The defence and triumph of a so-called fallen woman; the playing with class misalliance and wealth immorally gained: in these ways Baring-Gould was smuggling the contraband of dangerous ideas under the cover of the stereotype plot and characters of a sensational novel-romance. He was certainly not a *fin-de-siécle* aesthete or social-ist. He was out of step with Victorian values more by being behind his time than ahead of it. He placed his class loyalties very accurately in his reminiscences: 'With every wish to promote the well-being and emancipation of the working-classes, I should be sorry to see—what is approaching—the extinction of the old squirearchy, or rather their being supplanted by the *nouveaux riche*' (Baring-Gould 1925a: ix–x). Linked by sympathy with the squires who supported smuggling amongst the working classes (Lord Rolle was rumoured to support the historical Jack Rattenbury), Baring-Gould was a squarson whose long memory of past social arrangements enabled him to find fault with a bourgeois present. The limits of his thinking and of his powers as a novelist do not prevent him from writing a partly realistic romance that combines dramatic adventures with a sense of the interactions between locality, class and labour. In more ways than one, Baring-Gould knew his place.

## From 'Dirty Dartmoor' to a 'Wild and Wondrous Region'

Baring-Gould's fictions box the compass of his large and varied home county, but the lode-stone of his Devon inspiration was Dartmoor. This unique wilderness, containing heathland and granite tors on its heights and deep river valleys or cleaves at its edges, was estimated as consisting of 280,000 acres in 1848. Baring-Gould made many attempts to capture both the seity and variety of this region in his novels. *John Herring: A West of England Romance* (1883) explores South Tawton, Okehampton and links between the moor and Launceston in Cornwall. *Urith: A Tale of Dartmoor* (1891) explores Devil Tor, Tavistock and the Lyke-Way or corpse-road. *Guavas the Tinner* (1897) takes us to Yealm Steps, Crockern Tor and the so-called Abbot's Way. Princetown and Dartmoor prison feature in *Court Royal* (1886) and *Royal Georgie* (1901), the latter work also re-creating Widecombe and sketching Exeter in relationship to the moor. Baring-Gould's short stories, fictional and semi-fictional, use a wide range of

*10) Dewerstone Rock.*

This image of the The Dewerstone was one of a series of prints in Carrington's poem, 'Dartmoor' (1826). This illustrated edition influenced many Dartmoor enthusiasts, including the young Sabine Baring-Gould.

locations from Brent Tor to Holne Moor, and from Tavy Cleave to the Dewerstone (consult *Margery of Quether and Other Stories*, 1891, *Dartmoor Idylls*, 1896, and *Furze Bloom*, 1899). Finally, there is the prose work well described by Baring-Gould as a 'gossiping volume', which debates aspects of Dartmoor tradition used in many of the fictions, *A Book of Dartmoor* (1900).

The place that Baring-Gould loved above all others had long been regarded as neither beautiful nor useful. The wastes of Dartmoor were difficult to assimilate within the conventions of the educated, late-eighteenth and early-nineteenth-century gaze. The high parts of Dartmoor were neither mountainous enough to be considered sublime nor varied enough to be called pretty or picturesque. Dartmoor remained a place inaccessible both to travellers and to the human imagination. Some false etymology inherited from a translation of Camden did not help: according to this, the 'Dert' in 'Dertmoor' did not refer to the river Dart but simply meant 'dirty' (Carrington 1826: vi; Hemery 1982: 12). One turning point in the 'dirty' moor's literary and visual representation occurred in 1826, when N.T. Carrington's 'Dartmoor: A Descriptive Poem' was published, accompanied by eight vignettes, four prints and compendious notes on the moor by William Burt of the Plymouth Chamber of Commerce. Commerce and the muses of art and poetry came hand in hand to rescue Dartmoor: problems faced in 'improving' it agriculturally were related to the project of making it the subject of 'improving' literature. Both William Burt and Carrington's son, Henry, were sometimes defensive about their interest in the moor. Burt feared that the region would undeservedly remain a 'proverb for scorn' and refers to a 'kind of fashion to traduce Dartmoor' (1826: vi-vii). Henry Carrington commented 'Dartmoor is generally imagined to be a region wholly unfit for the purposes of poetry' (H. Carrington 1826: xi). The reviews of the poem suggest that Dartmoor remained a place under suspicion even though Carrington's poem was admitted to the world of the cultivated. Some readers felt that Carrington's work owed more to literature than topography, more to James Thompson's 'The Seasons' than to the true nature of Dartmoor. William Hazlitt records his and Henry Northcote's reactions to the poem as follows:

> Northcote showed me a poem with engravings of Dartmoor which were too fine by half. I said I supposed Dartmoor would

look more gay and smiling after having been thus illustrated, like a dull author who has been praised by a Reviewer. I had once been nearly benighted there and was delighted to get into an inn at Ashburton. 'That', said Northcote, 'is the only good of such places that you are glad to escape from them, and look back to them with a pleasing horror ever after . . . I have, however, told my young friend who sent me the poem, that he has shown his genius in creating beauties where there were none, and extracting enthusiasm from rocks and quagmires. After that, he may write a very interesting poem on Kamschatka'. (Hazlitt 1949: 123)

In spite of such reactions there was a growing awareness, partly inspired by Carrington's poem, that Dartmoor could offer delight and instruction to artists, antiquaries, geologists, natural historians and story-tellers. A dismissive reference to 'Dirty Dartmoor' was made as late as 1830 (Anon. 597) but by 1848 Samuel Rowe could salute the work of Carrington and Burt, and celebrate the many aspects of the moor in his influential tome, dedicated to the King and entitled *A Perambulation of the Antient and Royal Forest of Dartmoor* (Rowe 1985). Richard John King's travelogues of 1859 and 1864 suggest that Carrington had succeeded in putting the moor on the map for the literati and the tourist: 'The wanderer on Dartmoor should by all means make Carrington his companion. His poem has well been compared to certain wines, which can be drunk in perfection nowhere but among their native hills' (King 1874: 358). The dirty, dreary moor was now a refuge for all those tired of Victorian industrialization, a place to fascinate anglers, artists, seekers of folklore, dialect and ancient history. The uninteresting moor of William Gilpin's era had been metamorphosed into the wondrous region which Sabine Baring-Gould encountered, prior to its next shape in the public mind, as much to do with Dartmoor the prison as Dartmoor the place, in Conan Doyle's *Hound of the Baskervilles*.

Baring-Gould's father was happy to leave Dartmoor behind and search for the sublime amongst the Pyrenees. Baring-Gould was more influenced by his uncle, T.G. Bond, who lived near the moor, and gave his nephew a copy of Rowe's *Perambulation* in 1848. Baring-Gould prefaced his book on the moor with an explanation of the impression which Rowe made on his young mind: 'It arrested my

attention, engaged my imagination, and was to me almost as a Bible.'
Rowe's acknowledgement of Carrington and the impressive memorial
to the poet in Shaugh Prior church made Baring-Gould fully aware
of the local reputation of the 'Dartmoor Bard'. It was natural
to Baring-Gould, as to other Dartmoor enthusiasts, to quote
Carrington's description of the moor as a 'wild and wondrous region'
or to resort to Carrington as the best way to evoke the granite
outcrop called 'Bowerman's Nose'. Like Carrington, Baring-Gould
did not look at the moor with a tourist's gaze. Unlike Carrington, he
was free of the duty to seek the picturesque and the sublime. He was
more sceptical than Carrington of the idea of 'improving' Dartmoor
in agricultural or literary terms. What he sought, regardless of the
conventions of vision, was the seity of the moor which the traveller
could experience more easily than the writer could re-create: 'the lone
upland region possesses a something of its own—a charm hard to
describe, but very real . . .'. He had time to look clearly at the actual
moor and its people. As a teenage boy, he used every holiday as an
opportunity to mount his pony and head for the moor: 'I rode over it,
round it, put up at little inns, talked with the moormen, listened to
their tales and songs in the evenings, and during the day sketched
and planned the relics that I then fondly supposed were Druidical'
(Baring-Gould 1982).

As an adult, Baring-Gould's part in the archaeological discovery of
Dartmoor made him sceptical of the druidical speculations of Mrs
Bray of Tavistock. Nevertheless, the moor remained a place of wonder
for him, a region that reminded him of boyhood adventures and
gave him access to people and a culture normally excluded from the
world of the educated. His Dartmoor became an internalized image
that he could summon up in the most unlikely situations. Many went
to Rome to see its wonders; Baring-Gould used his time there
differently: 'When in Rome one winter, impatient at being confined
within walls, weary of the basaltic pavement, my heart went out to
the wilds of Dartmoor, and I wrote *Urith*. I breathed moor air, smelt
the gorse, scrambled the granite rocks in imagination, and forgot
the surroundings of an Italian pension' (1892b: 241). This led to the
creation of the novel *Urith* in 1891; in 1894, when visited by a
journalist, Baring-Gould's lifelong passion for the moor had not
abated. He is quoted as saying 'Nearly all my days just now are
spent on Dartmoor . . .' and is described closing the interview to
depart for 'a distant part of his beloved Dartmoor' (Dolman: 17, 20).

Nevertheless, Baring-Gould was aware that his paradise might be someone else's hell. He described the rector of Widecombe-in-the-Moor as 'cut off from all society, pinched between tremendous hills, with no pursuits, no neighbours, few books. He had no interest in the people, the place, the church; in the natural history, the antiquities of the Moor' (1925a: 126). This image is in every respect the complete opposite of Baring-Gould's character and interests. He was not pinched by the tremendous hills but embraced by them; the churches, natural history and antiquities of Dartmoor fascinated him.

## A Place and its People

### The Shape of the Land

Baring-Gould's numerous, topographical set-piece descriptions of the moor deserve to be anthologized in a separate volume. The three-page description of the western face of Dartmoor at the beginning of the story 'Little Dixie' is representative of his technique. It deserves to be read in its entirety but it is possible here to give an outline of his words. He begins with the conventional metaphor, from Gilpin onwards, for describing high moors: he compares the undulating surface of the heights to the roll of waves on the sea. He sophisticates the image, however: the western edge 'springs into the air like a seventh wave, and is tossed at points into serrated masses of granite, grey or white, as though the crest of the moor like a billow had broken into foam'. He then contrasts this 'long wave' with the 'cloven valley of the Tavy' which descends from 'fathomless bog' and 'barren wilderness' into the 'Garden of England'. Continuing the wave metaphor and employing the power of place-names, he describes how the 'main billow' contains a 'lesser wave' including Doe or Daur Tor, which he translates as 'the Hill of Waters'. At this point, he recognizes the hand of man in the landscape: the waters that fall from ledge to ledge on this Tor take the form of a Tinners' 'goyle': a water course that has been 'streamed' or 'turned over and tossed into the air, and its gravel passed through water, to force the granite sand and pounded crystalline rubble to deliver up its tin'.

Raising our eyes from the land to the sky, Baring-Gould now introduces 'The Roar of the Moor' and 'The Beam of the Moor' or the 'Strome'. The Roar is the east wind as 'it tears its way through the rock castles and crag towers, the granite windows and unclosed natural doors, piping, screaming, sobbing, muttering, growling—all these sounds at a distance' combining 'into one mighty organ note'. The beam is a belt of greyish-brown fog, which spreads in 'vaporous streamers' behind and above the 'upheaved wave' of the tor-crowned heights. He speculates that this 'Beam' in the sky is an equivalent to the beam once placed across a house door: 'when the Beam lies on the eastern horizon the door of Dartmoor is shut. One thinks more than once before ascending its flanks and facing the raging blast that is sweeping, nay mowing the great upland region, as with a scythe'. Only now does Baring-Gould pick out a human habitation in the scene: a farmhouse under Doe Tor is thumbnail sketched. It is a place that has 'shrugged its shoulders and drawn in its head behind turf banks and moorstone walls' (Baring-Gould 1896: 123). Baring-Gould's gaze roves on eastwards and upwards: in succession we see 'clatter' (or 'clitter', the granite debris found at the foot of tors), fertile green fields and the remains of a granite cross. Baring-Gould's telescope shows us the moor as a distant prospect and in close-up: he gives us glimpses of the seity that eludes the categories of sublime and picturesque.

## The People of the Moor: From Lady Darke to the Dartmoor Songmen

Baring-Gould's wilderness is not an empty prospect. His topographical descriptions are balanced by pen-portraits of the human beings who live amongst the topography. These portraits reveal their sitters both as individuals and in relation to their class and occupation. Carrington had largely explored Dartmoor as a wilderness and rural retreat; his references to the industrial aspects of the moor's history were not welcomed. Idealized notions of the rural do not dominate Baring-Gould's stories of the moor. His Dartmoor is thronged with people of many kinds, not just shepherds and farmers but china-clay workers, quarrymen, tin miners and convicts. Baring-Gould shows us the gradations in terms of land-ownership and scale of house between the squire and the yeoman farmer, between the yeoman and the man who owns rather than rents his land, between the small landowner and the labourer, the labourer and the vagrant. Near the apex of his Dartmoor social pyramid are some shadowy figures reputed to be the illegitimate descendants of the Prince Regent. Baring-Gould commemorates one of these in his book of Dartmoor. She is known as 'Lady' Darke. 'To the best of my knowledge no portrait of her remains' says Baring-Gould, but he gives us a verbal portrait of an imperious, eccentric character who boxes the local vicar's ears, practises black magic and is so contemptuous of her husband that when he dies, she has him buried in a pig-cloth used for salting bacon. 'She would do at one time a generous act and next a dirty trick, "just", as the people said, "as though she were a pixy" ' (1982: 183–89). After her death her most private room is opened: beneath a thick veil of cobwebs are bureaux stuffed with guineas and bank notes, and quantities of silver plate bearing the crest of titled men once at the court of the Prince Regent. A pale shadow of this Dartmoor version of Miss Havisham appears in Baring-Gould's novel *Royal Georgie*: it lacks the anecdotal clarity and startling qualities of its prose counterpart.

Baring-Gould is also able to portray the many who work at the base of the social pyramid. In 1894, a journalist recorded that Baring-Gould's passion for collecting folk-tunes 'has indirectly been of help to him in his work as a novelist. It has led him to make the acquaintance of many old Devonshire labourers whose memories are the chief repositories of the songs of the West Country' (Dolman: 20). In fact, Baring-Gould's interest in folk-music and the folk who made it permeates not only his novels (which often quote folk-songs in their titles and narratives), but his numerous short stories and anecdotes of Dartmoor. Baring-Gould's interest in folk-culture became part of a growing awareness of the lives of the working class and underclass, urban and rural, during the late nineteenth century. Gathering forces of social change, including the work of Joseph Arch the agricultural workers' leader, are the context for Baring-Gould's statement of 1895: 'The English labourer is now an important factor in politics; that he has been a factor in English music has not been recognised as it ought' (1895b, Vol. 1: xxiii). A staunch defender of rural hierarchy and resister of urban change, Baring-Gould nevertheless identified partially with the new interest in the labourer's voice. He acknowledged the worker's contribution to the creation of national music and valued folk songs as 'the expression of the minds, artistic sense, and feelings of the people . . .' (1925b: 211).

Baring-Gould left us several lists of the people who shared their songs, stories and working lives with him (1895d: vii–viii; 1905: viii). These lists have anecdotal qualities, giving us glimpses of whole lives in a few words. Here follows a selected inventory of the men and women, mainly of Dartmoor and its adjacent territory, who helped him to share in the life of the people. Sometimes his sources remain anonymous, a 'shepherd on Dartmoor', an 'old mason on the fringe of Dartmoor'. Sometimes they are sketched as a group in the Oxenham Arms at South Zeal, or in an informal gathering round the kitchen fire. More often, a thumbnail sketch links individual names, places, occupation and education. Consider James Parsons, a 'totally illiterate' hedger and song-man, Roger Huggins, mason, William Fry, labourer, Edmund Fry, thatcher, all of Lydford, Anne Roberts, 'formerly of Post Bridge in the heart of the moor', William Andrews, 'a fiddler at Sheepstor, on the edge of Dartmoor', William George Kerswell, 'a moorland farmer, an old man, near Two Bridges, in the heart of Dartmoor', J. Watts, 'quarryman, Thrushelton', John Bennett, 'a day labourer aged sixty eight' of Chagford, J. Gerrard, 'aged sixty eight, and nearly blind, a labouring man, illiterate, of Cullyton, near Chagford', Robert Hard 'an old stonebreaker' of South Brent who was found dead in a snowdrift, William Aggett, 'an old crippled labourer', 'very illiterate', of Chagford, James Coaker of Ring Hill, 'a blind man of eighty nine, in the heart of the Moor, very infirm', Mr J. Webb, 'captain of a mine hard by', Mary Sacherley 'an old illiterate woman, born and bred on the moor, and daughter of a very famous old song-man', John Helmore of South Brent, a miller 'ruined by the setting up of a steam-mill' who 'died at Ivybridge Workhouse in 1900', William Nankivell, 'an aged quarryman, who for years lived under Roos Tor, on the River Walla above Merrivale Bridge, absolutely illiterate, but with a memory laden with old songs'. Baring-Gould was the amanuensis for the songs of these Miltons who would otherwise be regarded as mute. He did not succeed in making a great Dartmoor novel from his unique knowledge of the life of the labourer. However, he did create as series of short descriptions and stories which take us closer to the lives of those many individuals sketched in his tantalizing lists of sources.

Baring-Gould began his collection of songs from the moor and the West Country in about 1888 but the interest originated during his boyhood excursions on Dartmoor and remained with him. He described himself when he asserted in 1894 that the professional musician who wanted to learn about folk-songs must 'put on an old coat and hat, and go on a tramp through England, lodging at little taverns, and associate with the labourers in the green fields and over the tavern table, about the tavern fire'. Defying Arnoldian assumptions, Baring-Gould claimed an advantage for the provincial or rural mind in this project: 'I venture to think that such a work as the collection of folk airs from the old singers would be impossible, or nearly so, to a man who had not lived the greater portion of his time in the country, and who did not know the ins and outs of the countryman's mind . . . I can rapidly unlock the hearts of our Devon and Cornish singers . . . in the West, for there we have a score of subjects in common: we know about each other and each other's friends and companions, about places associated with each other's old recollections—we are on common ground very soon' (1895a: vi, xi).

Baring-Gould faithfully collected the tunes sung by the Dartmoor labourers, but he often changed or censored the words of their songs because he found them improper. What he could not censor, however, were their force of personality and the colour of their tough lives, which emerge incidentally and anecdotally in his accounts of the collection of folk-songs. Baring-Gould, in these accounts, stands aside to let us hear the voices of the Dartmoor workers telling their story in their own words. He censored the saucy ballad 'A Sweet Pretty Maiden' but preserves an anecdote about how it was passed down the generations. 'One of my old singers [the miner Samuel Fone] said to me . . . "When my little sister, now dead these twenty years, was a child, and went up from Exeter to London with me in a carrier's van, Lor bless'y, afore railways was invented, I mind that she sang this here ballet [sic] in the wagon all the way up. We was three days about it. She was then about six years old." Baring-Gould adds that the ballad 'is not particularly choice and suitable for a child or a grown-up girl to sing, according to our ideas' (1905: x). Baring-Gould also encountered bawdy folk-song as a family affair when he visited a song-man at Belstone on Dartmoor: 'he sang a ballad to us, but dropped one of the verses, whereupon his daughter, a tall, handsome girl of about eighteen, shouted from the kitchen: "Fayther, you've left out someut," and she struck up and sang a most—to say the least—indelicate verse' (1925b: 190–91). Despite Baring-Gould's reservations about indelicacy, these anecdotes reach out from the culture of literacy, railways and individualism to touch the old world of carriers' vans and collective, oral tradition. On another occasion, Baring-Gould records:

A workman told me that there was in the parish of Northill [near Trebartha in Cornwall] an old man, a bit of a white-witch, who could sing. I made three excursions after him, driving a distance of eighteen miles, and the same distance back. On two occasions he was not to be found, on the third I caught him cutting fern on a bank. A fine old man with snowy hair and beard, dark eyes, and nose like the beak of a hawk. I at once asked him if he knew the song of the 'Oxen Ploughing'. He struck up at once. I sat on a heap of fern he had cut as bedding for cattle, and sang with him, till I had learned the song by heart, then I drove home the eighteen miles, singing it the whole way so as to make sure of the tune. (1895b, Vol. 2: xii)

Another source for Baring-Gould's collection of songs was an elderly woman he sometimes called Sally Satterleigh and sometimes Mary Satcherly. Her mind was a library where Baring-Gould knew many folk-songs were stored, but he discovered that this 'library' was only 'open' at certain times. 'She cannot be induced to sit down and sing—then her memory fails, but she will sing whilst engaged in kneading bread, washing, driving the geese out of the room, feeding the pig: naturally, this makes it a matter of difficulty to note her melodies. One has to run after her, from the kitchen to the pig-sty, or to the well-head and back, pencil and music-book in hand' (1895a: viii). The squarson pictured here, sitting on a heap of fern, following Sally to the well-head, enters the workers' world. He reveals the relentless nature of the labourers' work; he also pictures them as possessing a culture that survives in spite of and because of their lives of constant toil.

The tunes which Baring-Gould so patiently and respectfully sought were like the surface of Dartmoor, an extraordinary palimpsest of human experience over a vast stretch of time. A story told to Baring-Gould by a stone-breaker, John Goodrich of Thrushelton, suggests that those who had never been taught history by rote, nevertheless embodied it unconsciously. Baring-Gould explains how Goodrich was in a public house in North Devon in 1864

when at night a tramp entered soaked to the bone by the rain . . . Whilst in the process of throwing off the moisture in steam he sang and recited the story of 'Go from my window', that is quoted by Beaumont and Fletcher in *The Knight of the Burning Pestle*, 1613, and in Fletcher's *Monsieur Thomas*, 1639. It was licensed to be printed in 1587–8; and was parodied as a hymn in 1590 . . . The tune is found in Queen Elizabeth's Virginal Book. (1925b: 199)

Baring-Gould's scholarship allows him to link this anecdote about a nineteenth-century labourer with the culture of the Elizabethan and Jacobean court; but it is Baring-Gould's human qualities, his capacity to communicate with a stone-breaker, that inspires the memorable glimpse of culture coexisting with the everyday life of a vagrant. Sometimes the permanence of the common memory is in contrast to the transience of the labourer's life. The folk-song of 'The Garden Gate' reminds Baring-Gould of its singers:

> I have myself heard it sung by a little blacksmith who goes by the nickname of 'Ginger Jack', and from whom I have taken down a great many songs, new and old. Mr Sheppard also noted it down from a crippled stone-breaker [probably Robert Hard of South Brent], whose memory was richly furnished with old songs. Alas! the dear old man, for whom I had particular regard, is dead. He was found stiff in a ditch one bitter winter night. (1895b, Vol. 1: xxxii)

As well as these fascinating asides in his commentary on folk-songs, Baring-Gould has left us some short fictions and semi-fictions which portray individual Dartmoor workers in some detail. His pen-portrait of Jonas Coaker, a self-styled Dartmoor poet, is ambivalent. Jonas was born in 1801 and spent his life outside civilized habitation and civilized notions of time. When Baring-Gould met him in 1888 while seeking ancient folk-songs, Jonas was dwelling at Ring Hill in a lonely farmstead made out of granite blocks removed from Bronze Age hut circles. Jonas' long life is conveyed in a series of short anecdotes: he is reputed to have run non-stop from Postbridge on the moor to the city of Exeter in four hours; he was once publican of the remote Warren House Inn and locked out of his own pub by drunken miners; he became known as a poet by accident when a group of soldiers training on the moor were marooned by wet weather and had nothing better to do than read Jonas' verses. Baring-Gould is sceptical of Jonas' poetic powers and almost makes his epitaph a joke. Jonas spends his last days worrying about his own funeral and asking: 'When I'm dead, whativer shall I do wi' myself?'. Finally, however, Baring-Gould dignifies Jonas with an account of his funeral that becomes a Dartmoor prose-poem, combining pagan antiquity and nineteenth-century Christianity:

The day was Sunday, the 16th February, 1890. A frost was on
the short turf, the sky was clear. The miners from Hexworthy
were at Ring Hill in their best black; and away over the moors
in the glitter of the sun on the sparkling, hoary grass and
twinkling furze-bushes the old man was borne, followed by a
great train of all who had known and loved him; and as the train
swept over rolling hill, down into glen by brawling torrent,
mile after mile, by old cairns and primeval walled enclosures,
rose the hymn and psalm, swelling, ebbing, rising again—a
river of music—till, as the funeral procession reached the head
of Hameldon, a mighty wave of moorland, below which lies
the church of Widecombe, the music of the bells ringing for
afternoon service hushed the song of the bearers. (1896: 155)

Baring-Gould's tribute to Jonas is simultaneously a tribute to the
character of the moor and its people.

Baring-Gould gives us images of the labourer, who despite his
ingenuity, is at the mercy of economic forces. This is his thumbnail
sketch of the life and work of John Narracot, or Whistle-Jack, a man
who stands for countless others 'de-skilled' by 'progress' before and
since:

> He made brooms. He sheared sheep. He trapped moles. He
> thatched cottages and ricks. He composed verses. He was a
> rat-catcher. He was credited with being a poacher. Finally, he
> made and sold whistles. Broom cutting time was in winter.
> Mole catching in April. Shearing time in June. Patent poisons
> were destroying rats. Galvanised iron roofing was abolishing
> thatch . . . Poems Jack composed all year . . . But Board School
> education and the Press were reducing the number of those who
> cared to hear the rude compositions of Narracot. . . .' ('John and
> Joan', 1896: 9)

Baring-Gould's pen-portrait of Daniel Jacobs is a more detailed
study. He explains his personal involvement with Daniel: 'as I write
these words concerning him, the figure of the man with a wasted life
and forlorn old age rises up so vividly before my mind's eye, that he
seems to me to be still present, very real, and not a memory.'
Baring-Gould begins with Daniel's externals and takes you to his
soul. Daniel is a homeless and houseless cripple, to be found in the

ale house or the prison. His hair is white, his face is dirty and unshaven; he wears other men's cast-offs stained by peat water and covered in patches. His incongruous figure is transformed when he takes a shabby violin out of the green baize bag which he always carries and begins to play. Then 'every defect is forgotten in the study of his eyes . . . A far-off look comes into them . . . he is away in spirit in the music world . . . he is wrapped in his cloud of music, carried off in a whirlwind of harmonious sound—like Elijah transported heavenward in the chariot of fire'. Baring-Gould is aware of how different this portrait might have been. The young Daniel's musical abilities were spotted by a kindly local squire who would have helped him to develop his talent; unfortunately, Daniel's father is a strict Methodist teetotaller who will not tolerate the idea of his son making a living in such a sinful way. From that moment, Daniel's life deteriorates; the teetotaller's son becomes a drunkard. Like many others of his class, Daniel loses his way because he has been denied the opportunity 'to follow his natural bent, to develop the genius that was in him, to live in his proper artistic world' ('Daniel Jacobs', 1896: 63).

## The Idea of a Dartmoor Community

Baring-Gould could not save Daniel from his fate but he did create some short fictions that defended his perception of the Dartmoor community. Carrington and his supporters introduced Dartmoor to the public in a defensive, half-apologetic tone; Baring-Gould takes an aggressive attitude to those 'in-country' people who cannot understand the Dartmoor natives. He is willing to admit to the loneliness of life on the moor, but mainly from a resident's point of view. One story contains a vignette of a young woman called Joanna who longs to leave the moor and become a serving maid in fashionable Torquay. She complains to her unmarried brother: 'You are holding me here on to this desolate moor, where one sees no faces lookin' in at the winder but that of a bullock or a sheep or a Dartmoor colt, and I wants to be off—terrible' ('Green Rushes, O!', 1896: 224). This is not the moor idealized by an outsider: it is the moor seen from the inside, looking out. Relate this vignette to the anecdote of the Plymouth tailor, the outsider coming in. He enters the wilderness of the moor in order to attend a cousin's funeral, following a coach-driver's well-intentioned but fatally vague directions: 'You go along there, and you can't miss it!' At this point the tailor carries a black umbrella and is dressed in a black top hat and a glossy black suit. By the time Baring-Gould encountered him, the tailor has been 'pixie-led' for many hours. His shiny suit is bedraggled and he has lost his hat, his umbrella and his dignity, having spent most of the night lying in a bog, terrified by the baleful eyes of some curious sheep. Baring-Gould refreshes him with a Cornish pasty and shows him the way home but this does not convert the tailor. The anecdote ends with the Tailor's words: 'I solemnly swear to you, sir . . . nothing will ever induce me to set foot on Dartmoor again. If I chance to see it from the [Plymouth] Hoe, sir, I'll avert my gaze' (1982: 4–5).

Baring-Gould included both 'Dartmoor' the prison and 'Dartmoor' the community in his vision. The prison was originally built to house prisoners of war in the Napoleonic period and then abandoned. It was opened again to house criminals during Baring-Gould's childhood. Baring-Gould told stories about convicts escaping from the prison. In the short story entitled 'Caroline', a group of Dartmoor tin miners reluctantly shelter an escaped convict partly because he is a fellow miner. Due to the help of the miners, the convict works his way back to a respectable life. In this case, the moorland community not only contains the threat of crime but rehabilitates the criminal. Baring-Gould attaches this story to a specific location where: 'some crumbling walls . . . sustain as on crutches a gaunt, corroded water wheel. Near it are heaps that indicate mine works, and enclosures and relics of buildings that show where cottage, count-house and paddocks once were'. He re-creates the people who once brought life to this derelict scene, in a vignette of the mine-workers of the past emerging from beneath the earth: 'in their mining habits, stained red with tin; their slouched felt caps with dabs of clay in front, and in each dab of clay a tallow-candle' (1899b: 49, 51).

Parson Baring-Gould can tell a story at the expense of parsons, as long as the hero of his tale is the Dartmoor community. In one story, 'The Old Cross', he makes clever use of the art of the tall tale. H.G. Wells defined science fiction as beginning with one incredible assumption and from then on proceeding in an utterly logical, convincing manner. The tall tale, by contrast, begins with the credible and then becomes increasingly fantastic. The author winks at the audience; they know the tale is not literally true but collude in its fantasy because of its comedy and ingenuity. Baring-Gould begins his tale with a convincing description of a tangible, solid object and a typical Dartmoor feature: an ancient granite cross. 'On a long ridge of moor, a thousand feet above the sea, that forms a spur of Dartmoor . . . stands a very ancient cross—so rude, so shapeless that it probably belongs to hoar antiquity . . . It is of granite. It is covered with a crust of lichen, yellow, white and black' (1896: 239). Some pre-Christian superstitions associated with this cross inspire the local vicar to condemn it to destruction (compare the story of the Lew Trenchard Menhir). At the climax of his sermon against paganism, the parson tries to inspire his congregation to loathe the cross by telling them that he has seen the devil on top of it with his tail twined round it. The story then apparently digresses but actually prepares its central theme. The vicar goes for a walk on the moor, pausing to pick and eat one of the local delicacies: whortleberries. As he tramples among them, they stain and blacken his shoes and trousers. As he consumes the berries, his mouth becomes blackened with their juice. When a ferocious bull appears to interrupt his feast, the vicar flees desperately seeking a refuge; the only place to escape the bull is on top of the cross. The vicar's cries for help bring all his parishioners to the spot to see what seems to prove the sermon true: there is a black devil perched on the cross. When they recognize their own vicar, the man of God is reduced to a figure of fun, transformed into the devil he condemned and forced to value the very object he wished to destroy. This is a Dartmoor variation of the classic tale of the biter bit, or the wish that comes true in a way that horrifies the wisher. The ingenious fantasy of this tall tale retains a link with Dartmoor reality: it is an equivalent in fiction to Baring-Gould's practical work saving the antiquities of the moor. Baring-Gould saw Dartmoor only partly through the eyes of an educated rationalist; he also saw it through the eyes of the rural labourers of Devon. He gives us a glimpse of the origins of his writing mind as follows: 'There was an incredible amount of superstition among the people in the days when I was a child, and I heard such stories of ghosts, spectral flames, pixies and goblins, that it took me a good many years to clear my head of them' (1925a: 142). As a story-teller he did not 'clear his head' of these superstitions, and this enables him to approach the hidden territory of the labourer that others could not reach.

Baring-Gould's short story 'Snaily House' is optimistic about the moor's capacity to resist change. Two sisters on foot in a 'Northern Nannie' (or drenching rain storm from the north) come upon a carriage outside an inn. They seek refuge inside it and discover they are sitting where the greatest in the land once sat: 'The conveyance was of a very wonderful description. It was painted yellow, it had glass in front, and a leather apron . . . It was slung on immense C springs. The conveyance dated from the days of the Regency, when the Prince came to Dartmoor to visit Sir Thomas Tyrwhitt at Tor Royal. On the death of Sir Thomas, this had been sold along with the effects, and had passed into the possession of a little publican at Crockern Tor, named Leaman . . . On this day . . . Joe Leaman had driven a couple of gentlemen to Moreton Hampstead, who had come to the Moor on a scheme for the extraction of naptha from the peat' (1896: 71–72). Due to the sisters' fatigue and the fact that the wet weather causes so much condensation on the carriage windows, they do not notice Joe returning to drive the carriage away. Equally, he cannot see the women inside the carriage and sets off on the precipitous roads of the moor, carrying two panicking, unwilling passengers who find it difficult to signal their presence due to the peculiar interior design of their conveyance. The story of Joe and whether he will marry one or none of the sisters he has met by chance develops from here. In this one image, Baring-Gould has encapsulated an aspect of the history of the nation's relationship with the moor, and the way in which its topography and weather combine to mock pretensions to greatness and the schemes of businessmen. The carriage of the great is now important as the means by which the poor keep out of the wet and go courting.

Baring-Gould is less hopeful about the future of Dartmoor in an uncollected story entitled 'Sixpence Only', published in *The Graphic* in 1899. The basis of the tale is the unrecognized courage of the Dartmoor woman, Faith. The remote Dartmoor cottage where she lives alone with her mother is visited by two unexpected guests on the same night: an escaped convict seeking aid and a soap salesman who stays the night, unaware of his proximity to a dangerous man. The convict has evil designs on the salesman and his money which Faith thwarts, despite the salesman's condescending and ignorant remarks about the moor and its people. 'What an outlandish bit of England this is' he complains. In order to protect her mother and her guest she leads the convict away from the moor. He murders her before her heroic act can be made known. When she does not appear the following morning, the salesman interprets her absence as confirming his worst suspicions about unreliable Dartmoor folk: her second-rate hospitality is worth 'sixpence only' (Baring-Gould

1899c). This story sometimes rises above crude melodrama to convey a thought-provoking message: caught between the immoral convict and the commercially minded salesman, the true spirit of the moor and its people may die. In this and other fictions, Baring-Gould used his privileged position to speak up for the men and the women of his Dartmoor world.

## Baring-Gould's Place in the Modern World

Baring-Gould called a collection of his stories *Furze Bloom: Tales of the Western Moors*. The title expressed his loyalty to his region and his sense that landscape and people are intimately connected. He explained: 'as Scotland has the thistle, Ireland the shamrock, and Wales the leek as their emblems, we Western men of Devon and Cornwall should adopt the furze' (1982: 12). Some of Baring-Gould's contemporary readers shared his local patriotism and therefore had no doubt as to the value of his fictions. In 1889 *The Western Antiquary* referred to him as 'this popular Devonshire writer' (Anon. 1889: 131). A local reviewer of 1898 presented Baring-Gould as 'one who has done more than any other living writer to delineate the rugged character of the Cornish sea-faring folk and the no less sturdy sons and daughters of Devon' (Wright 1898: 376). This response is in the language of stereotype although Baring-Gould would have agreed to a connection between a 'rugged' Cornish coast and 'rugged' people. Like these readers, Baring-Gould was writing *from* more than *about* a region.

His affection for his region is not in doubt, but has the squarson something to teach the wider world and the modern world? His literary reputation is now much less known. Apart from authors with a knowledge of the West Country (John Betjeman, John Fowles and Charles Causley), few have noticed Baring-Gould's contribution to the tradition of regional writing. Baring-Gould paid attention to his place in a way that deserves our attention. It is possible to focus on his many works and achievements by using Wendell Berry's terms (see the Preface and Chapter 1 of this book). Baring-Gould, like other writers in this study, avoids the territory of abstraction to reach the territory underfoot, to meet the people on the cliff and on the moor. He is the least successful literary craftsman debated in this book, sometimes failing to transmute his unique local knowledge into successful fiction. He is, nevertheless, one of the most successful of the writers here in bringing hidden rural places and people before our gaze. He cannot follow Hardy into the territory of tragedy; instead, he creates an insightful comedy of local manners. A 'region' conceived as a 'community', to use those related keywords, can be found in Baring-Gould's work. He understandably regarded his collection of West Country folk-songs as his greatest achievement but this chapter shows that it is the asides in his accounts of folk-song that constitute some of his best work as a regional writer. This chapter also shows how his unique knowledge of the labourer contributes flashes of insight to his pen-portraits and short stories.

Publishing the unpublished, looking at the overlooked: in this way Baring-Gould made a unique contribution to teaching the world about the West Country. He maps it not just as a place but as a workplace, a region as the common man and woman experienced it. Baring-Gould was the amanuensis of West Country people; he was also the inventive teller of stories that preserve the essence of their personalities and their way of life. This chapter leaves the last word not to Baring-Gould but to a person we know because of Baring-Gould. The squarson was a man educated enough to learn from those assumed to be uneducated. One of his advisers on folk tradition was James Parsons, a hedger descended from a family of song-men. Baring-Gould was modest enough to leave us an anecdote of how this Westcountryman educated him: ' "Thicky wi'n't do . . . You've gotten that note not right. You mun know that I'm the master and you'm the scholar; and I wi'n't have any slurs or blunders. What is right is right, and what is wrong niver can be right to the world's end" ' (1925b: 197–98).

# 7

# To the Godrevy Lighthouse

*The view, in fact, seems to have been written by Virginia Woolf.*
Hermione Lee, looking at Godrevy from
Talland House, St Ives

*I can't resist the West.*

Virginia Woolf, 1936

In 1905, Woolf expressed her excitement about travelling westwards: 'It was with some feeling of enchantment that we took our places yesterday in the Great Western train'. The train was not a machine but a 'wizard' who would transport her from normal space and time to 'another world' and almost 'another age' (Leaska 1990: 281). Woolf (1882–1941) was like her Victorian predecessors in seeking the romance of place. She uses very similar terms here to the Hardy who wrote 'When I Set Out for Lyonnesse' (1870). On closer inspection, however, Woolf's explorations westward can be seen to exceed Victorian bounds. She provides a foil to the Victorian West Country and helps us to test how much of it we can take into the future. The Victorian West was created mostly by writers who were 'insiders', resident in their region for long or formative periods in their lives; Woolf is in some ways 'more like us': a holiday-maker, a wanderer, a permanent exile due to the mobility allowed by modern communications, transport and labour. The Victorian manuscript of the West Country was written mainly by authors who sought public attention: Woolf's relationship with her 'West' was a semi-private affair that only modern scholarship enables us to uncover. The Victorians explored West Country landscapes with Pre-Raphaelite concepts of realism in mind; Woolf explores visual perceptions of Cornwall in ways that were made possible after the Post-Impressionist exhibition of 1910. Many of the writers studied here were exploring the country of childhood, but none of them did it as intensely and deeply as Woolf, whose childhood holidays in Cornwall marked her more than her adult time elsewhere. Woolf created her childhood West post-Freud: she explores places in the mind and on the map in ways that were not available to her predecessors. Finally and importantly, the Victorian manuscript of the West Country was written in a patriarchal culture. The influential, literary version of the West includes many fictions about women but very few by women. Woolf extends our map in terms of gender, negotiating with a Victorian past in order to make a future. To find her voice, to create her place, Woolf had to exorcise the ghost of her own family's Victorian patriarch, Leslie Stephen.

### Eden and the Serpents

Woolf's letters reveal that she was sensitive to the topographical variations of the West Country as a whole. The word 'West', however, was mainly her sign for Cornwall as both a geographical and emotional territory. The Stephen family had a long love affair with Cornwall. Prior to his marriage to Julia Duckworth in 1878, Leslie Stephen (1832–1904) knew and loved Cornwall as a place for walking and creative work. He stayed at Falmouth in 1872 and at Newquay in 1879. He bought the lease of Talland House in St Ives from the Great Western Railway Company in 1881 and made it the holiday home of his family from 1882 until 1894. From there, accompanied by guests such as the American poet James Russell Lowell, they visited and adored many parts of Cornwall, including Land's End, Porthcurno, Gurnard's Head, Bosigran Castle and Trencrom Hill. This idyll ended for Leslie in 1895 when his wife Julia died, permanently changing his attitude to Talland House: 'Every corner of the house and garden is full of memories for me—I could hardly bear to look at it again, I think' (Bell 1977: 62). Since Talland now symbolized as much sorrow as joy, he deputized his stepson George Duckworth to sever the Stephen connection with the place.

The thirteen-year-old Virginia suffered like her father: the first of her many mental breakdowns occurred after her mother's death.

Unlike her father, however, she found that she could never leave St Ives and Cornwall either in imagination or in reality. As a child in London, Kensington Gardens served to remind her of Cornwall: the shells strewn on the Flower Walk recalled shells on the beach at St Ives; the toy boat which she sailed on the ornamental pond was a Cornish lugger. When, as an adult, she rented a house in Sussex, she named it 'Little Talland House'. During the last period of her life at Rodmell in Sussex, her own room contained a tile design picturing Godrevy Lighthouse at St Ives. When she visited Wales or Somerset, she compared her location unfavourably to the Cornish coasts. She returned to these coasts compulsively and consistently between 1905 and 1936. Leonard Woolf describes the destination of Virginia's 1936 journey as a Keatsian faery-land:

> We drove down into the west country by slow stages, stopping in Weymouth, Lyme Regis, and Becky Falls on Dartmoor, until we reached Budock Vean in that strange primordial somnolent Cornish peninsula between Falmouth and Helford Passage, where the names of the villages soothe one by their strangeness—Gweek and Constantine and Mawnan Smith . . . No casements are so magic, no faery lands so forlorn as those which all our lives we treasure in our memory of the summer holidays of our childhood. Cornwall never failed to fill Woolf with this delicious feeling of nostalgia and romance . . . As the final cure, we wandered round St Ives and crept into the garden of Talland House and in the dusk Woolf peered through the ground floor windows to see the ghosts of her childhood. (L. Woolf, Vol. 2, 1980: 300)

Virginia Woolf also visited St Ives and Talland in her imagination when she meditated on childhood photographs and as she wrote her many letters, her Cornish Journal, her short story 'A Walk by Night' (1905) and her autobiographical 'A Sketch of the Past' written in 1939. A thinly disguised version of St Ives, Talland House and her parents' Cornish activities appear in her famous novel of 1925–26, *To The Lighthouse*. Clearly, Cornwall is an important and unavoidable part of Virginia Woolf's geography. Although it held healing properties for her, it was not simply a place of romance. Leonard's attempted Cornish cure did not prevent his wife from committing suicide.

While the Stephen family shared a passion for Cornwall, there are significant variations in their interpretation of their chosen territory. Woolf certainly inherited her father's love of walking and of place. In 1905 she tramped the Cornish landscape in her father's manner, until 'the map of the land' seemed to become 'solid' in her brain (Leaska 1990: 285). In 1921 when she wrote a letter in praise of 'amazing' Cornish granite near Zennor, she was only repeating her father showing off what he called the 'granite country' of Cornwall to his friend Lowell (Nicolson 1975, Vol. 2: 463; Norton 1894, 2: 501). Woolf also liked to quote her father's vivid description of Talland House as being situated 'down at the very toe-nail of England'. Leslie's evocation of the St Ives home, written in 1882 long before death entered the garden, includes the two-year-old Virginia:

> We are here on a lovely blowing breezy day: the air is delicious
> —pure Atlantic breezes . . . and it is as soft as silk; it has a fresh
> sweet taste like new milk; and it is so clear that we see thirty
> miles of coast . . . We have a little garden . . . and yet it is
> a dozen little gardens each full of romance for the children
> —lawns surrounded by flowering hedges, and intricate thickets
> of gooseberries and currants, and remote nooks of potatoes and
> peas, and high banks, down which you can slide in a sitting
> posture . . . altogether a pocket paradise with a sheltered cove of
> sand in easy reach (for 'Ginia even) just below. . . . (Maitland
> 1910: 345, 384)

The adult Virginia also celebrated St Ives air and described the garden in ways similar to her father: 'It had, running down the hill, little lawns, surrounded by thick escallonia bushes . . . it had so many corners and lawns that each was named: the coffee garden, the fountain; the cricket ground; the love corner . . . the strawberry bed; the kitchen garden; the pond; and the big tree' (Schulkind 1978: 129–30). Leslie remembered Talland as a Summer idyll: according to Leonard Woolf, this sunlit happiness was also present in Virginia's memory and in her novel *To The Lighthouse* (L. Woolf 1980, Vol. 2: 119). It was her father's word 'romance' that Virginia used when she most wanted to express the power of Cornwall.

Virginia Woolf also learned her mother's kind of Cornwall. Leslie presents Julia as sharing in his passion for St Ives places: 'I can feel her sitting by me on the rocky point which bounds Porthminster

Bay, watching the seagulls in whom she delighted, or on the rocks by Knill's Monument—a favourite haunt of hers . . .' (Bell 1977: 63, 74). The posthumously published stories that Julia wrote for her children show hints of the Stephen aptitude for observing and recording a sense of place. A Cornish ambiance pervades parts of 'The Wandering Pigs' and 'The Monkey on the Moor', two whimsical stories containing references to beaches, cliffs, sea-thrift and granite features. 'The Wandering Pigs' contains a verbal thumbnail sketch of a house on the coast with a garden, lookout point, apple tree and path to the beach, exactly as at Talland. St Ives appears in 'The Monkey on the Moor' as a 'funny little fishing town stretching out into the sea, the houses so crowded together, it seemed as if people could not live in them' (Gillespie 1987: 61). This may be one of the seeds of Woolf's brilliant quintessence of St Ives created in 1939: 'It was a windy, noisy, fishy, vociferous, narrow streeted town; the colour of a mussel or a limpet; like a bunch of rough shell fish clustered on a grey wall together' (Schulkind 1985: 128). There is also evidence that Julia's St Ives was not simply a place to be observed but a place requiring participation. Julia Stephen's charitable activities were long remembered: one witness commented 'I cannot count the times when in the small, dingy crowded quarter of St Ives, her name was mentioned with affection and fervent gratitude' (Bell 1977: 63). This practical contribution to Cornish life is the origin for Mrs Ramsay's concern for the lighthouse keeper's boy in *To The Lighthouse*. The portrait of Mrs Ramsay also shows Woolf questioning the idea that a woman's role was to care for others.

Woolf grew from, but outgrew, her parents' Cornwall. She perceived that two ages clashed in the Stephen household: the Victorian and the Modern. Her father, she believed, had stayed living in the world of 1860 while his daughters and sons were living in 1910. This was the year that Roger Fry, art critic and Bloomsbury member, organized the controversial Post-Impressionist Exhibition. Speaking from the viewpoint of 1919 Woolf famously claimed: 'in or about December, 1910, human character changed . . . All human relations have shifted—those between masters and servants, husbands and wives, parents and children' (Woolf 1919: 189–90). By 1919, Woolf's parents were long dead but still exercising influence on her imagination, memory and relationship with Cornwall.

Virginia Woolf's parents influenced her voice but were not her ventriloquists. Julia and Leslie discovered Cornwall during their maturity. Woolf first experienced St Ives with a child's sense of wonder and, even as an adult, continued to see Cornwall through a child's eyes. There is a surviving fragment of Woolf's childhood thoughts about Cornwall. Initially with her brother Thoby's assistance, the precocious Virginia produced her own version of a weekly newspaper from 1891 until 1895, during the period of the St Ives idyll. This is an extract from the newspaper recording an event of 12 September 1892 when Virginia was nine years old: 'Master Hilary Hunt and Master Basil Smith came up to Talland House and asked Master Thoby and Miss Virginia Stephen to accompany them to the light-house as Freeman the boatman said that there was a perfect tide and wind for going there. Master Adrian Stephen was much disappointed at not being allowed to go' (*Hyde Park Gate News*, 12 September, 1892 quoted in Braybrooke 1991: 80). The tone of this early writing is intriguing: it is the language of formality but also of passions, it addresses children as adults but it hints at a child's incomprehension as to why wishes cannot be granted. The content of this early passage is also thought-provoking. This 1892 reference to Godrevy lighthouse, prominent in the panoramic view from Talland House, can be seen to contain the seed of *To the Lighthouse* written in 1925 to 1926. In the novel, it is young James who is prevented from visiting the lighthouse, partly due to his overbearing father Mr Ramsay, a partial portrait of Leslie Stephen. It is Mrs Ramsay, Woolf's fictional version of her mother, who after her death influences life in such a way as to make James's dream come true.

Woolf retained a child's vision of the place even when adult. She recalled Talland not only as a solid object but also 'like a child's drawing of a house' (Schulkind 1978: 129). In her father's adult world, the house and garden were small, the whole area amounting to a 'pocket paradise'. When Woolf remembered Talland it was within what she called the 'great cathedral space' of childhood, a huge place within which small details assume tremendous significance and every microcosm contains a macrocosm. When she returned to the area in 1905, the little details were more important than the relatively vast landscape in which they were set: 'at every turn of the road, we could anticipate some little characteristic—a water trough—or plank over the stream—which had impressed itself minutely upon our childish minds, & great was our joy when we discovered that our memory was right'. Virginia explained that to find 'these details unchanged' gave her more pleasure than to find 'the big hills in their places' (Leaska 1990: 283). Woolf remembered Talland in terms of the same small details. The 1905 visit seemed to reassure Woolf that memory was not invention: that the external reality of place could preserve experiences that might otherwise have been lost. It is more difficult to divide reality from fiction in her re-creation of Talland during the years 1938–39.

As she wrote about the house in her diary and 'A Sketch of the Past', the sketch became a complete picture, the past became present. Woolf explored every part of Talland in her imagination. She heard the latch clicking as she opened the large wooden gate and walked up the carriage drive past the flower-covered wall to the 'Look Out' place. There she saw the local railway signals and surveyed St Ives bay, its rocks and lighthouse. In the garden, she saw her mother walking up the path by the lawn and especially noted the rubbish heap, the escallonia leaves changing from green to grey, and an apple tree. Approaching the house, she saw the ants swarming on the step and a particular flower in the bed by the front door. In the hallway, she noted the looking-glass, and a slab outside the dining door where dishes could be placed. She entered the drawing room and saw the green plush sofa where she sat and scribbled stories while the grown-ups dined. She walked up the broad staircase to the nursery where a breeze rustled the pale yellow blind covering the window. Her gaze rested on the attic wall. She saw the nursery balcony which joined her first resting place with that of her mother: she focused on the passionflowers growing on the balcony wall, 'great starry blossoms, with purple streaks, and large green buds, part empty, part full'. The vision of the breeze-blown yellow blind and the sensuous passion flowers returned Woolf to an imagined womb, a place where one could delight in the first experience of rhythm, colour, light and sound. Woolf described her experience of this part of Talland as 'lying in a grape, and seeing through a film of semi-transparent yellow'. Talland was also the fruitful womb for the creative impulse. The rubbish heap and the single flower by the front door were small places where a writer's ambitions were born. She had once explained to her mother and her godfather James Lowell that the rubbish heap was the dwelling place of two creatures called 'Beccage' and 'Hollywinks'; looking intently at the flower and realizing its relation to the earth had given Woolf a sense of wholeness, of the many interconnections an artist might find in a complex, only apparently fragmented world (Schulkind 1978: 75–79, 82, 89, 129–30; Anne Bell 1984, Vol. 5: 192).

At this degree of focus, however, it is possible to discover that Woolf's Talland was a garden of Eden with serpents. Parts of the house had sad associations. Through the attic wall, Virginia had heard her stepsister sobbing about a love-affair. On the lawn she had fought with her brother Thoby and then ceased to fight, choosing to end the confrontation by suffering rather than inflicting violence. The apple tree in the garden bore the bitter fruit of knowledge: the grey-green creases in its bark were associated with the moment when she found out that a friend of her father had committed suicide. Most disturbing of all this territory was the hallway. Woolf once explained that she loved Cornwall because it was inextricably mixed up with her own earliest development: 'I like myself, before the age of 10, that is—before consciousness sets in' (Nicolson 1975, Vol. 2: 462). Talland was pre-conscious, paradisal unity with mother; it was the place where consciousness in the sense of awareness of delight began; it was also, however, the place where 'self-consciousness' in the sense of shyness, self-criticism and guilt began. Woolf associates this moment with standing on tiptoe to stare at her six-year-old face in the hallway mirror. She explains this 'mirror-phase' in her development in interesting ways: she had inherited a puritanical sense of unworthiness from her family; she and her sister Vanessa were happy tomboys, so taking an interest in one's looks was a betrayal of the tomboy code. These are partial clues; more revealing is the dream in which Woolf saw the face of an animal looking over her shoulder into this mirror. Perhaps this creature was her own awakening desire made to seem shameful by the 'animal' behaviour of her half-brothers, who according to Woolf and her biographers, sexually abused her. (For a careful account of this subject, see Lee 1996: 125–27, 153–59). This brings us back to the slab outside the dining room: like a dish of food to be consumed, it was here that Woolf remembered being placed by her half-brother Gerald, so that he could fondle her. Woolf preferred moments of being to non-being, moments of passion and insight to the living death of routine. Talland House was a place of what she called 'violent moments of being', a place of both pre-conscious bliss and conscious pain.

In the light of Virginia Woolf's own account, it may seem naive of her husband to think that a visit to Cornwall was the best hope of curing her last mental illness: after all she was visiting the site of her paradise *and* her Fall. How could paradise be regained? Like her parents, Woolf lived in a godless world: there was no providence to make a Fortunate Fall for her. There was, however, her love of her mother and her love of her art. The word that Woolf privileged in her description of her mother was 'central'; her mother 'was the whole thing; Talland House was full of her'. If she could only get past the troubling mirror in the hallway, the paradisal nursery awaited. The centrality and wholeness that she associated with her mother was linked to the wholeness of her vision of the flower: art could re-create what life had stolen from her. Indeed, art as well as memory played a part in the re-creation of St Ives. Woolf began her 'Sketch of the Past' admitting that her first memory was of a train journey with her mother returning *from* St Ives to London. She then asserts 'it is more convenient artistically to suppose that we were going to St Ives' (Schulkind 1978: 74, 92, 96). This evidence of invention does not mean that her desire to travel west was fictional: even when life forced her to travel east, her desire returned to Cornwall. Life alone would not permit her to return to Eden; life assisted by art enabled her to glimpse the garden of delights without being trapped by the horror in the hallway.

## From Life into Art

The pervasive nature of Woolf's Cornish memories is clearly evident in her private letters and memoirs but less overt in her fiction. She certainly intended that the novel *To The Lighthouse* would explore her Cornish childhood geography: 'to have father's character done complete in it; & mother's; & St Ives; & childhood . . .' (Anne Bell 1977, Vol. 3: 18). In practice, she set the published version of the novel near Scotland, attempting to develop the *peninsular* qualities of Cornwall and St Ives into the *insular* character of Skye and the Hebrides. The surface details of her setting are not convincing. The nearest city to the Hebridean holiday home is apparently not Glasgow but Edinburgh! Further confusion in her mind may be suggested by a letter in which she imagines her lighthouse in the Shetlands. When a reader wrote criticizing her local colour, Woolf confessed: 'I don't defend my accuracy . . . Lord Olivier writes that my horticulture and natural history is in every instance wrong: there are no rooks, elms and dahlias in the Hebrides.' Given that an accurate sense of place was a Stephen family inheritance, it initially seems odd that Virginia Woolf so inadequately disguises Cornwall as Scotland.

The exploration of her childhood helps us to understand this: Cornwall was a powerful place that inspired both joy and pain, a sense of hope and a sense of shame. She felt the urge to both reveal and conceal this territory. 'Secretly, all the romance of my heart is stirred by Cornwall', she wrote in 1928, revealing a secret to a fellow writer that she would not want others to know (Nicolson 1977, Vol. 3: 379, 517). To assimilate such a place satisfactorily in a work of art, it was necessary to disguise it from herself and her readers, distancing herself from her emotional involvement. Nevertheless, a sense of Cornwall or regions like it does emerge in the novel, just as Woolf's memories of St Ives constantly returned in her mind. Hugh Stoddart's 1985 television version of *To The Lighthouse* was justified in placing Woolf's novel back in the Cornwall where its real roots lie. Despite the surface anomalies, at a more profound level, the novel does express an intense sense of place, or rather of a type of place. For those familiar with Woolf's autobiographical writings, it is easy to recognize fictional, thinly disguised Scottish versions of the Stephen family, their guests and the local St Ives people who make a living from the sea or from servicing Talland House. For those familiar with Talland and its former occupants, it is easy to recognize allusions to the lawn, the cricket playing and tennis, the Jackmanna and passionflowers, the sound of the sea, the artistic activity of Virginia Woolf's sister Vanessa and the view of Godrevy lighthouse. For those who know neither the biography nor the place, the setting is still effective as a quintessence of many holiday homes by the sea.

As a fiction writer, Woolf did not intend to write works that could be conventionally regarded as regional or local. While visiting Cornish bookshops with Leonard in 1930, hoping to sell the works of the Hogarth Press, she remarked in her Bloomsbury manner on the Cornish novels of Crosbie Garstin: 'What is odd is that in Cornwall they live entirely by selling Cornish novels; one small shop yesterday had sold 2,000 by an unknown (to me) called Garstin' (Nicolson 1977, Vol. 4: 165). Criticized by Arnold Bennett for producing unbelievable characters in *Jacob's Room* (a novel partly set in Cornwall), Woolf responded by classing Bennett's regional writings with those 'materialists' who in their efforts to collect and compile details of external reality, missed the point of the novelist's true task:

to capture in words the sense of being alive and conscious. Woolf's fictional Cornwall is as much about the observer as the landscape observed. The thin Hebridean local colour is a sign of her attempt to escape from a place that meant too much for her to control, into a symbolic place that could be part of a new kind of novel. To create a design for her experimental work, to escape from the convention of a story into a voyage on the stream of consciousness, Woolf needed to be impersonal about the personal, to take the emotional territory of her childhood and transmute it into art. The signs of her striving for impersonality are evident. During the period of her novel's completion she noted: 'I am only an eye—yes, I observe the sea incessantly . . .'. She commented on her own writing: 'I am making more use of symbolism, I observe; & I go in dread of "sentimentality"' (Nicolson 1975, Vol. 3: 309; Anne Bell 1977, Vol. 3: 110).

Woolf's new approach can be appreciated in contrast to that of her father. Like his contemporaries, Leslie Stephen saw the prospects and wildlife of the South-Western coasts through spectacles provided by Charles Kingsley's novel *Westward Ho!* and his prose idyll entitled 'North Devon'. Leslie saluted Kingsley's achievement: 'he has done for Devon and Cornwall . . . what Scott did for the highlands' (Stephen 1909: 54). Kingsley's sense of the seabound peninsula and its maritime history emerges in Leslie's description of a West Country view of the ocean:

> The sea is always alive and at work. The hovering gulls and plunging gannets and the rollicking porpoises are animating symbols of a gallant struggle with wind and wave. Even the unassociative mind has a vague sense of the Armada and Hakluyt's heroes in the background . . . The very sight of a fishing boat, as painters seem to have found out, is a poem in itself. But is it not all written in *Westward Ho!* and in the *Prose Idylls*, in which Kingsley put his most genuine power? (Stephen 1902: 274–5)

Contrast this with Woolf's complex version of the West in *To The Lighthouse*. Where her father found a 'ripping yarn' and symbols of manly heroism, Woolf defied the conventions of story-line and made a symbolic lighthouse that combines many elements, including the male and the female. Where her father praised images of fishing boats such as the Newlyn School provided, Woolf saw the world in the light of Cezanne and the Post-Impressionists. The very structure of the sentence that suited her father was transformed by Woolf to serve her purposes as a woman writer.

## Godrevy Light

Virginia Woolf joined a long tradition of commentary on Godrevy Lighthouse, the gleaming white pinnacle perched on a tiny island that marks the horizon of St Ives bay. Godrevy Light was built in 1859: a Victorian response to ships wrecked on the lethal rocks off St Ives known as 'The Stones'. Keepers manned the light from the time of Woolf's childhood to the period when she wrote her novel in 1925 and revised it at Talland House in 1926. The intensity of the beam from Godrevy Light on a dark night was a memorable sight. Francis Kilvert in 1870 referred to the 'brilliant flash of the revolving light of Godrevy' (Kilvert Society 1978: 24). In 1934, Godrevy became unmanned and its bold, flashing beam was replaced by a light less vivid to observers on shore. Leonard Woolf describes how the original beam lit Virginia's nursery and had no doubt that it inspired her famous novel: 'the lighthouse in the book is the Godrevy light which she saw night by night shine across the bay into the windows of Talland House' (L. Woolf 1980, Vol. 2: 300). Godrevy was a place of danger and adventure before Woolf poeticized it. A group of tourists was marooned on the island of Godrevy in the 1840s due to bad weather and, in 1865, a man named Drury, curate of Gwythian Church, drowned amongst the rocks near the lighthouse. Francis Kilvert's diary suggests that Woolf's imaginative and experimental novel *To The Lighthouse* had a basis in many visitors' experience of St Ives: 'We meant to have gone across in a boat to Godrevy to see the lighthouse, but the sea was too rough for a boat to put out or to land at the rocks' (Kilvert Society 1978: 35). For Kilvert, Godrevy was a special place that provided a focal point for Cornwall as a romance:

> I seemed to see again the . . . white lighthouse, the spray on the rocks, the heaving bay, the sunny steeps, the cliffs, the seals, St. Ives, the bellbuoy . . . the rocks where poor Drury was lost . . . the distant view of Portreath, and the name kept on coming up, Godrevy, Godrevy. With a mournful cadence, Godrevy,

farewell. Unknown till yesterday. But now how dear, a possession for ever, a memory for ever. (Plomer 1961: 207–8)

Woolf's parents, Julia and Leslie, shared some of Kilvert's special
feelings for Cornish lighthouses. One of Julia's stories for her children
describes the brown sailed fishing boats of St Ives bay and a fishing
village with 'a long pier which ran out to sea' where one could view
'far off, rising straight out of the sea . . . a white lighthouse on whose
windows the sun was burning fiercely' (Gillespie 1987: 148). Leslie
Stephen, travelling home by ship from America in 1890, wrote to
his wife: 'I shall be glad to see the Godrevy lighthouse' (Spalding
1983: 11).

Virginia Woolf braved the waves and rocks to land on Godrevy
island in 1892, accompanied by a Mrs Hunt and other children.
Virginia's first brief account of the visit was written when she was
ten years old. Her cameo of the event begins as a romance, turns into
horror and ends as farce: 'On arriving at the light-house Miss
Virginia Stephen saw a small dilapidated bird standing on one leg on
the light-house. Mrs Hunt called the man and asked him how it had
got there. He said that it had been blown there and they then saw
that its eyes had been picked out. On the way home Master Basil
Smith "spued like fury" ' (Braybrooke 1991). The adult Virginia
developed the idea of a lighthouse viewed from changing perspectives
in her novel. Her 1905 short story, 'A Walk by Night', evokes both
the menace and romance associated with a lighthouse: 'Now and
again a far lighthouse flashed its golden pathway through the mist
and suddenly recalled the harsh shapes of the rocks' (Macneillie 1986,
Vol. 1: 80). When she departed from St Ives in 1905, the lighthouse
was a way of marking the difference between the West Country and
the City: 'The lights of London will be round me at this time of
evening tomorrow, as the lighthouse gleams now' (Leaska 1990:
285). In 1939, writing a 'Sketch of the Past', she could see the
lighthouse and its surrounding rocks clearly in her mind's eye.
Perhaps paintings of Godrevy helped her memory. Godrevy Light
earned the attention of painters before and during the writing of *To
The Lighthouse*. The Light was mainly painted by artists with local
connections and knowledge of the South West: William Gibbons in
1871, John Mogford in 1882, Garstin Cox in 1920 and R. Borlase
Smart in 1925 (Thomas 1978).

Woolf's lighthouse derives from and adds to a tradition centred on a solid object that belongs in a certain place, that is an expected part of certain coastal views. Woolf accepted that her novel's organizing symbol was rooted in reality. She apparently researched the details of her lighthouse in a literal-minded way. When The Seafarers Educational Society purchased two copies of her novel, Virginia was both amused and impressed. She wrote only half-jokingly to Vita Sackville-West: 'It's an awful thought that the merchant service will be taught navigation by me: or the proper use of foghorns and cylinders. It a compliment never paid to you poets.' Virginia added that she deserved her compliment because of the trouble she had taken to construct her version of the lighthouse. (Nicolson 1977, Vol. 3: 388). Mrs Ramsay's concern for the lighthouse keeper and his boy, the fact that the lighthouse can only be visited in certain weather conditions, the detailed descriptions of the light and its island can all be traced to the distinctive location of Godrevy. In this respect, Woolf was continuing the tradition of her father and other Victorian lovers of topography.

A lighthouse invites symbolic interpretations: it suggests images of humanity's struggle with Nature and a commitment to those in danger. A light kept burning in the night by a solitary keeper in order to save sailors from shipwreck requires more than prosaic description. Woolf's novel develops this symbolic function. While this symbolism relates to nineteenth-century notions of heroism, it also, within Woolf's novel, becomes a part of structural design. The mark that shapes vision in St Ives Bay becomes in fiction the mark around which Woolf organizes a mainly plotless work exploring the mazes, nooks and crannies of human consciousness.

The novel draws attention to the three strokes of the lighthouse beam, two short and one long. The three sections of the book replicate this beam: the middle section being a long ten years when the holiday home is abandoned; the first and last sections being about short but intense periods of human activity. The completed image of the lighthouse in the novel unites qualities conventionally considered male and female: the lighthouse is soft and romantic from a distance, hard and phallic when reached. It is a sign of a disagreement between mother, father and child in the opening section, and of a degree of unity between them at the end. Mr Ramsay's heroic and manly enterprise to reach the island is combined with Mrs Ramsay's wish to bring practical help for the keeper's boy. In 1930, Vanessa Bell created a tile design for Virginia's room at Rodmell, which is faithful to the nature of the lighthouse in the novel. The design is an oval seascape: on the left of the image is a sailing boat, with a triangular brown sail; on the right is a rocky headland; in the middle, balancing these two masses, is a an island with a lighthouse emitting a white beam down the centre of the picture. The boat represents the man and his children; the far-reaching beam that balances and unifies the overall design is the sign for Mrs Ramsay. The brown sail links the design to St Ives Bay but the composition of the image is true to the artistry of Woolf's novel.

## Making Scenes

In her biography of Roger Fry, Virginia Woolf quotes his opinion that Post-Impressionist artists do not seek to provide 'a pale reflex' of an 'actual appearance' that defies imitation; rather, they create the conviction of 'a new and definite reality'. Fry's artists do not imitate form but invent it. They make images which appeal to our imagination because they possess 'logical structure' and 'closely-knit unity of texture'. Paradoxically, they create the vividness of life by being unlike life (Bullen 1981: 167). Cézanne was a major figure in Fry's Post-Impressionist exhibitions and it is this artist that came to Woolf's mind when she considered how to portray her mother (Schulkind 1978: 99). Although it originates in real places and people, *To The Lighthouse* is much more than a long description of Talland House and Julia Stephen; it is an attempt, in Fry's terms, to provide an equivalent to life in fiction. Woolf was uncertain as to the best way to describe her work. It seemed too 'novel' to be a novel. Leonard Woolf described it as a 'psychological poem' (1979: 106). Some readers find that it leaves an impression in the mind that is less like a developing narrative than a picture that can be viewed in one gaze.

   Woolf wrote that it was impossible to escape from the power of her mother's central presence in life (Schulkind 1978: 96). There is moral perspective in the novel: Woolf both praises and questions Mrs Ramsay's ways. Nevertheless, Lily's final brushstroke is a tribute to Mrs Ramsay, and Mrs Ramsay is 'central' and pervasive in the book like a colour or a shape in the centre of a painting. This sense of centrality is conveyed in words evoking visual perception but more than gaze is involved. Lily strives impersonally for professional skill but what she wishes to represent in art is love. On Keats' famous

Grecian urn, the lovers are about to kiss but never kiss: they defy mortality but they cannot consummate their love. While reality is transient, art is permanent but unreal. In Woolf's book, astonishingly, Lily experiences both the artistic and emotional reality of her love for Mrs Ramsay, even after her death. Lily does not seek knowledge but unity and intimacy: she reaches this when she is close to Mrs Ramsay, either physically or through her art.

Woolf not only created a pictorial novel but within it evaluated the role of art. The novel is about people who 'make scenes'. Mr Ramsay, like Leslie Stephen, 'makes scenes' in an emotional, histrionic sense. Leslie Stephen compared himself to Carlyle, and connected his own behaviour to the Victorian notion that men of genius should be expected to become emotional under stress. Woolf seems to have felt that her father made a theatre of his own grief after the death of his wife, and forced the younger generation to play minor parts in a tragedy of which he was the suffering hero. Mr Ramsay is an interesting portrait, not only of the Victorian manly male, but of the emotional, male genius with attributes often stereotyped as female.

Mrs Ramsay, like Julia Stephen, makes scenes in a quieter but still powerful way. It is she who reconciles the apparently irreconcilable: she meets her children's conflicting demands; she brings people together at dinner parties or in marriage. Lily Briscoe makes scenes as an artist, reconciling the chaos of life within the order of art. She is a Post-Impressionist version of artists at St Ives who turn Cornwall and the sea into scenes on canvas. In the novel, all this scene-making is shown as transient, subject to chance and change. In the third and final part of the novel, Mr Ramsay the widower seems lost without a partner to share his scenes. Mrs Ramsay has died and her scenes of domestic bliss do not conclude as she intended: Lily remains celibate, and Paul and Minta's marriage, encouraged by Mrs Ramsay, ends unhappily. Lily fears that her picture will be ignored and left in attics: meaningless art because it has no audience. Nevertheless, there are moments when some scenes escape destruction. By the conclusion of the novel, Mrs Ramsay's plan to take James to the lighthouse and assist the lighthouse-keeper's boy is fulfilled under the leadership of Mr Ramsay, the person who had originally helped to thwart the plan. The male pays tribute to the woman's sensitivity and life of practical charity.

While Mrs and Mr Ramsay have created a scene in terms of action,

Lily commemorates it in art. She retrieves the picture she had abandoned ten years ago and which seemed doomed, like the Ramsay house and its human associations, to destruction. She completes it just as the remaining Ramsays reach the lighthouse. Her painting includes her visual sign for Mrs Ramsay, absent in life but present in her influence on the behaviour of others.

Mrs Ramsay is at the pivotal point of the novel, in the balance between art and life, life and death. It is her shawl that protects the frame of a picture in the house, and covers the animal skull which frightens the children. As ten years pass in the abandoned house, the shawl loosens from the skull: Mrs Ramsay's human love and protection lose the battle with death. Yet she returns, with Lily's artistic help, in the form of her family's actions and Lily's painting. The novel is critical of Mr Ramsay's bullying demands for pity, but it is also critical of Mrs Ramsay's 'do-gooding'. Lily has to resist not only the men telling her that women cannot paint but women like Mrs Ramsay who think that happiness can only be acquired in marriage. Nevertheless, it is Mrs Ramsay who inspires and enables the completion of Lily's vision on canvas. The novel reaches its climax with a moment that combines artistic discipline with human emotion, as Lily cries Mrs Ramsay's name. Woolf, influenced by the Hogarth Press' translations of Freud, considered her novel to be a writing cure equivalent to a 'talking cure'. The reconciliation between male and female, father, mother and children can be considered in this context. Part of Woolf's unfinished business with her parents was finished in the novel.

## The Dark Country

The visual qualities of this rich novel are complemented by its aural qualities, by melodic sentences that exceed conventional lengths and structures. Virginia Woolf's psychological poem grew from and outgrew her father's prose style. Like her father, Woolf loved Hakluyt and knew the allure of the Elizabethan West Country. However, her Elizabethan fiction, *Orlando*, has a protagonist who unexpectedly changes sex from male to female in the middle of the story. Woolf's famous writings defend the right of women to have a place of their own on the map and in history. In 1929 Woolf argued that the hitherto 'dark country' of women's experience was only being thoroughly explored in fiction for the first time. She not only questioned whether the content of literature was relevant to women but whether the very language in which it was written could express a woman's consciousness. The woman writer, thought Woolf, was like Hardy's Bathsheba who says 'I have the feelings of a woman but I have only the language of men'. (Bathsheba actually says: 'It is difficult for a woman to define her feelings in language which is chiefly made by men to express theirs' in Chapter 51, Hardy 1985: 412). Woolf theorized in relation to the woman writer 'the very form of the sentence does not fit her. It is a sentence made by men; it is too loose, too heavy, too pompous for a woman's use'. Woolf praised Dorothy Richardson for inventing a 'psychological sentence of the feminine gender', an 'elastic' form capable of 'stretching to the extreme, of suspending the frailest particles, of enveloping the vaguest shapes' (Barret 1979: 48, 50, 67).

*To The Lighthouse* is a 'psychological poem' that makes continuous use of the woman's sentence to evoke character in relation to place. The place in this case is very much a place by the sea. Woolf praised Hardy's Wessex and the Brontës' image of the Yorkshire Moors, arguing that the sense of place in such work not only consisted in 'the word-painter's gift' available in 'detachable descriptions' but in an 'element' that is 'rubbed deep into the texture and moulds every part' (Lyon 1986: 193). Such an 'element' pervades *To The Lighthouse* and is connected to an 'element' in the natural world: the sea. Woolf shared in her father's feeling for the lure of the sea. She once announced 'How any one, with an immortal soul can live inland, I can't imagine' (Nicolson 1975, Vol. 1: 418). 'The sea is to be heard all through it', she said of her experimental novel *To The Lighthouse*. Woolf prided herself on possessing a 'St Ives sea sense' (Anne Bell 1977, Vol. 3: 34, Vol. 5: 327). Her novel is attached covertly to St Ives and overtly to the sea. The novel records the external details of seaside living but the sounds and motion of the sea are most vividly present in the woman's sentence that pervades the novel. Open the novel at any page and you are likely to find examples of such sentences. Lily, for example, thinks in section nine of part 1:

> And, what was even more exciting, she felt, too, as she saw Mr
> Ramsay bearing down and retreating, and Mrs Ramsay sitting
> with James in the window and the cloud moving and the
> tree bending, how life, from being made up of little separate
> incidents which one lived one by one, became curled and whole

like a wave which bore one up with it and threw one down with
it, there, with a dash on the beach. (Woolf 1973: 55)

The Leslie Stephen figure, here and elsewhere in the novel, embodies Victorian, manly values; he quotes poetry about the Crimean
War and charges straight up and down. Lily's mind, by contrast, is
expressed in a sentence that is sea-like in many ways: it encompasses
and combines diverse things in a single motion; it moves rhyth-
mically around and about; it builds gradually in momentum and
ends in a climactic splash. Woolf also uses this myriad-eyed, maze-
like sentence to look simultaneously into several minds. Consider the
closing section of 'Time Passes', invoking not only the sea and the
lighthouse but the way they are perceived by two minds at one
moment in time:

> Gently the waves would break (Lily heard them in her sleep);
> tenderly the light fell (it seemed to come through her eyelids).
> And it all looked, Mr Carmichael thought, shutting his book,
> falling asleep, much as it used to look years ago. (Woolf 1973:
> 162)

The entire narrative, rather than proceeding like an arrow to its
target, moves gently but powerfully like a tide back and forth over
the same issues and feelings. It was a method that Woolf was to
develop even more powerfully in *The Waves*.

In 1936, Leonard Woolf attempted to take Virginia out of the
fallen world of her mental depression back to the paradise of
the West. As he watched her staring into the dark windows
of Talland House, he speculated that she saw a double of herself
which mocked what she had experienced as a child (L. Woolf
1980, Vol. 2: 300–1). The West Country and Talland House could
not, to use Leornard's word, 'cure' her, because of the serpents in its
paradise. While *To The Lighthouse* suggests that she was capable of
working through some of her many childhood traumas, as the
ominous notes in Leonard's description suggest, she could not sustain
her flight from the darker side of her life. During the final bout of
madness before her suicide, Woolf thought her mother was in the
room and began talking to her. It is tempting to speculate that in
one corner of her mind, paradisal unity with her parent was still
possible. Then it could be argued that in art and hallucination she

*11) St Ives.*
The roof-tops of St Ives looking towards Godrevy Lighthouse
on the horizon.

recovered her happy past, although in life her happiness could not be
sustained.

Many of those interested in Woolf's life cannot read *To The
Lighthouse* without imagining its Cornish origins; they cannot visit St
Ives without viewing it through Woolf's spectacles. Unwittingly,
Woolf contributes to the process by which the modern West Country
is known. Despite her efforts to disguise her powerful feelings about
Cornwall, her fiction has been put in its place by the tourist trade,
scholarship, biography and the televised version of her novel.

How should Woolf's work be placed within the argument of this
book? Virginia Woolf's territory by the sea differs in interesting ways
from all the other writers' territories explored here. Woolf inherited
a knowledge of the tradition of regional writing from her father,
the admirer of Kingsley and Hardy. From her father she acquired the
habit of paying attention to the land and its people; like him,
she knew the territory underfoot as only a walker can know it.
Consult her letters, journal and autobiographical writing for evidence

that she had the interests and abilities required by a conventional topographical writer. Woolf planned a major work on the 'nature and characteristics' of Cornwall but never carried out her intention (Nicolson 1975, Vol. 1: 206). Instead, she wrote a Modernist novel that, in Fry's terms, re-creates rather than imitates the world. Developing away from her father's tradition, she might have ended in the territory of abstraction and art that Wendell Berry distrusts. It is limiting to consider her only as a 'mind'; this chapter shows her to be a writer whose fiction takes the reader to a more than intellectual place. Her novel is a world of thoughts but it is also a world where senses and feelings interact with a particular location. It would caricature the evidence of this book to argue that the male writers invade and conquer their territories, while Virginia Woolf more tenderly touches her world. It *is* cogent to argue that her unique, sea-like sentences, caressing her place into life for readers, open up possibilities for those like Lopez, who want to maintain a sensitive equilibrium between the territory within and the territory without. Woolf's work suggests subtle ways of relating words to the world. Her novels enable us to rethink the Victorian exploration of people and places so as to allow full scope for the inventive powers of the mind. This discovery and celebration of the inner self does not have to result in a severance between region and observer. The travel writing of D.H. Lawrence and the place-conscious fiction of Jean Rhys also suggest that it is possible to use Woolf's methods without cutting the connection between people and place.

# 8

# The Lie of the Land or
# the Land as a Lie?

*I cannot say how shocked I am to see*
*The variations in our scenery . . .*
*But as for Dorset's flint and Purbeck stone,*
*It's old thatched farms in dips of downs alone—*
*It should be merged with Hants and made to be*
*A self-contained and plann'd community.*
*Like Flint and Rutland it is much too small*
*And has no reason to exist at all.*
*Of Devon one can hardly say the same*
*But 'South West Area One' 's a better name*
*For those red sandstone cliffs that stain the sea*
*By mid-Victoria's Italy—Torquay.*
*And 'South West Area Two' could well include*
*The whole of Cornwall from Land's End to Bude*

John Betjeman, 'The Town Clerk's Views' 1948

*when they proscribe the diverse uses and impose the rootless uniformities pray for us*

David Jones, 'The Tutelar of the Place' 1974

The death of regional identity and regional writing in Britain has
often been announced. In the mid- to late nineteenth century, Hardy
and Baring-Gould thought that they were describing a vanishing
rural way of life, a regional identity that they had to preserve in texts
because it would not survive in any other form. John Betjeman
lamented the passing of regional character in the 1940s and 1950s.

In 1967, Daphne du Maurier praised her chosen literary territory in a book entitled '*Vanishing* Cornwall' [my italics]. The umbilical connection once noted by Baring-Gould between local building materials and houses, local costumes and trades, is no longer a feature of our world. Has an umbilical connection between writers and places also been broken? Stella Gibbons satirized the weaknesses of regional writing in *Cold Comfort Farm* so effectively that it became difficult for writers to rescue the tradition. One critic's work suggests that this text of 1932 is a sign of the end of a tradition (Keith 1988: 173–5). From the perspective of 1941, Phyllis Bentley presents the English tradition of regional fiction originating with the Brontës in the 1840s, peaking in the novels and stories of Hardy (from 1872 to 1913) and of Bennett (the *Clayhanger* trilogy was published between 1910 and 1916), and declining finally in the 1940s, when wartime evacuation and national patriotism combined to suppress regional identity.

Bentley predicted the death of literary regionalism when she considered the impact of the 'motor-bus' and radio communication. Today we have much more pervasive forms of transport, communication and technology to consider. It might be argued: never has there been less regional difference and never has there existed more technology to create it synthetically on the radio or television screen. When a film-maker can 'borrow' a house from one part of the country and a landscape from another, combining them together in a way that deceives the eye, who needs an existing regional identity to create a romantically different place? The power of computer graphics is substituted for the power of place, although this technology is then used to invent *ideas* of distinctive locations and their particular histories. Instead of seeing the lie of the land, we see the land as a lie. As geographical regions are erased or transformed by relentless urbanization, they are invented again in images constructed for urban entertainment. The radio which Bentley saw as the enemy of regionalism now preserves the idea of rural ways in 'The Archers'; popular television series such as 'Emmerdale Farm' perform a similar role in the world of visual messages.

Regionalism is like a person pronounced dead who refuses to lie down. Consider the dates in the title of a recently published work: *The Regional Novel in Britain and Ireland 1800–1990* (Snell 1998). The concept of a region in political and literary terms remains useful: poised between individual spot on the map and capital city, between centre and periphery, it enables us to hold in the mind both the local and the wider world. Regional assemblies offer the possibility of bringing decision-making closer to the people affected by the decisions. 'Small is beautiful': the region is small enough to be on the human scale, to enable us to see people and places in their particular contexts. The telescope held at the centre is replaced by the magnifying glass at regional level. The idea of a region also enables us to preserve respect for the shape of the land and a sensitivity to the debatable boundaries formed by topography, history and linguistic inheritance. Underneath the screen of a 'virtual reality' is the territory underfoot, often ignored, often mistreated because it is ignored. D.H. Lawrence declared in 1921 that the 'mechanical age' tries but fails to overcome 'the spirit of the place'. Lawrence predicted that this spirit 'will smash our mechanical oneness into smithereens, and all that we think the real thing will go off with a pop, and we will be left staring' (1985: 55). E.M. Forster also asks us to consider what happens when 'The Machine Stops', when we leave the synthetic 'muzak' of the shopping mall to encounter the music of the wind on the heath.

In a computerized rather than a mechanical age, is it possible to share these writers' visions? Their ideas originate in a reality that Seamus Heaney still finds convincing: 'when we look for the history of our sensibilities I am convinced . . . that it is to . . . the stable element, the land itself, that we must look for continuity' (Heaney 1985: 149). Regions change, regions die, regions are invented in artificial ways, but the fundamental source for the idea of a region remains: the land is the 'stable element' connecting the differing work of the many writers interpreting it, the many people living and working within it. A modern novelist, speaking for a modern multi-cultural Britain where exiles have 'imaginary homelands', argues that people are now rooted in ideas rather than places (Rushdie 1991: 124). Taking his argument a step further, we can say that there are no longer communities defined by places, but communities defined by interests. They can share their thoughts on an internet that is nowhere and everywhere. But this international conversation without walls includes, as one of the ideas in which we can root ourselves, recognition of the importance of understanding and caring for places. These places and their communities exist outside the computer screen although they can demand recognition in the form of websites.

In this context, the regional writers of the past still have a message for the present. The land outside the computer screen is like a text that we can forget how to read. Regional writers prevent this form of illiteracy and forgetfulness. They are valuable as archivists of lost traditions, as decoders of pre-existing 'placewrit' (to use Barnes' word). They also instil life into 'old ground'. A particular type of invention is a feature in the work of Hawker, Kingsley, Blackmore, Hardy and Baring-Gould. Their fictions have become part of the reality represented on the map, the signpost and the website. King Arthur lives at Tintagel, 'Westward Ho!' ceases to be a novel title and becomes a coastal resort, Jan Ridd's home is a local farm house, Casterbridge effectively subsumes Dorchester, mainly or partly because of the power of the word to remake the world, to intervene in geography and history. The literary West Country inventories facts and events but it also invents a region: it is proof of humanity making itself at home in an environment. It is Nature connected to Nurture; Nature nurtured to satisfy the human need for story-telling rooted in past and place. However, these writers' inventions become accepted as realities because they suit the soil in which they were planted; they were created with a pre-existing reality in mind. Such writers do not use the trickery of technology to create their worlds but the human imagination interacting with the land.

The writers in this book take you to a varied terrain which they respect: they are careful to preserve the topographical personalities of their locations. These writers also show how it is possible to resist the pressure of a dominant discourse about the rural, regional, provincial and peripheral. They do so by deriving strength from the territory and people about them. When their gaze is clearly on their territory, when they are attentive to their world, the particulars in their minds enable them avoid or re-interpret the language of the centre. Using dialect, place-names and knowledge of local lore, they escape from generalization, aloofness and distance into detail, intimacy and immediacy. They write 'from' rather than merely 'about' their places. This study shows that peripheral West Country fiction owes some of its origins to the needs of the centre. The connections between Hawker's Arthur and the national debate on the definition of a gentleman, between Kingsley's *Westward Ho!* and the Crimean War, Blackmore's *Lorna Doone* and a royal romance: all this suggests that the Victorian, literary West Country was defined within national pressures. This study also shows, however, that these West Country fictions cannot be dismissed as the servants of national and imperial ideology or the products of internal colonialism. Hawker, Blackmore, Baring-Gould, Hardy and Woolf, in a variety of differing ways, defy centralizing uniformity by gaining the wisdom of the 'Tutelar of the Place.'

Can the Tutelar still tell us who we are? The inhabitants of modern Britain source their identity in many ways. Some seek it in region and some in nation, some in the 'Rule Britannia' of the past and some in the 'Cool Britannia' of today, some as subjects of the Crown and some as citizens of Europe and the world. The prospect of maintaining a multiple identity may seem liberating; alternatively, the very multiplicity of choice can create confusion and self-doubt. Amongst this choice of identities, the land itself provides continuity. Seamus Heaney picks up Carson McCullers' idea that in order to know who are, you need a place to come from. Heaney sees the poets Ted Hughes, Philip Larkin and Geoffrey Hill creating regions in their poetry defensively because their identity and culture is under threat (Heaney 1985: 135, 150–51). As Yeats and his colleagues created Celtic places to counter British domination, Hughes, Larkin and Hill create regions to counter the forces of globalization. Britain's previous imperial role has ended but a new one has not been successfully found. In this vacuum, these poets' territory becomes 'precious' (Heaney's word) to them as a valid source for a new identity with old roots. Their defensive reaction, their revaluing of the land, need not lead to the territory of prejudice. There is a dangerous point in the argument for regional identity where it can slide into an argument for racism or be related to nationalism of the negative kind. If 'our' place is special, if it has borders, then there are some who must be kept out. Most of the fiction discussed here enables inclusion not exclusion. Regional fiction at its best, as this book attempts to show, is the means by which anyone willing to pay attention to the world can become a 'native'. It is the passport to a place, not the means of fencing it in. In the terms of the epigraph to Chapter 1 of this book, an international audience can *see* a place because it has been effectively *described* or made accessible by regional writers. Through the tricks of the writer's trade, through empathizing with character and entering narrative, the reader (local or not) can make a region of the land become 'solid' in the mind.

The lie of the land, the land and the people within it, needs to be freed from associations with notions of racial superiority or a militant nationalism. Once freed from this it is a source of identity open to all who are willing to pay attention (in Wendell Berry's terms) to their world. There is an element of controlled forgery in such an identity. You are making yourself and making yourself at home in a landscape. Regional writers show how it is possible to do this, wherever your point of origin. They show also, however, that this forging of an identity and home needs to take account of pre-existing tradition and topographical personality. To do it successfully, you need an inclusive gaze, including respect for history and fiction. Stories should suit their locations, as when Jane Austen created the 'exact spot' where Louisa Musgrove fell. It is also necessary to be interested, unlike Tennyson and like Blackmore or Hardy, in the 'exact spot', where the Duke of Monmouth landed and fought a battle in 1685.

This is not just a spot in time but a territory that is still present. Charles Kingsley passed his custodianship of a spot on the earth to us in the following way. Reputedly a manly and muscular Christian, Kingsley sometimes looked tenderly at locality and Mother Earth. When he returned after forty years to the landscape of his childhood to address the Devonshire Association, his words were full of local reference, and the attraction of a place that defied shallow ideas of progress:

> I find still unabolished the Torridge and the Hubbastone, and Tapeley, and Instow, and the Bar, and the Burrows, and the beloved old Braunton Marshes and Sandhills, and doubt not that the raised beach under Saunton is as safe as it has been any time this 20,000 years, and that not an ounce of rock has been worn off the Morte stone since I first steamed past it as a boy. We abolish many things, good and evil, wisely and foolishly in these fast going times; but, happily for us, we cannot abolish the blue sky, and the green sea, and the white foam, and the everlasting hills, and the rivers which flow out of their bosoms.

Then Kingsley turns away from his rural and regional Eden towards the uncertain future. Love for his own locality helps him to focus on an issue of relevance to all localities:

> And we, who, with all our boasted scientific mastery over nature, are, from a mechanical and carnal point of view, no more than a race of minute parasitic animals burrowing in the fair Earth's skin, had better, instead of boasting of our empire over

Nature, take care lest we do not become parasites too trouble-some to Nature, by creating in our haste and greed, too many great black countries . . . in which case Nature, so far from allowing us to abolish her, will by her inexorable laws abolish us. (Kingsley 1871: 377–8)

Kingsley's fear of industrialization and faith in the permanence of a God-given Nature mark him as a religious Victorian. But he combines his local pride with humility towards the natural environment, anticipating twentieth-century concerns. The empire-builder who dedicated *Westward Ho!* to Rajah Brooke is not an Imperialist in his attitude to locality and the natural world, he does not boast of 'our empire over Nature'. He reaches towards an understanding that indifference to place is a step on the road to the pollution of place and that as humanity poisons its environment it poisons itself. The literature of the West Country, like literature rooted in other places and regions, can play a part in restoring our human connection to a world that needs imagination as well as science if it is to survive.

# Further Reading: Other Journeys

This book is part of a long conversation between literary critics, creative writers, historians, sociologists, philosophers and geographers about the nature of place and region. Readers who wish to join this conversation may find some of the signposts in this short section useful. In the following account, brief bibliographical details are given of books included within the following list of works cited; more bibliographical details are provided for books not included in this list.

Begin at the beginning by looking at works of reference that contain some famous and lesser known examples of the links between writers and regions, people and places. Daiches' and Flower's *Literary Landscapes* or *Narrative Atlas* (1979) gives you a long list of territories, urban and rural, to explore. Other similar sources are *The Oxford Literary Guide to the British Isles*, edited by Dorothy Eagle and Hilary Carnell (Oxford, Oxford University Press, 1977), and Ian Ousby's *Blue Guide to Literary Britain and Ireland* (London, A.C. Black, 1990). These introductory reference works understandably do not attempt to address the many theoretical questions raised by their subject but they do benefit, in the context of the argument made in this publication, from paying attention to the shape of the land. So does Margaret Drabble's *A Writer's Britain: Landscape in Literature* (London, Thames and Hudson, 1979), which takes you through many kinds of territory, including 'Sacred Places'.

Works attempting to define the origins and nature of the regional novel are of interest to both literary critics and historians. Phyllis Bentley's study, *The English Regional Novel* (1941), remains the best short introduction to its subject and deserves to be reprinted. Still valuable is Lucien Leclaire's comprehensive *General Analytical Bibliography of the Regional Novelists of the British Isles 1800–1950* (Paris, 1954). Fascinating materials and compelling arguments are found in W.J. Keith's *The Rural Tradition: A Study of the Non-Fiction Prose Writers of the English Countryside* (University of Toronto Press, 1974) and *Regions of Imagination* (1988). The former study includes a careful introduction to Henry Williamson's work in North Devon; the latter study ends with an epitaph for the regional novel, making the dates in the title of K.D.M. Snell's recent work interesting: *The Regional Novel in*

*Britain and Ireland 1800–1990* (1998). Snell introduces and edits a collection of essays which provide both practical information and a recognition of the need for an inter-disciplinary approach. Use the references listed in Snell and Keith as a guide to those humanistic or cultural geographers who have recognized the literary contribution to the sense of region and place. Also consult *Humanistic Geography and Literature: Essays on the Experience of Place* (London, Croom Helm, 1981), edited by Douglas Pocock. Philip Crang is a contemporary geographer who explores some interesting ways of conceptualizing a region in 'Regional Imaginations', an essay in a collection edited by Ella Westland (*Cornwall: the Cultural Construction of Place*, Penzance, The Patten Press and Institute of Cornish Studies, University of Exeter, 1997). For a diverse choice of individual theoretical approaches, read Westland and Snell's collections in combination with the essays edited by Ronald Draper (*The Literature of Region and Nation*, New York, St Martin's Press, 1989).

The relationship between time and place has been interestingly debated. The theorist Mikhail Bakhtin has proposed the word 'chronotope' to indicate recognition that *topos* cannot be considered without *chronos*, that place cannot be considered outside of time. Consult Vernon McGee's *M.M. Bakhtin: Speech Genres and Other Essays* (Austin, University of Texas Press, 1987: 42, 46–54). A modern critic has inverted this term: regionalism should be considered 'topochronically', a word which puts space and place first although it then recognizes the inescapable influence of time and history. Consult David Jordan's *Regionalism Reconsidered: New Approaches to the Field* (London, Garland Publishing, 1994: 22). Also consult the other essays in this useful collection for issues around regionalism, bioregionalism and travel writing.

On the complex debate about the relationship between places outside and inside the mind, consult Simon Schama, *Landscape and Memory* (London, Harper/Collins, 1995). Readers who want to theorize the relationship between landscape and class can turn to Widdowson's account of Wessex and Wiener's account of rural literature generally (see Bibliography). Raymond Williams' seminal *The Country and the City* (1985) is one of their inspirations. Supplement this with Williams' essay 'Region and Class in the Novel' in *Writing in Society*, London, Verso, n.d. (1983?). Williams combines cultural studies and literary criticism with sensitivity. Raphael Samuel rivals him as a cultural historian in the posthumously published collection of essays *Island Stories* (Vol. 2, 1996–98). The essays 'Unravelling Britain', 'Country Visiting' and 'North and South' refreshingly unite autobiographical reflection with a grasp of historical context. The question of national, racial and linguistic identity in relationship to regional identity is a complex area worth careful consideration. Samuel's essays can be read together with Declan Kibberd's substantial study, *Inventing Ireland*

(London, Verso, 1996) and Michael Wood's *In Search of England: Journeys into the English Past* (London, Viking, 1999). Also consult the essays edited by Tony Curtis: *Wales, the Imagined Nation: Essays in Cultural and National Identity* (Bridgend, Poetry Wales Press, 1986) and by Ian Bell: *Peripheral Visions: Images of Nationhood in Contemporary British Fiction* (Cardiff, University of Wales Press, 1995).

Seamus Heaney successfully juggles with many themes: poetry and place, ideas and land-shapes, regions of earth and regions of language, the territory underfoot as a source of symbols and as solid reality. Consult his inspiring essays: 'The Sense of Place', 'Englands of the Mind' (1985), 'The Placeless Heaven: Another Look at Kavanagh' (*The Government of the Tongue*, London, Faber, 1988) and 'Frontiers of Writing' (*The Redress of Poetry*, London, Faber, 1995). Jeremy Hooker's *Writers in a Landscape* (Cardiff, University of Wales Press, 1996) takes you on a journey from Richard Jefferies to Hardy and J.C. Powys before exploring Wiltshire as represented in V.S. Naipaul's *The Enigma of Arrival*. This novel also interests Salman Rushdie: see his essay 'V.S. Naipaul' in *Imaginary Homelands* (1991). In the same collection, the essay 'The Location of Brazil' discovers a kind of sense of place at the cinema. Hooker, Rushdie and Said (see his *Culture and Imperialism*, London,Vintage, 1994) may help you to see place and identity in a modern, multi-cultural context.

Another direction takes you to an exciting place where literary criticism and ecological thinking meet. Garry Snyder's bridges text and topography in *The Real Work* (New York, A New Directions Book, 1980) and *The Practice of the Wild* (New York, North Point Press, 1990). Barry Lopez's *Crossing Open Ground* (1988) is in this tradition and helps to inspire Wendell Berry's ingenious essay 'Writer and Region' (1987) which helped me to write this book. Richard Kerridge's collection, (*Writing the Environment: Ecocriticism and Literature*, London, Zed Books, 1987) continues the debate in several directions, combining poetry and philosophy (Heaney and Heidegger) in interesting ways.

Criticism of individual authors is also relevant. Very little has been published on Hawker and Baring-Gould. Their neglected work is recognized in short essays by Betjeman, Fowles and Causley (consult my text and Bibliography). I discuss Baring-Gould's little known novel *Court Royal* in 'Dickensian Influences on the Life and Work of Sabine Baring-Gould', *The Dickens Quarterly*, June, 1998, Vol. 15, No. 2: 123–32. Little has been published on Charles Kingsley as a fiction writer: Susan Chitty's short book (*Charles Kingsley's Landscape*, 1976) remains an excellent introduction informed by local knowledge. Philip Dodd uses Kingsley's work in his essay 'Gender and Cornwall' within Snell's collection. Blackmore is also relatively neglected but consult the relevant chapter by Keith in *Regions of Imagination* and Sally Shuttleworth's introduction to the OUP World's

Classics edition of *Lorna Doone* (Blackmore, 1994). M.K. Sutton's book (*R.D. Blackmore*, Boston, Twayne, 1979) remains relevant, especially on the relationship between place and myth in *Lorna Doone*. There is an enormous literature on Thomas Hardy, including much work on Hardy and Wessex: consult my text and Bibliography for some starting points. Kay-Robinson and Desmond Hawkins combine a detailed knowledge of topography and Hardy's texts. Gattrell and Widdowson provide different approaches, the former using textual scholarship and the latter employing theoretical perspective. Ralph Elliott's *Thomas Hardy's English* (New York, Blackwell, 1986) may be used to explore the relationship between language, dialect and region. Woolf has been the subject of much recent biographical interest but as far as I know, has not been considered in the context of her father's links with topographical writings (see my text). Develop my reading of *To The Lighthouse* by consulting the references to Woolf and Cézanne in Stephen Kern's *The Culture of Time and Space 1880–1918* (Cambridge Massachusetts, Harvard University Press, 1983). Also helpful is Diane Filby Gillespie's *The Sisters' Arts: The Writing and Painting of Virginia Woolf and Vanessa Bell* (New York, Syracuse University Press, 1988).

There are many creative writers omitted from this study who have contributed to the literary West Country as loosely defined here. The literary invention of Devon could include reference to Blackmore's lesser known novels as well as exploration of works by George Gissing and Eden Phillpotts. Representations of Dorset and Somerset appear frequently in the work of the extraordinary Powys family: in the novels of J.C. Powys and T.F. Powys, as well as the essays of Llewelyn Powys. Another study could include reference to Arthur Quiller-Couch (or 'Q') and representations of Cornwall in the work of fiction writers and poets such as Arthur Caddick, Daphne du Maurier, Winston Graham, John Betjeman, Charles Causley and Jack Clemo. The series of *Cornish Studies* published by the Institute of Cornish Studies and the University of Exeter Press helps to uncover some of this territory. The main practical problem for a reader who wants to focus on a region is that the more you examine it as a body of knowledge, the bigger it gets. This is also a reason for continuing to explore it.

# Bibliography

Anon. (1830) 'The Moors', *Blackwood's Edinburgh Magazine*, Vol. 28, October: 575–607.

Anon. (1852) Review of Wilkie Collins' *Rambles Beyond Railways*. *Household Words*, 13 March, Vol. 4, No. 103: 598.

Anon. (1855a) 'Clavering St. Mary, and a Talk About Devon Worthies', Fraser's Magazine, Vol. LII (November): 534–48.

Anon. (1855b) Review of *Westward Ho!*, *Fraser's Magazine*, Vol. 51, May: 506–17.

Anon. (1860) 'Inconveniences of Being a Cornishman', *All the Year Round*, Vol. 4, 1 December: 188–92.

Anon. (1863) 'The Doones of Exmoor', *The Leisure Hour*, Vol. 12, No. 610, 5 September: 561–64; No. 611, 12 September: 577–79; No. 612, 19 September: 593–95; No. 613, 26 September: 609–12; No. 614, 3 October: 625–28; No. 615, 10 October: 641–44; No. 616, 17 October: 65–59; No. 617, 24 October: 673–75.

Anon. [James Hannay?] (1865) 'Provincialism', *The Cornhill Magazine*, Vol. 11, May: 673–81.

Anon. (1869) Review of *Lorna Doone*, *The Athenaeum*, No. 2154, 17 April: 534–35.

Anon. (1870) Review of *Lorna Doone*, *The Saturday Review*, 5 November: 603–4.

Anon. [attributed to Mrs Oliphaunt], (1871) Review of *Lorna Doone* in 'New Books', *Blackwood's Edinburgh Magazine*, Vol. 109: 43–47.

Anon. (1872) *The Annual Register: A Review of Public Events at Home and Abroad for the Year 1871*. New Series.

Anon. (1877) 'Living Novelists No. 10', *London*, 29 September: 211–12.

Anon. (1889) 'Correspondence', *The Western Antiquary*, Vol. 8, No. 6–7: 130–1.

Anon. (1895a) 'The Rev. S. Baring-Gould at Home', *Sunday Magazine*, Vol. 24, September: 599–606.

Anon. (1895b) 'The Author of "Onward Christian Soldiers": The Rev. S. Baring-Gould at Home', *The Young Man: A Monthly Journal and Review*, Vol. 9, September: 289–94.

Anon. (1901) Review of Baring-Gould's *The Frobishers*, *The Athenaeum*, No. 3832, 6 April: 429.

Anon. (1965) Mystery Holly on 'Mad Vicar's' Grave, *The Independent* (local paper), 3 January: 8.

Arch, J. (1986) *From Ploughtail to Parliament: An Autobiography*, Cresset Library.

Archer, W. (1901) 'Real Conversations: Conversation 1—With Mr Thomas Hardy', *The Critic*, Vol. 38, April: 309–18.

Ashe, G. (1980) *A Guidebook to Arthurian Britain*, London, Longman.

Baring-Gould, S. (1888a) Preface to *Red Spider: A New Edition*, London, Chatto and Windus: v–vi.

Baring-Gould, S. (1892a) 'Cruel Coppinger', *The Western Antiquary*, Vol. 11, May-June: 154–57.

Baring-Gould, S. (1892b) 'Colour in Composition', *Atalanta*, Vol. 6, December: 239–42.

Baring-Gould, S. (1895a) Introduction to *A Garland of Country Song*, London, Methuen: v–xi.

Baring-Gould, S. (1895b) *English Minstrelsie: A National Monument of English Song*, ed. Sabine Baring-Gould, 8 vols, Edinburgh: T.C. & E.C. Jack.

Baring-Gould, S. (1895c) 'The Last of the Smugglers', *Cassell's Family Magazine*, 22 June: 483–88.

Baring-Gould, S. (1895d) Preface to *Songs and Ballads of the West*, London, Methuen: vii–xliii.

Baring-Gould, S. (1896) *Dartmoor Idylls*, London, Methuen.

Baring-Gould, S. (1897) *A Study of Saint Paul: His Character and Opinions*, London, Isbister.

Baring-Gould, S. (1899a edn) *The Vicar of Morwenstow*, London, Methuen.

Baring-Gould, S. (1899b) *Furze Bloom: Tales of the Western Moors*, London, Methuen.

Baring-Gould, S. (1899c) 'Sixpence Only', *The Graphic*, 13 May, 593–94; 20 May, 625–6.

Baring-Gould, S. (1900a) *Winefred: A Story of the Chalk Cliffs*, London, Methuen.

Baring-Gould, S. (1900b) *The Book of the West: Devon*, London, Methuen.

Baring-Gould, S. [1905] Introduction, *Songs of the West: Folk Songs of Devon and Cornwall Collected from the Mouths of the People*, new and revised edn, London, Methuen: v–xii.

Baring-Gould, S. (1924) *My Few Last Words*, London, Skeffington.

Baring-Gould, S. (1925a) *Early Reminiscences 1834–1864*, London, John Lane.

Baring-Gould, S. (1925b) *Further Reminiscences 1864–1894*, London, John Lane.

Baring-Gould, S. (1981 edn) *A Book of the West: Cornwall*, introduced by Charles Causley, London, Wildwood House.

Baring-Gould, S. (1982 edn) *A Book of Dartmoor*, London, Wildwood House.

Baring-Gould, S. (1993 edn) *A Book of Folklore*, West Sussex, Praxis Books.

Barnes, W. (1830) 'On the English Language', *Gentleman's Magazine*, 100, Part 2, November: 395.

Barnes, W. (1832) 'On Compounds in the English Language', *Gentleman's Magazine*, 102, Part 2, Supplement: 590–93.

Barnes, W. (1840) 'The Saxon Dialect of Dorsetshire', *Gentleman's Magazine*, 13, Part 1, January: 31–33.

Barnes, W. (1848) *Poems of Rural Life in the Dorset Dialect*, London, John Russell Smith.

Barnes, W. (1868) *Poems of Rural Life, In Common English*, London, Macmillan.

Barnes, W. (1886) Fore-notes to *A Glossary of the Dorset Dialect with a Grammar*, 1886, London, Trubner: 1–7.

Barrett, M. (ed.) (1979) *Virginia Woolf: Women and Writing*, London, The Women's Press.

Barrie, J.M. (1889) 'Thomas Hardy; The Historian of Wessex', *Contemporary Review*, Vol. 56, July: 57–66.

Barrie, J.M. (1890) 'Mr Baring-Gould's Novels', *Contemporary Review*, Vol. 57, February: 206–14.

Bell, A., (ed.) (1977) *Sir Leslie Stephen's Mausoleum Book*, Oxford, Clarendon Press.

Bell, Anne, (ed.) (1977–84) *The Diary of Virginia Woolf*, 5 vols, London, Hogarth Press.

Bentley, P. (1941) *The English Regional Novel*, London, PEN Books, Allen and Unwin.

Berry, W. (1987) 'Writer and Region', *Hudson Review*, Vol. XL, Spring: 15–30.

Betjeman, J. (1997) *Coming Home: An Anthology of his Prose 1920–1977*, selected and introduced by Candida Lycett Green, London, Methuen.

Billing, M. (1857) *Directory and Gazeteer of the County of Devon*, Birmingham, M. Billing's Steam Press.

Blackmore, R.D. (1855) 'Sicilian Hours', *Dublin University Magazine*, August: 201–7.

Blackmore, R.D. (1898) *Tales from the Telling House*, London, Sampson Low, Marston.

Blackmore, R.D. (1994 edn) *Lorna Doone: A Romance of Exmoor*, edited with an introduction by Sally Shuttleworth, Oxford, Oxford University Press.

Borlase, W. (1882) Introduction, *The Western Antiquary*, Vol. 1: 5–7.

Braddon, E. (1876) *John Haggard's Daughter*, 2 vols, London, Macmillan.

Bradshaw, D. (ed.) (1994) *The Hidden Huxley*, London, Faber.

Bray, J. [written *c.* 1860] (1975) *An Account of Wrecks on the North Coast of Cornwall 1759–1830*, ed. A.K. Hamilton Jenkin, Truro, The Institute of Cornish Studies.

Braybrooke, N. (ed.) (1991) *Seeds in the Wind*, Oxford, Oxford University Press.

Brendon, P. (1983 edn) *Hawker of Morwenstow: Portrait of a Victorian Eccentric*, London, Anthony Mott.

Broadley, A. (1911) *Napoleon in Caricature 1795–1821*, 2 vols, London, Bodley Head.

Buckle, G. (1926) *The Letters of Queen Victoria*, 2 vols, Second Series, London, John Murray.

Bullen, J. (ed.) (1981) *Roger Fry: Vision and Design*, Oxford, Oxford University Press.

Burrit, E. (1868) *A Walk from London to Land's End and Back*, London, Sampson Low and Marston.

Burrows, M. (1926) *Robert Stephen Hawker: A Study of his Thought and Poetry*, Oxford, Basil Blackwell.

Burt, W. (1826) Preface and Notes to *Dartmoor: A Descriptive Poem* by N.T. Carrington, London, Hatchard.

Byatt, A. and Warren, N. (eds) (1990) *George Eliot: Selected Essays, Poems and Other Writings*, Harmondsworth, Penguin.

Byles, C. (1906) *The Life and Letters of R.S. Hawker*, Bodley Head, New York.

Carlyle, T. (1898) *Latter-Day Pamphlets*, London, Chapman and Hall.

Carrington, H. (1826) Preface to *Dartmoor* by N.T. Carrington, 2nd edn, London, John Murray: xi–xxiii.

Carrington, N. (1826) *Dartmoor*, London, John Murray.

Chanter, C. (1856) *Ferny Combes: A Ramble after Ferns in the Glens and Valleys of Devonshire*, London, Lovell Reeve.

Chanter, C. (1860) *Over the Cliffs*, 2 vols, London, Smith, Elder.

Chanter, J.F. (1903) 'R.D. Blackmore and "Lorna Doone"', *Transactions of Devonshire Association*, 35: 239–50.

Chanter, J.F. (1907) *A History of the Parishes of Lynton and Countisbury*, Exeter, James G. Commin.

Chanter, J.R. (1884) 'Blackmore's Lorna Doone', Supplement to *The Western Antiquary*, 3rd Series, Part 11: 221–24.

Chitty, S. (1976) *Charles Kingsley's Landscape*, Newton Abbot, David and Charles.

Clark, A. (ed.) (1898) *Brief Lives: Chiefly of Contemporaries, Set Down by John Aubrey, between the years 1669 & 1696*, 2 vols, Oxford, Clarendon Press.

Collier, J.F. (1889) 'The Song of the Western Men', *The Western Antiquary*, Vol. 8, No. 6–7, Dec–Jan: 130–1.

Collins, M. (1875) *Sweet and Twenty*, 3 vols, London, Hurst and Blackett.

Collins, W. (1851) *Rambles Beyond Railways*, London, Richard Bentlay.

Colloms, B. (1975) *Charles Kingsley: The Lion of Eversley*, London, Constable.

Cooper, T. (n.d. [1853]) *Guide: A Short Historical Sketch, Lynton and Places Adjacent including Ilfracombe*, London, John Russell Smith.

Courteney, M. (1890) *Cornish Feasts and Folklore*, Penzance, Beare and Sons.

Cox, Charles J. (1905) 'The Doones of Exmoor', *The Athenaeum*, No. 4061, 26 August: 274–75.

Coxe, A. (1984) *A Book About Smuggling in the West Country 1700–1850*, Padstow, Tabb House.

Craik, D.M. (1884) *An Unsentimental Journey Through Cornwall by The Author of 'John Halifax, Gentleman'*, London, Macmillan.

Cross, T. (1994) *The Shining Sands: Artists in Newlyn and St Ives*, Tiverton, West Country Books.

Daiches, D. and Flower, J. (1979) *Literary Landscapes of the British Isles: A Narrative Atlas*, London, Paddington Press.

Dolman, F. (1894) 'Novel-Writing and Novel Reading: A Chat with the Rev. S. Baring-Gould', *Cassell's Family Magazine*, Vol. 22, December: 17–20.

Drabble, M. (1975) *Arnold Bennett: A Biography*, London, Futura.

Dugdale, F. (1911) 'Blue Jimmy: The Horse Stealer', *The Cornhill Magazine*, Vol. 30, February: 225–31.

Dunn, R.W. (1956) *R.D. Blackmore: The Author of Lorna Doone*, London, Robert Hale.

Easson, A. (ed.) (1991) *Elizabeth Gaskell: The Critical Heritage*, London, Routledge.

Eliot, G. (1855) Review of *Westward Ho!*, *Westminster Review*, NS, Vol. 7, July-October: 288–99.

Esquiros, A. (1865) *Cornwall and its Coasts*, London, Chapman and Hall.

Fenn, W. (1880) 'Favourite Sketching Grounds: Clovelly', *The Magazine of Art*, Vol. 3, London, Cassell: 87–91.

Fortescue, J. (1887) *Records of Staghunting on Exmoor*, London, Chapman and Hall.

Fowles, J. (1964) 'On Being English but Not British', *The Texas Quarterly*, 7, No. 3, 154–62.

Fowles, J. (1975) Foreword to *Hawker of Morwenstow* by Piers Brendon, London, Anthony Mott: 15–21.

Fowles, J. and Godwin, F. (1978) *Islands*, London, Jonathan Cape.

Fox, C. (1882) *Memories of Old Friends: Being Extracts from the Journals and Letters of Caroline Fox of Penjerrick, Cornwall, from 1835–1871,* 2 vols, ed. Horace Pym, London, Smith, Elder.

Freud, S. (1986a edn) 'The Theme of the Three Caskets', *Art and Literature*, Vol. 14 of *Pelican Freud Library*, trans. James Strachey, Harmondsworth, Penguin: 235–47.

Freud, S. (1986b edn) 'The "Uncanny"', *Art and Literature*, Vol. 14 of *Pelican Freud Library*, translated by James Strachey, Harmondsworth, Penguin: 339–76.

Froude, J. (1894) *Short Studies on Great Subjects*, 4 vols, London, Longmans, Green.

Garvin, J.L. (1925) 'One Hundred Years of Lorna Doone', *Littel's Living Age*, Vol. 326: 142–46.

Gattrell, S. (1988) *Hardy the Creator: A Textual Biography*, Oxford, Clarendon Press.

Gifford, E.L., n.d. [1870?] *The Maid on the Shore*. [Unpublished typescript of this novel exists in Dorset County Museum, Dorchester.]

Gillespie, D. and Steele, E. (eds) (1987) *Julia Duckworth Stephen: Stories for Children, Essays for Adults*, Syracuse, Syracuse University Press.

Golby, J. ed. (1986 edn) *Culture and Society in Victorian Britain 1850–1890*, Oxford, Oxford University Press in association with the Open University.

Gosse, E. (1890) *The Speaker*, 13 September, Vol. 11: 295.

Griggs, L. ed. (1956–71) *Collected Letters of Samuel Taylor Coleridge*, 6 vols, Oxford, Clarendon Press.

Hamilton-Jenkin, A.K. (1932) *Cornish Seafarers: The Smuggling, Wrecking and Fishing Life of Cornwall*, London, J.M. Dent.

Hardy, F. (1986 edn) *The Life of Thomas Hardy 1840–1928*, London, Macmillan.

Hardy, T. (1920) *The Dynasts: An Epic Drama*, London, Macmillan.

Hardy, T. (1979 edn) *The Return of the Native*, introduced by George Woodcock, Harmondsworth, Penguin.

Hardy, T. (1985 edn) *Far From the Madding Crowd*, introduced by Ronald Blythe, Harmondsworth, Penguin.

Hardy, T. (1986 edn) *The Trumpet Major*, introduced by Roger Ebbatson, Harmondsworth, Penguin.

Harrison, J. (1984 edn) *Early Victorian Britain 1832–51*, Glasgow, Fontana/Collins.

Hathaway, E. (1994) *Smuggler: Jack Rattenbury and His Adventures in Devon, Dorset and Cornwall 1778–1844*, Swanage, Shinglepicker Press.

Havinden, M. *et al.* (eds) (1991) *Centre and Periphery*, Exeter, University of Exeter Press.

Hawker, R. (1845) *The Field of Rebhidim: A Visitation Sermon*, London, Edwards and Hughes.

Hawker, R. (1866) 'Cruel Coppinger', *All the Year Round*, Vol. 16: 537–40.

Hawker, R. (1893) *The Prose Works of Rev. R.S. Hawker*, London, William Blackwood.

Hawker, R. (1922) *Stones Broken from the Rocks: Extracts from the Manuscript Notebooks of Robert Stephen Hawker*, selected by E.R. Appleton, ed. C.E. Byles, Oxford, Basil Blackwell.

Hawker, R. (1928 edn) *Cornish Ballads and Other Poems*, ed. C.E. Byles, London, John Lane.

Hawkins, D. (1986 edn) *Hardy's Wessex*, London, Macmillan.

Hazlitt, W. (1949) *Conversations of James Northcote*, London, Frederick Muller.

Heaney, S. (1985) *Preoccupations*, London, Faber.

Hemery, E. (1982) *Historic Dart*, Newton Abbot, David and Charles.

Howitt, W. (1835) 'A Daydream at Tintagel', *Visits to Remarkable Places*, London, Longman, Orme, Brown and Green.

Howitt, W. (1838) *The Rural Life of England*, 2 vols, London, Longman, Orme, Brown and Green.

Hughes, T. (1892) *The Scouring of the White Horse: The Long Vacation Ramble of a London Clerk and What Came of It*, London, Macmillan.

Hurley, J. (1973) *Legends of Exmoor*, The Exmoor Press.

Hutchins, J. (1973 edn) *The History and Antiquities of the Country of Dorset*, 4 vols, Trowbridge, Wiltshire, Redwood Press.

James, H. (1983 edn) *English Hours*, introduced by Leon Edel, Oxford, Oxford University Press.

Jamieson, A. (1992) 'Devon and Smuggling, 1680–1850, in *The New Maritime History of Devon*, Vol. I, ed. Michael Duffy *et al.*, London, Conway Maritime Press in association with the University of Exeter, Vol. I: 244–50.

Jefferies, R. (1948) *Field and Hedgerow: Being the Last Essays of Richard Jefferies with an Introduction and Notes by Samuel J. Looker*, London, Lutterworth Press.

Jones, D. (1974) *The Sleeping Lord and Other Fragments* London, Faber.

Jordan, T. (1678) *The Triumphs of London*, London, printed for John and Henry Playford.

Jordan, T. (1683) *The Triumphs of London*, London, printed for John and Henry Playford.

Kay-Robinson, D. (1972) *Hardy's Wessex Re-appraised*, Newton Abbot, David and Charles.

Kegan Paul, C. (1876) 'The Wessex Labourer', *The Examiner*, July: 793–94.

Keith, W. (1969) 'Thomas Hardy and the Literary Pilgrims', *Nineteenth Century Fiction*, Vol. 24, No. 1: 80–92.

Keith, W. (1988) *Regions of Imagination: The Development of British Rural Fiction*, London, University of Toronto Press.

Kerr, P. (ed.) (1997) *The Crimean War*, London, Boxtree.

Kilvert Society (1978) *Culvert's Cornish Holiday: Further Extracts from Kilvert's Diary*, Hay on Wye, Kilvert Society Publications Department.

King, R. (1874) *Sketches and Studies: Descriptive and Historical*, London, John Murray.

Kingsley, C. (1859) *Miscellanies*, 2 vols, London, John W. Parker.

Kingsley, C. (1871) President's Address in *Transactions of the Devonshire Association*, Vol. 4, Pt 2: 377–95.

Kingsley, C. (1877) *Two Years Ago*, London, Macmillan.

Kingsley, C. (1878a edn) *Westward Ho!*, London, Macmillan.

Kingsley, C. (1878b edn) *Yeast: A Problem*, London, Macmillan.

Kingsley, C. (1890 edn) *Glaucus or The Wonders of the Shore*, London, Macmillan.

Kingsley, C. (1891) *Prose Idylls: New and Old*, London, Macmillan.

Kingsley, C. (1892 edn) *Hereward the Wake: 'Last of the English'*, London, Macmillan.

Kingsley, C. (1901) *True Words for Brave Men*, London, Macmillan.

Kingsley, F. (ed.) (1891) *Charles Kingsley: His Letters and Memories of His Life*, 2 vols, London, Macmillan.

Kingsley, H. (1894a edn) *Ravenshoe*, London, Ward, Lock.

Kingsley, H. (1894b edn) *Geoffrey Hamlyn*, London, Ward, Lock.

Kingsley, H. (1895 edn) *Reginald Hetherege and Leighton Court*, London, Ward, Lock.

Knox, R. (1862 edn) *The Races of Man*, London, Renshaw.

Lawrence, D.H. (1985 edn) *D.H. Lawrence and Italy*, introduced by Anthony Burgess, Harmondsworth, Penguin.

Leaska, M, (ed.) (1990) *A Passionate Apprentice: The Early Journals*, London, Hogarth Press.

Lee, F. (1876) *Memorials of the Late Rev. Robert Stephen Hawker*, London, Chatto and Windus.

Lee, H. (1996) *Virginia Woolf*, London, Chatto and Windus.

Lerner, L. and Holstrom J. (eds) (1968) *Thomas Hardy and his Readers: A Selection of Contemporary Reviews*, London, Bodley Head.

Looker, S. and Porteous, C. (eds) (1966) *Richard Jefferies: Man of the Fields*, London, Country Book Club.

Lopez, B. (1988) *Crossing Open Ground*, New York, Charles Scribner's Sons.

Lyon, M. (ed.) (1986) *Virginia Woolf: Books and Portraits*, London, Triad.

MacDermott, E. (1973 edn) *The History of the Forest of Exmoor*, Newton Abbot, David and Charles.

Macneillie, A. (ed.) (1986) *The Essays of Virginia Woolf*, 6 vols, London, Hogarth Press.

Maitland, F. (1910) *The Life and Letters of Leslie Stephen*, London, Duck- worth.

Maskell, W. (1872 edn) 'Bude Haven', *Odds and Ends*, London, James Toovey.

Masson, D. (1859) *British Novelists and their Styles*, London, Macmillan.

Maxted, I. (1998) TS letter to the author, 27 July.

Millais, J.G. (1899) *The Life and Letters of John Everett Millais*, 2 vols, London, Methuen.

Millgate, M. (ed.) (1996) *Letters of Emma and Thomas Hardy*, Oxford, Clarendon Press.

Monk. G. (1961) *Lew Trenchard: Lew House, Lew Trenchard Church and Baring-Gould*, Plymouth, Clarke, Doble and Brendon.

Morris, M. (1892) 'Culture and Anarchy', *Quarterly Review*, 174, April: 219–26.

Motion, A. (ed.) (1994) *William Barnes: Selected Poems*, Harmondsworth, Penguin.

Murray, J. (1865) *A Handbook for Travellers in Devon and Cornwall*, London, John Murray.

Nicolson, N. (eds) (1975–81) *The Letters of Virginia Woolf*, 6 vols, London, Hogarth Press.

Norton, C. (ed.) (1894) *Letters of James Russell Lowell*, 2 vols, London, Osgood, Mcilvanie.

Oakeley, Atholl (n.d.) *Doone Valley of 'Lorna Doone'*, Williton, Somerset.

O'Connor, F. (1972) *Mystery and Manners*, London, Faber.

Olmsted, J. (1979) *A Victorian Art of Fiction: Essays on the Novel in British Periodicals 1830–50*, London, Garland.

Orel, H. (ed.) (1967) *Thomas Hardy's Personal Writings*, London, Macmillan.

Page, J. (1895) *The Coasts of Devon and Cornwall and Lundy Island*, London, Horace Cox.

Page, N. (ed.) (1983) *Tennyson: Interviews and Recollections*, New Jersey, Barnes and Noble.

Payn, J. (1856) 'A Dull Day on Exmoor', *People, Places and Things*, London, S.O. Beeton: 146–60.

Pearse-Chope, R. (1908) Cruel Coppinger, Appendix F in R.S. Hawker, *Footprints of Former Men in Far Cornwall*, ed. by C.E. Byles, London, Bodley Head: 301–4.

Perrett, W. (1903) *The Story of King Lear from Geoffrey of Monmouth to Shakespeare*, Weimar.

Pinion, F. (1984 edn) *A Hardy Companion: A Guide to the Works of Thomas Hardy and their Background*, London, Macmillan.

Plomer, W. (ed.) (1961) *Kilvert's Diary*, London, Jonathan Cape.

Powys, J. (1964 edn) *Wolf Solent*, Harmondsworth, Penguin.

Powys, J. (1967 edn) *Autobiography*, London, Macdonald.

Powys, L. (1937) *Somerset Essays*, London, Bodley Head.

Powys, L. (1983 edn) *Dorset Essays*, Bristol, Redcliffe.

Prichard, T. (n.d. [1873?]; 1991) *The Comical Adventures of Twm Shon Catty Commonly Known as The Welsh Robin Hood*, Wales, Llanerch Publishers.

Purcell, W. (1957) *Onward Christian Soldier: A Life of Sabine Baring-Gould with an Introduction by John Betjeman*, London, Longmans.

Purdy, R. (1954) *Thomas Hardy: A Bibliographical Study*, London, Oxford University Press.

Purdy, R. (ed.) (1978–88) *The Collected Letters of Thomas Hardy*, 7 vols, Oxford, Clarendon Press.

Pyke, E., (ed.) (1967) *Human Documents of the Victorian Age*, London, Allen and Unwin.

Rawle, E.J. (1903) *The Doones of Exmoor*, Taunton, The Athenaeum Press.

Reynolds, S. (1911 edn) *A Poor Man's House*, London, Methuen.

Roberts, G. (1840) *An Account of the Mighty Landslip at Dowlands and Bindon Near Lyme Regis*, Lyme Regis, Daniel Duster.

Rogers, W. (n.d.) *Notes on Bideford*, Vol. 3 in Westcountry Studies Library, Exeter.

Rowe, S. (1985 edn) *A Perambulation of the Ancient and Royal Forest of Dartmoor*, Exeter, Devon Books.

Rowse, A. (1986 edn) *The Little Land of Cornwall*, Gloucester, Alan Sutton.

Rushdie, S. (1991) *Imaginary Homelands*, London, Granta Books.

Ruskin, J. (1903–12) *The Works of John Ruskin*, ed. Cook and Wedderburn, 39 vols, London, George Allen.

Samuel, R. (1996–98) *Island Stories*, 2 vols, London, Verso.

Schulkind, J. (ed.) (1978) *Virginia Woolf: Moments of Being*, St Albans, Triad Panther.

Schulkind, J. (ed.) (1985) *Virginia Woolf: Moments of Being*, revised and enlarged edition, London, Hogarth Press.

Smithard, W. (1905) 'A Talk with the Wessex Novelist at Casterbridge', *The Daily Chronicle*, 8 February: 4.

Snell, F.J. (1903) *A Book of Exmoor*, London, Methuen.

Snell, K. (ed.) (1998) *The Regional Novel in Britain and Ireland 1800–1990*, Cambridge, Cambridge University Press.

Spalding, F. (1983) *Vanessa Bell*, London, Weidenfeld and Nicolson.

Stephen, L. (1902) *Studies of a Biographer*, London, Smith, Elder.

Stephen, L. (1909) *Hours in a Library*, 3 vols, London, Duckworth.

Super, R. (ed.) (1973) *Matthew Arnold: Lectures and Essays in Criticism*, Ann Arbor, University of Michigan Press.

Tennyson, H. (1897) *Alfred Lord Tennyson: A Memoir*, 2 vols, London, Macmillan.

Thackeray, W. (1946) *The Letters and Private Papers of William Makepeace Thackeray*, ed. Gordon N. Ray, 4 vols, London, Oxford University Press.

Thomas, C. (1978) *To The Lighthouse: Catalogue of an Exhibition*, Redruth, Penwith Books.

Thomas, D. (1966) *A Regional History of the Railways of Great Britain*, Newton Abbot, David and Charles.

Thomas, E. (1932 edn) *The South Country*, London, E.P. Dutton.

Thornton, W. (1899) *Reminiscences and Reflections of an Old West-Country Clergyman*, Second Series, Torquay, Andrew Iredale.

Travis, J. (1993) *The Rise of the Devon Seaside Resorts 1750–1900*, Exeter, University of Exeter Press.

Tuckerman, H. (1853; 1982) *A Month in England*, Gloucester, Alan Sutton.

Tugwell, G. (1857) 'Wanderings on Exmoor', *Fraser's Magazine*, Vol. 56: 489–98.

Ward, H. Snowden (n.d.) *The Land of Lorna Doone*, London, Sampson Low.

Warren, T. and Page F. (eds) (1989 edn) *Tennyson: Poems and Plays*, Oxford, Oxford University Press.

W.E.H.F. (1871) 'The Royal Marriage Act', *Gentleman's Magazine*, Vol. 6: 272–76.

White, W. (1855) *A Londoner's Walk to the Land's End*, London, Chapman and Hall.

Widdowson, P. (1989) *Hardy in History: A Study in Literary Sociology*, London, Routledge.

Wiener, M. (1993 edn) *English Culture and the Decline of the Industrial Spirit 1850–1980*, Cambridge, Cambridge University Press.

Williams, M. (1978 edn) *Thomas Hardy and Rural England*, London, Macmillan.

Williams, R. (1985 edn) *The Country and the City*, London, Hogarth Press.

Williams, R. (1988 edn) *Keywords: A Vocabulary of Culture and Society*, London, Fontana.

Woolf, L. (ed.) (1979 edn) *A Writer's Diary*, St Albans, Triad Panther.

Woolf, L. (1980) *An Autobiography*, 2 vols, Oxford, Oxford University Press.

Woolf, V. (1919) 'Modern Novels', *Times Literary Supplement*, 10 April: 189–90.

Woolf, V. (1973 edn) *To The Lighthouse*, Harmondsworth, Penguin.

Worth, R. (1875) *The West Country Garland*, London, Houlston.

Wright, W. (1898) 'Romances of the West Country Written by The Rev. S. Baring-Gould', *Doidge's Western Counties Illustrated Annual*: 376–90.

# Selective Index of Places, People, Texts and Themes

Book titles and page references for illustrations are in italics. Stories and poems are in quotation marks.